Screen Christologies

Religion, Culture and Society

Series Editors:
Oliver Davies,
Department of Theology and Religious Studies,
University of Wales, Lampeter,
and Gavin Flood,
Department of Religious Studies,
University of Stirling

Religion, Culture and Society is a series presented by leading scholars on a wide range of contemporary religious issues. The emphasis throughout is generally multicultural, and the approach is often interdisciplinary. The clarity and accessibility of the series, as well as its authoritative scholarship, will recommend it to students and a non-specialist readership alike.

Screen Christologies

Redemption and the Medium of Film

CHRISTOPHER DEACY

UNIVERSITY OF WALES PRESS
CARDIFF
2001

British Library Cataloguing-in-Publication Data
A catalogue record for this book is available from
the British Library.

ISBN 0-7083-1712-X paperback
     0-7083-1713-8 hardback

Typeset by Mark Heslington, Scarborough, North Yorkshire
Printed in Great Britain by Dinefwr Press, Llandybïe

Contents

Preface

In this book I examine the manner in which a process of redemption analogous to that located in Christian thought is operative through the 'secular' medium of film.

At the crux of my work lies a consideration of why the category of *film noir* constitutes a fertile site of redemptive significance. I demonstrate that the oppressive and fatalistic images and narratives delineated in such films bear witness to what the Christian tradition categorizes as the basic human condition, and from which redemption constitutes a vital possibility.

Particular consideration is given in this light to the cinema of Martin Scorsese, whose often alienated and dysfunctional *noir* protagonists may be seen to undergo a process of being redeemed, reborn and resurrected through violence, destruction (often self-destruction) and a confrontation with the propensity towards sin that characterizes human existence.

I suggest that the *noir* protagonist is a model or exemplar of redemptive possibility in the manner of the Christian under-standing of the Person of Christ. For Christ's own redemptive significance, according to the Antiochene christological tradition, emanates not from his divine, transcendent qualities as the Son of God but from his inherently human and fallible condition as the Son of Man.

The prevalence of redemptive motifs in *films noirs* opens up the possibility that the medium of film is a significant conveyor and agency in contemporary western society of religious hopes and values. The significance this has for the academic study of religion, which has traditionally eschewed the popular media as a serious repository of religious activity, is considerable, and, I suggest, warrants a radical and new evaluation of contemporary religiosity.

Acknowledgements

This book started out as a Ph.D. thesis, and there are some people I wish to thank for enabling me to undertake this research. To my supervisor, Dr Chris Arthur, for his constructive help and guidance at all times, and to Professor Paul Badham and those other members of staff in the Department of Theology and Religious Studies at the University of Wales, Lampeter, who ensured that I was provided with the necessary resources. In particular, the allocation of office space within the department while I was a postgraduate student was of enormous benefit. Thanks are also due to the Catherine and Lady Grace James Foundation and to the University of Wales for their financial help at various stages over the three years, and to my parents and grandparents whose help, support and encouragement has been unceasing and extremely generous.

At the time of writing, I am approaching the end of a two-year Special Research Fellowship from the Leverhulme Trust to carry out postdoctoral research on religion and film. If it had not been for their support, I would not have been able to produce this book. Having the opportunity to work on two (albeit complementary) books simultaneously has ensured that the last two years have been nothing short of eventful, and I am extremely grateful to the Leverhulme Trust for recognizing the value and significance of this project, and for having the confidence in me to carry it out.

Research on the interaction between religion and film is increasingly the way forward for scholars working in the relevant academic disciplines – theology, religious studies and film studies – and I am grateful to all those who have enabled me to make a contribution to this field. A final thank you must go to all those at the University of Wales Press for their hard work and diligence in putting this book into print. While this is primarily an academic text, I hope the insights made in the pages that follow will be of use to anyone who has a passion, like me, for participating in the experience of going to the movies.

1

Cinema as a contemporary site of religious activity

Film as a fertile site of religious significance

According to Plato, 'All mankind, Greeks and non-Greeks alike, believe in the existence of gods.'[1] Even if Plato's assertion is deemed to have less resonance in the twenty-first century than it did in the fourth century BCE,[2] it is difficult to disagree with Brian Morris's assessment that some form of religion is universal to humankind, even to the extent that 'We have yet to discover any society that does not articulate some notions about the sacred and about spiritual beings.'[3] As Carl Jung postulates, humankind 'has everywhere and always spontaneously developed religious forms of expression',[4] and, since the beginning of time, the human psyche has 'been shot through with religious feelings and ideas'.[5] Although the form and nature of religiosity has varied greatly over the centuries, religious hopes, sentiments and aspirations may be found to be as integral to, and pervasive in, contemporary Western culture as they have been at any previous time in humankind's history. Of course, from a contemporary perspective, there are prominent differences between the role and efficacy of religious expression today and that of previous centuries. In today's world, in particular, we have less recourse to religion as a social institution, in the respect that one may no longer look to the Christian Church for interpretations of all spheres of human activity. In the Middle Ages, in marked contrast, Christianity was firmly entrenched as the religion of Europe, with the Church and the political structure inextricably bound up so as to supply the 'God-given' social framework within which each human being found his or her appointed place and travelled on his or her path to heaven or to hell, respectively. Nevertheless, even though such an all-embracing, unified vision no longer exists and, as Margaret Miles puts it, Christian churches 'have relinquished the task of providing life-orienting images',[6] there is a substantial extent to which *secular culture* has, as it were, 'filled the void', and taken on many of these functions.

At the very least, no one would seriously doubt that the Western religious consciousness underwent a significant reshaping in the latter half of the twentieth century, following a decline in traditional organized religion and the emergence of New Age movements. Although many look back upon the Enlightenment as a time when European society was emancipated from the so-called 'shackles' of religion, this does not even begin to make sense of the situation in modern America, where, as Conrad Ostwalt attests, many commentators 'point to the vitality and variety of religion in a secular U.S. society', in which 'religion is being popularized, scattered, and secularized through extra-ecclesiastical institutions'.[7] Despite reaching its culturally definitive form for the West in Christianity, scholars in the fields of theology and religious studies are being faced with a new challenge – one that involves coming to terms with the fact that people's hopes, aspirations, fears and anxieties, and all the vicissitudes of human life and endeavour, as traditionally expressed in the Christian religion in the language of sin, estrangement, atonement and redemption, are being articulated through radically different vehicles of expression and outside traditionally demarcated boundaries of religious activity.

Perhaps, though, this is not so far removed from the thinking of Paul Tillich, for whom, notwithstanding Christ's unique status as redeemer through whom 'all saving and healing processes'[8] may be said to function, it is not the case that 'there is no authentic encounter with divine grace, no genuine healing of our brokenness or overcoming of our estrangement, to be found or discerned anywhere else'.[9] It is thus possible, in effect, for human beings to be inundated with religious stimuli without ever having attended a church service or belonging to a religious community or organization. Rather, religion is implicit in all aspects of human life. Ultimately, there is no occurrence in human affairs that is removed from at least a potential religious interpretation, to the extent that, for Tillich, everything that the human thinks, feels, and performs achieves its greatness and depth because of the active presence of a *religious* dimension to life. If the fields of theology and religious studies are thus to take human history and human experience seriously, then such media as television and

popular film must be accorded what Michael Paul Gallagher categorizes as 'a privileged witness in today's culture'.[10] While it would
be misleading to go so far as to suggest that traditional religious
activity has been totally superseded by the agencies of secular
culture – as Peter Williams acknowledges, 'institutional religion
shows no sign of disappearing, and even experiences periodic
resurgences'[11] – in an age in which popular film, in particular, can
be seen to be so pervasive, the overwhelming evidence suggests
that some of the roles traditionally associated with religious
discourse have been displaced by, and transposed through, such
media.

Without disputing that the dialogue between religion and film is
only at a relatively embryonic stage of development, the academic
study of religion actually *necessitates* interdisciplinary study. As
Walter Capps indicates, *multiplicity* is integral to religion, and

> the variety of subjects, methods, intentions, and insights that comprise
> religious studies requires the effective interaction between sub-fields
> and disciplines. Stated in bolder terms, religious studies is not the
> sociology of religion, or philosophy of religion, or history of religion, or
> anthropology of religion, and so on, but is comprised of the co-
> operation between all of these.[12]

As regards religious traditions themselves, furthermore, any
judicious and authoritative study of religion must take into
consideration the empirical fact that they are not 'static or
monolithic phenomena'[13] but are inextricably bound up with
the advancements and achievements made across the whole range
of human activity. As humans evolve, the various scientific and
social progressions and discoveries that are made will have a
concomitant effect upon religious institutions, doctrines and
representations. For instance, it was as a consequence of Darwin's
evolutionary theory, as expounded in *The Origin of Species*, that
Christianity in the nineteenth century was prompted to reassess
its understanding of the nature and providence of God. Whereas
in the Newtonian world it had still been possible to relate God
the Creator to the 'world machine', it was now deemed difficult
by many contemporary Christians to associate God with a process
of such infinite length and such apparently chaotic and erratic
development. Due to such advances within the scientific
community, it would not be inappropriate to categorize the period

since the Enlightenment as one in which, albeit with varying degrees of emphasis, Christians have continually been confronted with challenges to what, in John Macquarrie's words, may be identified as 'the historical trustworthiness of the New Testament',[14] and to the very basis and kernel of the Christian faith. In short, 'religions arise, develop and change in time and in response to specific historic and social situations'.[15] As humankind evolves, traditional religious doctrines and assumptions will necessarily be subject to revision, and even to transformation.

Provided that academics take this capacity for change and development into account, there is scope for religious motifs and expressions to be located in all manner of unexpected places. Indeed, in Capps's words, scholars are often 'taken by surprise by hosts of topics that are not within the range and focus of that at which they have been trained to look'.[16] As regards the medium of film, therefore, while a certain scepticism and ignorance may prevail within some sections of the academic community as to the viability of examining such media as a potential site of religious significance, no credible account of the place and function of religion in the twenty-first century would dismiss at least the possibility that the film industry is one of many contemporary 'secular' agencies that has challenged (some would go even further and say *superseded*) religious institutions in the scramble for what Conrad Ostwalt identifies as 'societal attention and participation'.[17] According to Ostwalt, indeed, 'it might even be argued that the movie theater has acted like some secular religion',[18] wherein, in a manner that is analogous to traditional institutions such as the Church, groups of people file into a theatre at a specified time, choose a seat, and prepare with others for what could be said to amount to a religious experience. Without going so far as to say that the cinema *has* replaced the sanctuary, and that the cinema screen *has* replaced the pulpit, the experience which a film such as Martin Scorsese's *Raging Bull* (1980) can have upon an audience, by way of enabling one to *confront* Jake La Motta's need for redemption and to see in one's own life 'the beginning of a trajectory up to some kind of salvation',[19] would suggest that such a process is not untenable.

At the very least, it would be imprudent for the theologian or the religious studies scholar to overlook – let alone dismiss out of hand – Margaret Miles's assertion that the representation of values in contemporary culture may be seen to occur most persistently not in the church or the synagogue but in the movie theatre.[20] In her words, American people – including those who hold religious affiliations of some kind – 'now gather about cinema and television screens rather than in churches to ponder the moral quandaries of American life'.[21] While there are, invariably, detractors and opponents of this position, who will posit that this is not, strictly speaking, a religious but merely a *pseudo*-religious activity, and that there can only, at most, be a *reflection* in such media as film of religious possibility, rather than that film, in itself, has the potential to constitute a religious site, what *is* clear is that religion is a multifaceted and heterogeneous sphere of activity. It would, in effect, thus be spurious to dismiss out of hand the potential veracity of Miles's claim. Among various sociologists and anthropologists of religion, indeed, there is no such thing as a *false* religion. According to Emile Durkheim, for instance, all religions meet particular needs and concerns that are part and parcel of human life,[22] and, in the words of Max Weber, 'every need for salvation is an expression of some distress', and that 'social or economic oppression is an effective source of salvation beliefs.'[23] The category of films known as *film noir* may not, strictly speaking, be an *overt* site of religious significance in the manner of traditional Christian agencies, but, throughout history, it is apparent that a number of religious movements have developed at times of social crisis, such as when a hitherto isolated, often agricultural, community has come into rapid contact with an aggressive and technologically more advanced culture.[24] While *film noir* may not exactly be what Weber had in mind when he declared that 'there is no known human society without something which modern social scientists would classify as religion',[25] it is no coincidence that this particular body of films arose in the 1940s and 1950s at a time when America was undergoing a social crisis of unprecedented proportions, precipitated by the upheavals of the Second World War.

Indeed, films do not develop in a vacuum but, rather, they emanate in, and respond to, concrete and particular historical circumstances, to the extent that to be properly understood at least some reference must be made to the society and culture within which they were conceived. Accordingly, the fact that the world of *film noir* consists of individuals 'fighting for survival in an ambiguous and uncertain world' and speaking for 'the troubled spirit of post-war America'[26] may be seen to concur with the broad thrust of Weber's claim that religious needs are inclined to develop at times of cultural crisis, when a culture has been faced with considerable turbulence and chaos. It should not therefore be deemed extraneous or merely peripheral to the theologian or student of religion that, to use Foster Hirsch's words, 'In its pervasive aura of defeat and despair, its images of entrapment, the escalating derangement of its leading characters, *noir* registers, in a general way, the country's sour postwar mood.'[27] Moreover, as Weber observed, religious movements have usually sprung up in *urban* contexts, with the major processes of social – and, as a corollary, religious – change and growth centring in urban populations. Hence, it is especially significant that, throughout the 1940s and into the 1950s, *film noir* 'played upon basic themes of aloneness, oppression, claustrophobia, and emotional and physical brutality, manifested in weak men, various gangsters and detectives . . . who lived – or cringed – in an *urban* landscape that defied clear perception and safe habitation'.[28]

As a consequence, rather than detached or abstract individuals, the protagonists in *film noir* have the capacity to be intimately related to the disaffected and disquieted sensibility of the film audience at a time of cultural disillusionment and chaos. This is especially brought out in Scorsese's *Taxi Driver*, which – while bearing witness to universal human themes pertaining to the alienated and 'fallen' human condition – is grounded in a particular social and historical urban milieu. Indeed, the film was produced in 1975, at a time when American culture had undergone what Kolker identifies as 'a depressive reaction'[29] and 'a helpless withdrawal from social and political difficulties,'[30] due in large measure to America's involvement in the Vietnam War (of which the protagonist, Travis Bickle, is a veteran) and the recognition brought about by the Watergate scandal – in which 'involvement in criminal activity, misuse of funds and a massive cover-up conspiracy'[31] forced the resignation of President Nixon – that political and economic institutions were open to corruption and abuse. Fear and despair could be said to have characterized the American inner cities and, on the eve of America's bi-centenary of 1976, national morale was at its lowest ebb.[32] Within this context, it is significant that many contemporary films illustrated 'impotence and despair, and signalled disaster, a breakdown of community and trust so thorough that it left the viewer with images of lonely individuals, trapped, in the dark, completely isolated.'[33]

Sociologists and anthropologists are thus right to postulate that 'religion is never an abstract set of ideas, values or experiences developed apart from the total cultural matrix and that many religious beliefs, customs and rituals can only be understood in reference to this matrix'.[34] If *Taxi Driver* and other *films noirs* of the 1970s, such as *The Long Goodbye*, *Chinatown*, *Night Moves* and *The Conversation*, which will be covered in the pages that follow are, as this book will propose, amenable to a religious interpretation, it is feasible that the authentic urban backdrop of such films contributes greatly to such a reading. In particular, such a hypothesis has particular resonance when it is understood in the light of Steve Bruce's analysis that 'so long as life is nasty, brutish, and short'[35] – and the urban jungle of New York City is the epitome of such a condition – then 'we will be in the market for religion'.[36] If the historical context had been different, one can assume that an alternative form and expression of religious possibility would have emerged. It is no coincidence, indeed, that in the First World War, some three decades before *noir* first emerged, a different form of religiosity, and a different interpretation of redemption, was in operation due to the quite different circumstances of the period. In contrast to the bleak and despairing vision of the *noir* universe, many contemporaries of the First World War, at least in intellectual circles, saw the conflict in Europe as something which was, or at least had the capacity to pre-empt, something creative and good. According to the French poet, Paul Claudel, for instance, it was expected that France would experience the day of resurrection during the great battles which lay ahead,[37] and Maurice Barrès was confident that the War would 'bring about a resurrection'.[38]

In essence, therefore, while acknowledging that film will not be deemed by all scholars to constitute an exemplary and perfectly realized model of contemporary redemptive activity, there are, I believe, strong grounds for reading many motion pictures in these terms. Of course, it is still possible to encounter sociologists and anthropologists as well as academics in other fields who consider it appropriate to examine western religion in terms of the 'secularization thesis', according to which religions are being 'increasingly eviscerated by the secular forces in the modern world'.[39] On such a basis, it is believed that one can tabulate and plot the ever-diminishing influence of religion on contemporary spheres of human life. However, I would argue that such models depend upon a seriously flawed understanding of religion. In response to such a model, this book will posit that religious activity is in no way extrinsic to, or on the periphery of, contemporary western culture. The function and, above all, the *need* which religious agencies have traditionally performed is undiminished, and has merely found expression in new – albeit unconventional – instruments and agencies. Certainly, 'many traditional'[40] as well as 'current formulations',[41] and perhaps even 'entire traditions',[42] of religion 'will radically change or even disappear'[43] from western society, yet, as Don Cupitt indicates, this 'does not alter the fact that at the deepest level religious needs and impulses are as great as ever'.[44]

In many respects, the possibility that a secular agency such as film may carry and convey religious ideas and values has previously been acknowledged by scholars, even if the extent of the process has only been fully realized and taken seriously in recent years. According to Durkheim, for instance, writing in 1912, although 'the former gods are growing old or dying',[45] religion in an altered form is likely to continue in western society. While he anticipated that religious activity might be found in terms of ceremonial activities and in the celebration of humanist and political values such as freedom, equality and social co-operation which contain certain implicit religious suppositions, rather than in terms of the mass media, the anticipation that such secular concerns are amenable to a religious interpretation is not fundamentally at odds with what I am seeking to demonstrate in this book. Indeed, for Durkheim, such 'secular' activities as flag-waving and coronations and the rendition of songs such as 'Land of Hope and Glory' amount to civil religions,[46] and are analogous in essence to the ostensibly religious activities of institutionalized religion. Consequently, both traditional religious and secular agencies may be involved in the same kind of activity. At the time of writing, Durkheim concluded that no obvious replacement to 'the old gods' had emerged. While many commentators are inclined to posit that, if major, mainstream religions are in decline then it follows that a new religious *tradition* will fill the gap – Stark and Bainbridge, for instance, look to the Mormons[47] – I believe that the medium of film is actually capable of fulfilling this function. Credence for this is achieved by the fact that, while the collapse of mainstream churches, certainly in Europe, has theoretically made a large number of people available to join new religious movements and traditions during recent decades, 'relatively few have taken up the offer'.[48] In the 1980s alone, over five million people left the mainstream churches in Britain, and yet the total membership of new religious movements did not exceed five or six thousand.[49] If there is a religious instinct in humankind, the evidence thus suggests that it should not simply be discerned and looked for in terms of membership of ostensibly religious *institutions*.

While not all films which are produced by Hollywood are carriers of religious significance, it is in the medium of film that prominent expressions of religiousness and fertile models and exemplars of redemptive activity can be seen to abound. So long as Hollywood continues to function as 'a house of illusions,'[50] whereby, 'demanding nothing of the viewer', it seems to offer 'the power to understand without the need seriously to think or change',[51] then David Jasper's diagnosis that Hollywood cinema cannot make a serious contribution to theological and religious reflection will stand. However, in terms of the serious potential for religious reflection that is embodied and manifested within and through the images, narratives and protagonists of many films – particularly *films noirs* – the medium of film is capable of performing a powerful function in contemporary culture. Although the concept of redemption has a particular grounding and foundation within the categories of the Christian tradition, to the effect that in any judicious examination of the redemptive significance of film, a certain familiarity and acquaintance with the rudiments of Christian theology is imperative, this is not to say that the *experience* of redemption is in any way restricted in its scope, as this book will demonstrate. For, it is the intrinsically *human* nature and orientation of redemption that renders it such a powerful and pervasive motif in religious discourse, emanating as it does from the concrete and empirical reality of human existence, and, in particular, the universal human experience of sin, alienation and suffering. Whether or not an actual film audience will come to formulate a correlation between the protagonist in a *film noir* and the figure of Jesus Christ, humiliated and enduring immense physical suffering on the Cross, it is the inherently human experience that the protagonist undergoes, and which has the capacity to resonate with the lives and experiences of the *audience members*, that enables such films to be read in theological terms. Ultimately, therefore, there are viable grounds for supposing that redemption has the capacity to be apprehended and encountered in the secular sphere, and, in particular, for seeing in the medium of film robust indications and manifestations of religious activity.

2

The cultural and religious significance of film

The cultural significance of film

The medium of film undeniably performs a pivotal function in contemporary western society. As Peter Horsfield attests, we are living in a mediated consumer culture in which people organize and express themselves in relation to the demands of the mass media.[1] In the United Kingdom alone, cinema attendance has progressively risen since the mid-1980s: in 1998 alone, a total of 135.5 million admissions were made to its 759 theatres (encompassing 2,564 screens) and £514.73 million was taken at the British box office.[2] Together with the mass ownership of television – and, as we enter the twenty-first century, the development of digital broadcasting, with the attendant opportunity for, literally, hundreds of television channels to be accessed in every household in the country, twenty-four hours a day – it does not seem too wide of the mark to presume that the realm of the media has now come to be the primary realm for articulating and embodying the beliefs and values of individuals and communities in western society. At the very least, whereas in the nineteenth century popular novels and presses largely held the public's imagination, there is now a substantial sense in which images are replacing written texts in their ability to capture the human imagination and to shape our world-views. A random glance at the Internet Movie Database (IMDB) provides ample evidence of the immense, and diverse, appeal of film, and the profound effect any one film can engender among global audiences. Not only is every single motion picture ever made listed on this site, but it is a rare occasion indeed when any selected film does not contain at least a dozen or so 'user comments'. While not all films on this site may be particularly praised or appreciated, the fact that, by the time *American Beauty* had won five Academy Awards in March 2000, nearly one thousand reviews of the film had been posted on the IMDB by non-professional filmgoers and enthusiasts, and more than two thousand such reviews had appeared of *Star Wars Episode One: The Phantom Menace* by the beginning of September 2000, is indicative of the cultural appeal the medium has the capacity to command.

The viability of a religious interpretation of film

Without disputing, however, that film has a significant cultural dimension, it is less easy to establish that a film may be performing a religious function. Since no two individuals will read the same film in the same way, what may be construed as a film of prodigious religious significance by one person may be categorized and apprehended by another as a film of merely biographical, historical or cultural value, which no more than delineates individuals or communities involved in some form of religious practice, ritual or struggle. A film such as *The Exorcist* (1973)[3] may be interpreted as a religious picture by virtue of the fact that three of its characters are Roman Catholic priests and its subject-matter is the alleged demonic possession of a twelve-year-old girl living in Georgetown, USA. Alternatively, without even acknowledging that the film broaches certain fundamental religious themes pertaining to the classic supernatural conflict between the forces of 'good' and 'evil', embodied in the figures of the young girl, Regan (Linda Blair), and the Christian Church, many other audience members might be more inclined to classify *The Exorcist* as a horror movie, whose ostensive aim is to shock, frighten and, ultimately, entertain audiences. Even among audience members who share a particular religious sensibility there will be no consensus of opinion as to how to interpret even an overtly religious film, as the controversy surrounding the release in 1988 of Martin Scorsese's *The Last Temptation of Christ* testifies, when many evangelical and fundamentalist Christians objected to Scorsese's presentation of Jesus Christ as a fully human individual struggling to come to terms with his messianic vocation.[4] The fact that the picture is in many respects christologically and doctrinally orthodox, and was actually intended by Scorsese as a means of forcing people 'to take Jesus seriously' and at least to 're-evaluate His teachings'[5] exemplifies the potential difficulty involved in any exploration of the religious nature and interpretation of film.

Given the diverse and complex nature of audience attitudes and dispositions, it is thus evident that any judicious and meaningful assessment of the degree to which film is amenable to a religious reading can realistically only be tentative and provisional in form. Nonetheless, while no single interpretation or categorization of a given film or film genre is universally valid, it is at least apparent that there are certain underlying themes intrinsic to some pictures into which discordant and heterogeneous audiences can at least potentially tap, and which thereby open such films to a possible religious interpretation. For example, although no two viewers of *Born on the Fourth of July* (1989) will 'read' the picture in the same manner, and notwithstanding the diversity of possible interpretations on offer, Oliver Stone can be seen to draw in his film on a number of cultural codes – particularly those of a religious and geographical orientation – which possess 'great connotative and symbolic power for members of the audience'.[6] Consequently, although Stone's message is aimed primarily at an American audience, its portrayal of the effects of the Vietnam War has the potential to affect anyone who has experienced twentieth-century warfare, and who can come to perceive that, in White's words, 'the mixture of patriotism and militarism is a cultural contradiction that can only be resolved with a personal transformation'.[7] Through showing that the young warrior, Kovic, is tormented with guilt for his militarism, and the anguish he feels at having killed a fellow soldier in Vietnam – to the extent that Kovic comes to confess his guilt to the family of the deceased comrade – Stone could be said to be

> inviting the American people to 'confess' that they have killed their own sons and innocent people in Vietnam with their misplaced patriotism. The elderly mother of the boy killed forgives the hero with words of 'absolution' [such that] the confession has a sacramental power of healing, reconciliation and interior peace that gives the young man new purpose in life. Stone is inviting his audience to be 'healed' by identifying with the hero and to 'recover' the deepest values of the American culture, finding national meaning not in militarism but in peacemaking.[8]

The audience is in a position to enter into a reworking of the cultural codes upon which Stone draws because of his use of religious symbolism to illustrate and construct these codes. For, even where audiences may fail to make a specific connection with Stone's anti-militaristic message – insofar as they have no personal understanding of, or relationship to, the issues surrounding the Vietnam War – the symbolism he uses necessarily has a much wider and more universal significance, with which audiences familiar with religious – and specifically Christian – symbols and images can engage. Thus, in touching different life-situations among different audience members, there is a degree to which Stone's picture, which is ostensibly a war film, is able to facilitate the reconciliation of contradictions of meaning which lie at the heart of the everyday lives of individual members of the audience. Hence, while White doubts 'that many people rushed out to become pacifists after seeing the transformation'[9] of Ron Kovic,

> I suspect that the formula of humble admission that 'I was wrong in my whole worldview and that I will find peace and personal integration by publicly confessing this to the people I have offended' did nestle into the imaginations of people and may have found some application in whatever major meaning contradictions they were facing at the time.[10]

Consequently, then, as with White's illustration of how *Born on the Fourth of July* imparts to a multifaceted audience certain fundamental themes, such as the concept of atoning for one's sins, which they can then transpose into the context of their own life-situations, this book will demonstrate that the depiction in many motion pictures of flawed, 'everyman', and authentically human characters could be said to fulfil a religious function by means of offering new religious paradigms as to how heterogeneous audiences have the potential to negotiate meaning and value in their lives.

The religious significance of film

That the medium of film is at least amenable to a religious reading is demonstrated by the fact that, over the years, some film-makers and theorists have sought to lay emphasis upon the degree to which film is adept at carrying and conveying religious hopes and values. The editorial of the autumn 1995 edition of the journal *Media Development* states, for example, that film can deal with the realm of the metaphysical better than any other medium,[11] and it cites in this regard a number of directors who 'have been able to problematize the perennial questions of life and to express them through codes that have both a particular and a universal appeal'.[12] Further, according to Marjeet Verbeek, writing in the same journal, film art is able to represent what is in our daily experience unrepresentable,[13] and has the potential to evoke the spirituality of humans and to 'open their rationality for the Other, the Transcendent'.[14] Hence, the French director Robert Bresson could be said to have explored themes pertaining to the super-natural and spiritual by exposing 'those extraordinary currents, the presence of something or someone . . . which confirms that there is a hand guiding everything'.[15] In this respect, with refer-ence to Bresson's *The Diary of a Country Priest* (1950), Michael Bird argues that his actors almost refrain from acting, and pose as transparent figures behind whom a spiritual significance can be discerned.[16]

Such a spiritual presence would further seem to be in operation in the 1991 picture *Grand Canyon*, in which Lawrence Kasdan could be said to be presenting the persistence of narrative coincidences which are 'inexplicable and seem to point to some-thing beyond themselves'.[17] It would seem to be a supernatural thread that holds things together, and the suggestion is that Los Angeles may really be the City of Angels, with 'the danger of Los Angeles life' lending 'the American Dream . . . the haunting quality of afterlife'.[18] Furthermore, religious themes are clearly in abundance in Steven Spielberg's *Close Encounters of the Third Kind* (1977), insofar as the picture's 'spectacle of brilliant alien technology' could be considered analogous to 'biblical accounts of celestial phenomena',[19] with 'the fiery clouds of biblical texts' becoming 'the boiling clouds and blinding light of Spielberg's film'.[20] Hence, despite the predominantly scientific and rational ethos that pervades contemporary western society, such a film has been deemed by some to give credence to the religious hope that we can 'still hope for salvation from above', in a world where 'we cannot save ourselves'.[21]

In actuality, however, without disputing that this is one possible interpretation of the meaning and function of film, it is apparent that such a position is by no means universally held, either inside or outside the academic discipline of religious studies. Among film theorists and critics, in particular, the religious nature and orientation of film is substantially overlooked, if not altogether dismissed, as a viable or authoritative interpretation. As Gaye Ortiz points out, indeed, whenever a new text on theology and film is published – and she indicates that there were at least five in 1997 alone – 'the academics in film studies titter and scornfully dismiss churchy types who dare to bring God into the rarified presence of cinematic discourse'.[22] Consequently, to quote Joel Martin, if religion is dealt with in film studies at all it is as a purely 'peripheral phenomenon in contemporary social organization',[23] where the forces of secularization are taken for granted. For example, in an introduction to a series of books on films, Edward Buscombe and Phil Rosen indicate that the discipline of film studies has been enriched 'in interaction with a wide variety of other disciplines',[24] among them literary studies, anthropology, linguistics, history, economics and psychology, while altogether omitting reference to the potential role played by the fields of theology and religious studies.

Likewise, in his introduction to *The Oxford Guide to Film Studies*, published in 1998, John Hill acknowledges 'the diversity of theoretical, critical, and cultural perspectives that have been a feature of film study'[25] over the years, and notes that since the 1960s 'film studies has borrowed heavily' from such other fields as 'semiotics, structuralism, psychoanalysis, Marxism, feminism, post-structuralism and deconstruction, and, more recently, cultural studies and postmodernism',[26] but he conspicuously neglects to attach any influence to the territory of theology or religious studies. Even when conceding that certain 'less well-known perspectives' have been 'especially influential in shaping the study of film' and for addressing 'issues that dominant strands of film study may often have neglected',[27] Hill refers only in this regard to the influences of Impressionism and hermeneutics. Ultimately, therefore, so long as an overtly Christian agenda is at work, according to which film is deemed to have no function beyond that of fostering a Christian sensibility, then the discipline of film studies will be predilected to continue to overlook, if not actually ignore, the potentially fruitful insights of theology or religious studies. As Paul Giles puts it, in the introduction to his study of *American Catholic Arts and Fictions*, published in 1992, 'it is still not easy to discuss religion within a contemporary cultural context',[28] since the prevailing ethos is that the academic study of the arts and culture 'is, *per se*, a rationalistic enterprise',[29] with no room for what is perceived to be 'the mumbo jumbo of spiritual belief'.[30]

However, even among theologians and religious historians, this emphasis on the explicitly Christian function of film is in no sense a widespread conviction. As Margaret Miles concedes, in her examination of *Seeing and Believing: Religion and Values in the Movies*,[31] it is hard to convince friends and even scholars of religion about the merits of studying the medium of film in the socio-cultural context of America since they tend to regard the enterprise as a 'lark'[32] and as a departure from 'serious' academic work. Scripture will usually be approached by theologians as the written word, born in an oral tradition, and which has endured for some two thousand years, while cinema is an audio-visual 'word', little more than one hundred years old, and which belongs to a social-cultural and entertainment – rather than liturgical, devotional or academic – setting, and within a highly structured socio-economic system of production and distribution. Cinema's 'word', moreover, is ontologically different from the 'word' of scripture which, among practising Christians at any rate, is often assumed to have been divinely sanctioned, if not divinely inspired. On the whole, as Lloyd Baugh points out, it is commonly assumed that 'These are two worlds that have little in common.'[33]

Furthermore, not only have few books been written on film by religious studies scholars,[34] but the limitations of the majority of those that have been written are all too apparent. For, until the last few years at any rate, books on the religious orientation of film have not only adopted a very narrow line of enquiry, construing as religious only those films which embrace a specifically religious agenda, but, broadly speaking, the underlying assumption is that only a 'highbrow' film can be truly religious. Consequently, the only films that tend to be taken into consideration as sites of religious significance are biblical epics and gospel stories, European films and established American classics, rather than more mainstream, popular and contemporary works. For example, in his chapter, 'Toward a theological interpretation and reading of film', in John May's *New Image of Religious Film*,[35] Joseph Marty argues that the cinema possesses a religious dimension insofar as it 'develops and enriches the human, awakening the living but forgotten forces of homo religiosus, and thus approaches a spiritual dimension',[36] while concentrating exclusively on the works of European and/or non-commerical directors such as Ingmar Bergman, Federico Fellini and Denys Arcand, whose self-consciously religious films – though renowned and critically acclaimed – are not indicative of the tastes and sensibilities of the majority of contemporary film audiences. Although cinema is capable of, in Marty's words, binding us 'with the poetic and religious expression of humanity',[37] and summoning and supporting elements that belong to the religious dimension that is innate in every person,[38] the absence of non-specifically religious films from his discussion would at least suggest that unless a film's content is explicitly religious then it is not amenable to a potential religious interpretation.[39]

Yet a film does not have to contain specifically religious material in order to be deemed religious. Indeed, it may be more appropriate to speak of the 'religious interpretation of film' than of the interpretation of religious film. Is not film a mirror of human experience, which attempts to deal, like religion, with questions pertaining to the meaning of human life? Consequently, to quote Michael Paul Gallagher, 'The theology that takes human history and human experience seriously is one that needs to embrace film as a privileged witness in today's culture.'[40] In his words, 'theology needs to be pushed out of its sacred enclosures, to plug itself into other languages and other forms of knowing', and to engage 'other questions than those that belong to its own territory'.[41] Even in seemingly non-religious films, therefore, despite the absence of a specifically or self-consciously religious agenda, the theologian should not overlook the possibility that a plethora of themes and imagery may be in existence which are at least amenable to a potential theological or religious reflection. The fact that a number of 1990s Hollywood films – including *Waterworld* (1995), *Twelve Monkeys* (1995), *Contact* (1997), *Deep Impact* (1998), *Armageddon* (1998) and *End of Days* (1999) – grappled with the theme of the apocalypse, and delineated the threat of the end of the world[42] (whether as the result of human, cosmic or even supernatural forces), could be interpreted as a sign that the medium is engaged, at least to some extent, in religious dialogue, and could even be said to be functioning religiously. At the very least, film may be said to have 'discovered and tapped into a secular, popular apocalyptic imagination that is prevalent in our contemporary culture',[43] such that, although some may claim that the forces of secularization have taken root in contemporary western society, this has demonstrably not resulted in the total eradication of religious consciousness.

Hence, in spite of the fact that many theologians may be inclined to view the popular media as something ultimately without depth and as unbefitting the attention of the theologian, popular films have come to be construed as possessing what Margaret Miles designates as a 'quasi-religious power'.[44] Recognition of this power can be seen in the fact that some film critics have recently encountered and examined in popular films such perennial religious themes as grace, forgiveness, alienation, the apocalypse and redemption, even though the *content* of such films is not explicitly religious. Examples of such religious themes in films which are not ostensibly religious in nature will form the bedrock of this book. While concurring, therefore, with John Hill's contention in his introduction to *The Oxford Guide to Film Studies* that the guide is liable 'to provoke thought and encourage debate, and to stimulate further research' in what amounts to 'a field in which a variety of approaches coalesce and compete and in which basic questions remain unsettled',[45] it is questionable, in light of the absence of any acknowledgement of the potential role played by religion in the study of film, that 'the result is a book which . . . successfully conveys the variety of ways in which film has been studied and the genuine debate that has characterized the field'.[46]

Rather, provided that there is no attempt to *impose* on films theological ways of thinking and talking and theological solutions, there is no reason why a proper dialogue between film studies and theology and religious studies should not be possible. On the part of theology, indeed, Carl Skrade is right to point out that there is 'something basically dishonest and unfruitful in any attempt to "use" . . . films as a propaganda device for mouthing warmed-over formulas'.[47] Joseph Marty comes perilously close to this position in his exclusively theological assertion that through the incarnation 'God is with us at every moment and in every place',[48] to the effect that the cinema is a potentially rich site of religious 'encounter and dialogue'[49] and 'sanctification',[50] where 'one must discern and await the annunciation of the Good News'.[51] At the same time, however, Marty's conclusion that 'the Catholic Church is not the only repository of the religious and the sacred'[52] is a much more tenable position, and is broadly compatible with my claim that, ultimately, the 'secular' medium of popular film may be seen to be performing a religious function in contemporary western culture by addressing and confronting fundamental issues and themes which are distinctively and quintessentially religious in form.

3
Models of redemption evident in film

Redemption and escapism

In terms of how the medium of film is able to be read as a site of
potential redemptive activity, the most obvious starting-point is a
consideration of those films of a fantasy and wish-fulfilment
persuasion which at least appear to offer redemption from the
present experience of suffering. Indeed, in a world imbued with
evil and suffering on many different levels, a number of theorists
have indicated that the 'fantastic' images presented on the screen
have the power to redeem and 'liberate the imagination from the
tedium'[1] of physical reality. For example, redemption could be
said to function through the Hollywood musicals of the 1930s and
1940s, which insert a certain energy and spontaneity into the
repetitiveness of everyday social reality, whether by means of Fred
Astaire's escape into the 'perfect' world of dance or Gene Kelly's
making the imperfect world more perfect by *making* it dance.[2] In
the context of poverty and the quest for capital at the time of the
Depression, furthermore, it is significant that *Gold Diggers of 1933*
(1933) features a 'show' on stage, which is presented 'as a
"solution" to the personal, Depression-induced problems of the
characters',[3] and – by extension – the problems of the audience
watching the film. The films of Frank Capra, John Ford and
Henry King also fit into this vein, in that 'the work of all three is
permeated by nostalgia for a vanished America, an idealized pre-
urban America, where a purer, better, freer way of life was lived'.[4]
Capra, in particular, diagnosed the cause of the American malaise
around the time of the Depression 'in the disappearance of good
neighbourliness', such that if one's 'friends rallied round and
people loved and helped one another'[5] then many of the tensions
and conflicts in contemporary American culture could be
resolved.

In more recent years, the films of Woody Allen frequently bear
witness to the power and magic of the cinema, and to the

possibility of redemption thereby achieved. In *Hannah and her Sisters* (1986), Allen plays a neurotic and hypochondriac character called Mickey who comes extremely close to committing suicide due to his inability to find the meaning in life, having consulted a number of religious and philosophical traditions for the answer. Needing 'a moment to gather my thoughts, and be logical, and put the world back into rational perspective', Mickey enters a movie house, where he finds himself watching the Marx Brothers' screwball comedy *Duck Soup* (1933), which he had seen and enjoyed 'many times in my life, since I was a kid'. Significantly, as he becomes increasingly engrossed in the picture, he explains in voice-over mode,

> And I started to feel how can you even think of killing yourself? I mean, isn't it so stupid? . . . look at all the people up there on the screen. You know, they're real funny, and what if the worst *is* true? What if there is no God, and you only go around once and that's it? Well . . . don't you want to be a part of the experience? And I'm thinking to myself . . . I should stop ruining my life searching for answers I'm never going to get, and just enjoy it while it lasts . . . And then, I started to sit back *and I actually began to enjoy myself.*

An experience of redemption could thus be said to be engendered in the cinema auditorium by the spectacle on the large, letterbox-shaped screen, in that the audience is given the opportunity to immerse – if not actually lose – itself in a fantasy and 'magical' experience, where powerfully stunning and spectacular images are exhibited. In this regard, as Joseph Marty attests,

> The spectator, comfortably seated in the dark, has his outer perceptions minimized while the screen comes to life and the sound wraps around him. His liberty and his consciousness are lulled because he is fascinated by the shadows, the lights, the rhythm, the actions or the passions presented.[6]

The process could be seen in terms of Bryant's understanding that 'the "stuff" of everyday life can be taken up and magically transformed' and that 'base metals are turned into gold'.[7] Indeed, the British film author and critic David Thomson even recollects in the first chapter of his book on *America in the Dark: Hollywood and the Gift of Unreality* to being 'mystified' in his youth by what he calls 'the serene persistence of film'.[8] He paints a bleak picture of

1940s London, where he grew up, which he refers to as being 'solid with construction tenement houses like matches in a box', where there were few large buildings besides the churches and in which 'the most glamorous places were the bus garages where the red monsters whose numbers I craved stewed the smell of rubber and petrol in the gloom . . . *except for the cinemas*'.[9]

In Thomson's words, the cinemas 'seemed exotic places', which – in contrast to the grey, anonymous sprawl surrounding them – 'were ornate, decorated and extravagant'.[10] Whereas the shops and businesses in his locale rarely changed ownership or line of business, and their window displays seemed 'locked in place and had not much "display" about them', he recalls that the cinemas were 'restless and volatile, lively yet unstable',[11] not only opening every day but remaining open after dark, 'twinkling with lights and turning the night into dark velvet'.[12] Referring to his young self as 'a shy but inquisitive intruder at the entrance tunnel to a hall of desirable things', and who designated the darkness of the cinema auditorium his 'secret garden',[13] Thomson evidently believes that the cinema broadened and matured his young imagination and facilitated his growth into adulthood. Moreover, the influence upon Thomson of the cinema was such that,

> I learned the pleasure of looking for the week's fresh posters, but I also found that, inside the cinemas, excitement with the movie I was about to see was surpassed by the raised expectations of the coming attractions. I always wanted it to be next week, and I see that it was in the cinema that I began to be discontent with now and immediate reality . . .[14]

It is especially significant that cinema had such a profound effect upon Thomson at a time when, as he indicates, 'the world did not seem religious'.[15] His testimony suggests that the cinema has the *capacity* to perform a functional equivalent to traditional religious activity, especially in the life of someone for whom traditional religious observances were not a prime influence.[16]

Redemption as the antithesis of escapism

Without disputing that the experience of watching an escapist film is theologically significant, this model of redemption, though persuasive, is open to a number of fundamental, pivotal objections. A religious dimension may be involved, but the efficacy of this model of 'redemption as escapism' is, I believe, seriously undermined by the fact that, within Christian theology, although a vast, and heterogeneous, range and variety of interpretations of redemption abound, at no point is this state identified as a realm of wish-fulfilment, magic or fantasy, where one can simply enter in order to escape the pressures and traumas of present existence on earth. Rather, whether it is identified as a this-worldly or other-worldly, individual or social, present or future, physical or spiritual, evolutionary or revolutionary phenomenon, redemption in the Christian tradition is understood to constitute a state or condition of existence that can be attained only after a person has made a fundamental and decisive break with their past lives, and, specifically, entered into a new covenant, or relationship, with God, by means of the incarnation of Jesus Christ. While the cinema is undoubtedly a vehicle that has the capacity to engender a transformation in the quality of human existence – as the testimony of David Thomson, M. Darroll Bryant and Woody Allen has convincingly evinced – the specifically *redemptive* orientation of such a transformation is much less certain. 'Base metals' may be 'turned into gold' as a consequence of watching a film, but this is a qualitatively, and ontologically, distinct experience to, say, that of receiving what the Fourth Evangelist identifies as the 'bread of life'[17] and the 'living water',[18] whereby, according to Christ in John 6: 35, 'he who comes to me shall not hunger, and he who believes in me shall never thirst'.

If there is a redemptive dimension to the medium of film, then such a process must ultimately entail a transformation in the nature and quality of existence of the most radical and rudimentary kind, analogous in essence to the redemption that the Christian scriptures believe is possible through Christ, and must not consist of a merely transitory and ephemeral experience, in the manner of Hollywood escapism. In contradistinction to the transformative experience of redemption that is intrinsic to the Christian faith, Hollywood film is often little more than 'superficial, stereotyped' and, ultimately, 'dishonest'[19] in the way it understands the human personality, a point further attested by Hortense Powdermaker who, in 1950, wrote that no one in Hollywood is interested in 'the reality of emotions and with truthfulness of meaning'.[20] Rather, in Powdermaker's words,

Man, according to Hollywood, is either completely good, or bad. His personality is static, rarely showing any development either in growth or in regression. The villain is a black-eyed sinner who can do no good and who cannot be saved; while the hero is a glamorous being, who can do no wrong of his own volition, and who is always rewarded.[21]

Although Powdermaker's analysis is too general and simplistic in nature to function as an accurate critique of every single motion picture produced by Hollywood – not every Hollywood film is as intellectually unsatisfying as her analysis would suggest – her broad argument does convey a certain resonance. For, what is clearly missing in so much of Hollywood cinema is 'a realistic concept of the human personality, a complex being who can love and hate' and 'who has human frailties and virtues'.[22] In contradistinction to the Christian understanding of humankind as essentially fallen and estranged in nature, a certain deception and illusion may be seen to prevail in the world of Hollywood cinema, wherein only the exceptional film attempts to portray 'real human beings living in a complicated world',[23] and whose overwhelming output is said by Maltby to be no more than 'banal, repetitive, and predictable'.[24]

Redemption as the antithesis of escapism: an illustration

One example of a film whose escapist sensibility may be seen to present obvious difficulties from a theological point of view is Woody Allen's *Hannah and her Sisters*. Indeed, on the surface at any rate, Allen's film would seem to bear out the notion, posited at the beginning of this chapter, that the 'magic' of cinema has an especially redemptive quality. As Mickey's voice-over explains, the experience of watching *Duck Soup* in a movie house one afternoon set his imagination free from the burdens and afflictions of existence that had earlier prompted him to attempt suicide. However, with regard to the upbeat ending of *Hannah* – in which Mickey subsequently settles down with a compatible partner (Dianne Wiest) and learns, contrary to earlier medical information, that he is able to become a father – it is claimed that Woody Allen 'was not happy' with this part of the film, on the grounds that 'life never worked out as neatly for people as that'.[25] In the original script for the film, the 'benign'[26] or – as some critics perceived – 'fairy tale' ending[27] was missing, in favour of a more ambiguous conclusion, in which the various romantic and psychological upheavals and entanglements of a middle-class Manhattan family spread over the course of three Thanksgiving festivals are not altogether resolved. As a consequence of the 'more benign ending' which was subsequently added, Allen has spoken in interviews of his dissatisfaction with the end product, and has tended to speak ambivalently about the picture, even to dismiss its artistic merits.[28] In a similar vein, Martin Scorsese has conceded that the relatively 'happy' ending of his commercially successful film, *The Color of Money* (1986), can have the effect of cheating audiences as much as exciting them. For, in delineating 'easy' emotions – the protagonist Eddie Felson's (Paul Newman) triumphant announcement at the end, 'I'm back', is, as Keyser attests, more on a par with E.T.'s voyage home, Rocky's victorious call to Adrian and Indiana Jones's inevitable triumphs than with the more complex 'resolutions' of his other pictures – Scorsese acknowledges that they are to some extent being *shortchanged*.[29]

Moreover, as Woody Allen implicitly recognizes with regard to many of his contemporaries who grew up during the so-called Golden Age of Cinema, and who are still immensely affected and influenced by the films they watched in their youth, there is a profound *danger* in many fantasy and escapist films. For, as he explains with reference to such a picture as *Yankee Doodle Dandy* (1942), through which

> you would leave your poor house behind and all your problems with
> school and family, [where] they would have penthouses and white
> telephones and the women were lovely and the men always had an
> appropriate witticism to say and things . . . always turned out well[30]

he knows many people of his age who have

> never been able to shake it, who've had trouble in their lives because of
> it, because they still – in advanced stages of their lives, still in their 50s
> and 60s – can't understand why it doesn't work that way, why
> everything that they grew up believing and feeling and wishing for and
> thinking was reality was not true and that reality is much harsher and
> uglier than that.[31]

A similar consideration is implicitly espoused by Margaret Miles in her examination of *Seeing and Believing: Religion and Values in the Movies*, in which she points out that, in seeing her first movie, *The Glenn Miller Story* (1953), at the age of seventeen, she had 'a riveting experience'[32] and that 'a new world was opened to me. In the world of the movies people did and said daring things, looking beautiful all the while, and confident, somehow, that everything would come right in the end.'[33] Miles concludes her recollection of this experience, however, with the qualification that 'It has taken me forty years to put the movies in perspective.'[34] If, indeed, the effect of a film is, to quote David John Graham, 'only to make us come out feeling nice and agreeing with what we have seen', then, as a corollary, there is a danger that, in the long run at least, 'our horizons' will not have been 'expanded',[35] and a dichotomy will have been set up between the fictional world of film and the empirical world of everyday reality.

Woody Allen dramatizes this conflict between the fantasy and fairy-tale ethos of Hollywood cinema and the potentially harmful effects of such films upon the film audience in his 1985 picture *The Purple Rose of Cairo*. The film's protagonist, Cecilia (Mia Farrow), is a waitress living at the time of the Great Depression, whose husband, Monk (Danny Aiello), is unemployed, indolent and inclined to hit her, to drink heavily and to fraternize with other women. Ultimately, as Girgus points out, 'Cecilia's story in this world leaves little room for anything besides pathos, loneliness, and despair.'[36] However, there is one source of joy in her otherwise unfulfilled life, which comes from frequenting her local movie house. Indeed, Hollywood could even be said to function 'as a substitute for her miserable life'.[37] As demonstrated by her intimate knowledge of the lives of Hollywood stars and details pertaining to their films, which she reveals in conversation with her sister in the diner in which she works, Girgus suggests that Cecilia possesses 'a nearly pathological fixation on a world of escapist fantasy'.[38] After watching the same picture, 'The Purple Rose of Cairo', on at least five consecutive screenings, a character from the film, 'Tom Baxter' (Jeff Daniels), literally walks out from the screen in order to join Cecilia in the 'real' world. Not surprisingly, in view of her infatuation with Hollywood, she falls in love with Tom and his 'perfection'. Nevertheless, when 'Gil Shephard' (Jeff Daniels), the actor who plays Tom Baxter, arrives on the scene, Cecilia manages, at least temporarily, to forget her own dependence on the fictional world of Hollywood films, and to choose Gil over Tom, explaining to the latter, 'See, I'm a real person. No matter how . . . tempted I am, I have to choose the real world'. A realization that the world of Hollywood cinema is ultimately second-best to the empirical world goes some way towards presenting a critique of the false and deluded hopes that such films commonly impart.

On a deeper level, however, rather than opting for the 'real world', in choosing Gil over Tom there is still a sense in which Cecilia is choosing 'the epitome of the unreal',[39] insofar as Gil's profession consists in the making and selling of *dreams*. The illusory nature of the world Gil inhabits is borne out by his abrupt decision to return to Hollywood 'to project dreams onto the screen for others'[40] in lieu of keeping an appointment with Cecilia, thereby leaving her, once again, alone and dejected. Even so, in spite of having experienced at first hand the transitory and illusory nature of Hollywood, Cecilia in the final scene is observed seeking escape and solace from the misery of her world – to which the cinema's false hopes and dreams have in no small measure contributed – by once again attending the local movie house and immersing herself in a Hollywood musical. Hence, as Commins perceives, while Cecilia listens to Fred Astaire singing 'I'm in heaven', in a scene from *Top Hat* (1935), she sits, correspondingly, in her own personal 'hell'.[41] The notion that any 'personal liberation' or redemption can feasibly be offered by Hollywood films is thus 'sheer fantasy'[42] as far as Cecilia's life is concerned – her inability to recognize this only exacerbating the illusion – and there is, if anything, a substantial degree to which the false and deluded hopes they have the potential to engender embody, rather, the *antithesis* of redemption.

In a comparable manner, when, in *It's a Wonderful Life* (1946), the film's protagonist is driven to the point of suicide by the financial ruin that befalls his small, family loan firm – and the subsequent, wrongful charge of fraud – redemption would *appear* to be in operation when an angel intervenes and reveals to him how differently his small Massachusetts town would have turned out had he never existed. For George Bailey (James Stewart) comes to regain his optimism upon learning that, if it had not been for him, his brother would have drowned many years ago, since he would not have been around to save him; the local, good-hearted pharmacist would be rotting in gaol because he was not there to prevent him from inadvertently mixing in poison while preparing a prescription; his wife would have become a lone, despairing old maid; and his father's small loan society would be in the hands of Potter (Lionel Barrymore), the unscrupulous local magnate. However, in actuality, it is apparent that the 'alternative' America he encounters in this nightmare scenario is a substantially accurate and authentic representation of contemporary America, in that, as Žižek indicates, the features of the bursting, violent small town, populated by rude drunkards and noisy nightclubs, and whose communal solidarity has dissolved, 'are those of the contemporary grim social reality'.[43] In short, the nightmare vision he experiences is not unlike 'a vision of the *noir* city'.[44] Consequently, Bailey's realization that this life is 'wonderful' after all, as delineated by the film's 'roaringly sentimental resolution'[45] in which his benevolent friends and neighbours rejoice around a piano – thereby suturing him 'back into the community after his spell in a wilderness of self-doubt'[46] – could be said to constitute a fabrication of reality, which belies actual human experience in which goodness often goes unrewarded and injustice prevails. The film's message would thus appear to be that life is not as inauspicious as George Bailey initially believed, and yet his 'rebirth'[47] is only achieved when the director, Frank Capra, engages in 'a nostalgic fantasy of the "eternal" American community',[48] drawing upon a representation not of the 'twentieth century American town'[49] but of an idealized 'Golden Age', wherein the 'small-town and the individual's place within it'[50] is sanctified. As Krutnik attests, however, such a vision 'was no viable model for mapping the complex social landscape of postwar America',[51] in which – unlike Capra's 'hero' – not everyone had somewhere secure and hospitable in which to return.

It is most ironic, therefore, that some forty years after making *It's a Wonderful Life*, Capra believed that 'The gloom of the world is but a shadow. Behind it, yet within reach, is joy. There is a radiance and glory in the darkness, could we but see, and to see we have only to look. I beseech you to look!'[52] As Stephen Brown indicates, Capra's aim had been to capture on screen the innate beauty, extraordinariness and, ultimately, the 'magic' of existence, which he believed any reasoning person could infer from simply observing the world. In this regard, it is appropriate that the film's opening shot is of snow descending beautifully over Bedford Falls, followed by a pan upward to the heavens where the stars, in the infinity of space, look gently down on God's creation.[53] As the anonymous poem, *Desiderata*, which is often associated with Capra's picture, affirms, 'with all its sham, drudgery and broken dreams, it is still a beautiful world'.[54] Such a depiction may of course be seen to tie in with the classical teleological argument for the existence of God, wherein the assumption is made that the regularity, intricacy and perfect interrelationships of nature – in essence, the evidence of design – proves that there must exist a Designer, and who, by inference, is the God of classical Christian theology. In William Paley's words, indeed, 'There cannot be design without a designer', and 'arrangement, disposition of parts, subserviency of means to an end' and the 'relation of instruments to a use imply the presence of intelligence and mind'.[55] The world, according to Paley, is, in effect, a vast machine, and consists of 'infinitely complex parts, each working for the well-being of the whole'.[56] Hence, rather than an indifferent, even hostile, universe, of the kind which led George Bailey to attempt suicide as a means of escaping the anguish and misery of existence, Capra attempts to convey in *It's a Wonderful Life* that the goodness of God can be 'read off' and inferred from the perfect design of the cosmos. Although Bailey needs to have an angel, Clarence (Henry Travers), sent to him in order for him to realize the intrinsic goodness of God's creation, there is nevertheless a sense in which Clarence performs the function of enabling the *audience* to bear witness to God's beautiful handiwork by encouraging us, as Brown discerns, to look 'properly at our world',[57] and so to come to an affirmation that 'It's a Wonderful Life' after all.

In actuality, however, there are a number of fundamental difficulties with Paley's and, by inference, Capra's hypothesis. Indeed, some twenty-three years before Paley's *Natural Theology* was published in 1802, David Hume had put forward a fervent critique of the design argument, in which he cast doubt on the assumption that the world has been created by a god – let alone the providential, all-loving deity of Capra's imagination – on the grounds that 'we have no direct experience either of other worlds or world-designers',[58] and so are in no position to assert that the world has been *made*, in the manner of an artefact, rather than simply evolved into being, in the manner of a vegetable. Indeed, knowledge of God, to which Capra suggests we can readily adhere, 'could only be established', to use Heron's words, 'if either God himself were immediately accessible to our awareness' – which in the 'closed' world of modern science he is not – 'or "God" were a category demonstrably necessary, like those of space and time, to the ordering and shaping of our understanding',[59] which again is not the case. Are there not, moreover, what David Hume construes as 'many inexplicable difficulties in the works of nature',[60] which Capra's talk of the 'magic', beauty and extraordinary design of the world fundamentally overlooks? To quote Hume, this world, for all one knows, 'is very faulty and imperfect, compared to a superior standard, and was only the first rude essay of some infant deity who afterwards abandoned it, ashamed of his lame performance'.[61] Serious problems are thus raised by Capra's simple assumption that 'ultimate reality, being under the control of good rather than evil, supports, if not guarantees'[62] the ability of humankind to undergo an improvement in its condition, once the beauty and majesty of God's creation have been recognized and understood, to the effect that, as Brown attests, Bedford Falls may be seen to constitute, on Capra's interpretation, 'an optimistic paradigm of the Kingdom of God'.[63] Rather, in actuality, *It's a Wonderful Life*, in its emphatic avowal that things can be better in this life, bears witness to a naive theological interpretation of redemption.

That the optimistic, life-affirming spirit of Capra's *It's a Wonderful Life* is not amenable to a viable redemptive interpretation was even implicitly acknowledged by Capra himself in later years, as Capra's cinematic vision became increasingly bleaker in nature. Whereas in the 1930s the inference in Capra's films was that 'if enough moral people arose then they would form a power structure capable of converting immoral society'[64] – as reflected by the narratives of *Mr Smith Goes to Washington* (1939), *Mr Deeds Goes to Town* (1936) and *Meet John Doe* (1941), wherein the power of one lowly, unintimidated person against corporate cynicism wins the day – even by the time of *It's a Wonderful Life* it is less manifest that 'wrong' deeds, if exposed, will be righted. When, for instance, there is a run on the bank, the immediate response among George Bailey's customers is to demand their money back, and the threat posed by Potter is not diminished. Indeed, as Jonathan Romney points out, in an article in *Sight and Sound*, 'Potter, who still has the mislaid $8,000, remains undefeated', and so the film concludes 'with a strange, unarticulated sense of incompletion'.[65] If there are any transformations in the quality of human behaviour, they are no more than tentative and transitory in essence. Rather, redemption, if it comes at all, can only be seen to function if it is imposed from the outside. Brown concludes his discussion of *It's a Wonderful Life* by remarking that 'Humans cannot effect their own transformation by themselves. This present life can only be wonderful if we believe in God's promise through the risen Christ to be with us to the end of time, working with us.'[66] Contrary to the spirit of Capra's films, therefore, it came to be recognized that a propensity for good moral conduct, and the showing of benevolence towards one's fellow human beings, would not by itself usher in the Kingdom of Heaven on earth.

As Romney attests, *It's a Wonderful Life* even seemed to be something of an anachronism in its own day, with contemporary newspaper and magazine critics such as Bosley Crowther of the *New York Times* dismissing the picture as 'a figment of simple Polyanna platitudes'.[67] In terms of its box office takings, further, Romney points out that Capra's film was 'eclipsed . . . by a far more sober anatomy of America's mood after World War Two',[68] namely, William Wyler's *The Best Years of our Lives* (1946). Even James Stewart, the actor who played George Bailey, came to 'doubt the value of such flippant films', to the extent that 'he considered quitting'[69] his profession, following his work leading bombing raids over Germany in the Second World War. Stewart's recognition of the problems inherent in such escapist pictures thus resulted in his tendency to 'take darker roles'[70] in subsequent years, as reflected in his performances in the psychological thrillers of Alfred Hitchcock,[71] and psychological Westerns of Anthony Mann.[72]

Inevitably, for some – even for most – audiences, it may well be the case that, to use Richard Maltby's term, 'Hollywood seduces us'[73] and that the movie theatre continues to function as 'a place where we are encouraged to accept the fantasies we see in front of us'[74] as a substitute for the reality of the empirical world in which we live. After all, film is open to multiple readings, and audiences will, invariably, read the same 'text' in a variety of ways. Films indubitably serve an important function in contemporary society, but they are simply not treated by most audiences as carriers and conveyors of religious possibility. Rather, films are part of the international *entertainment* industry, with so-called 'blockbuster' films in particular competing for global marketing shares alongside soft drinks, sportswear and popular music, often within the same commercial, multinational enterprise.[75] Their ostensive aim, in short, is to entertain audiences, and make money. As Nick Roddick acknowledges, in his review of the contemporary state of British cinema, in the December 1998 edition of *Sight and Sound*, 'The concept of film as a mass-audience form – as something made for a multiplex – is where we are: culturally, economically and aspirationally.'[76] Some films may not stand up to intellectual or theological scrutiny, but they were never conceived with that function in mind. Rather, the experience of watching a film at the cinema is, in Maltby's words, simply

> an alternative leisure-time experience to eating at a restaurant or spending an evening with friends in a bar or a pub. Like food or drink . . . the entertainment of 'going to the movies' is a transient experience; when we finish consuming a movie, we have only a ticket stub to show for our transaction.[77]

It could therefore be said that, given its function as a primarily escapist and entertainment medium, to study the medium of film from an academic perspective 'is to perform a perverse, unnatural act'[78] insofar as 'it involves reading movies "against the grain" of their declared absence of seriousness'.[79]

Nevertheless, without seeking to dismiss the fact that the success and popularity of a film can depend in large part on the degree to which the audience is not required to think too heavily, and that an escapist film can actually perform a positive, rather than a *detrimental*, function on this basis, on a theological level, *vis-à-vis* the concept of redemption, such films *do*, however, pose considerable difficulties. As a brief overview of the films of Frank Capra and the testimony of Woody Allen have illustrated, while films *may* be read as models of escapist activity, it remains the case – albeit the minority case – that their ultimate value and beneficence have not been taken for granted by film makers and spectators, and it is here, I believe, that a viable redemptive interpretation of film becomes possible. In many cases, moreover, films which work 'against the grain' of the sugar-coated fantasy, escapist ethos of Hollywood cinema do actually perform well at the box office, and may even turn in a sizeable profit for the studio that produced them, as a number of recent films have demonstrated which bear witness to a number of discernible religious themes and insights, among them *The Last Temptation of Christ* (1988), *Schindler's List* (1993) and *Seven* (1995). There is at least a market, therefore, for serious, controversial and thought-provoking films in today's cinema, which, while not automatically opening up such films to a *redemptive* interpretation, certainly goes some way towards indicating that film cannot simply be categorized – or, indeed, dismissed – as an expressly *entertainment* and *escapist* medium, wherein the possibility of redemption is lacking. The fact that *Schindler's List* was directed by Steven Spielberg, the director of *Raiders of the Lost Ark* (1981), *E. T. the Extra-Terrestrial* (1982) and *Jurassic Park* (1993) best illustrates this point.[80]

Of course, while escapist films do not constitute the most felicitous site of redemptive activity, it does not thereby follow that redemption is any more applicable to other categories and genres of film, many of which might, at first sight at least, appear to be *devoid* of redemption due to their portrayal of, at worst, *hostile* and, at best, *ambiguous* worlds. Upon thorough scrutiny, however, I aim to establish that, despite the apparent paradox, there is a powerful sense in which a process of redemption analogous to that located in Christian theology is operative through the downbeat and pessimistic complexion of films – so-called *films noirs* – that, since the Second World War in particular, have come to form an integral part of contemporary American cinema. For this to be so, an attempt must, of course, be made to overcome the quite serious problem of how a theological concept – a complex and heterogeneous one at that – such as redemption, which has particular historical and doctrinal connotations, can be applied to this category of films in a way that is any more feasible and effective than that of the escapist body of films that has so far characterized this discussion, and in relation to which a redemptive reading has proven to be so unsuitable. Whether such *films noirs* emanate from the studio system, as part of a strictly commercial enterprise, or, as is increasingly common, as part of an independent, more personal aesthetic, I will examine the extent to which there is a tenable and legitimate correlation between the characteristically alienated and fatalistic landscape of such films and many of the insights and precepts pertaining to the concept of redemption as adduced within the Christian tradition.

4

Film noir *as a repository of theological significance*

A definition of *film noir*

While escapist films are not, strictly speaking, open to a redemptive reading by virtue of their fantasy and wish-fulfilment sensibility, *film noir* is susceptible to a very different kind of interpretation. Scholars are often in disagreement as to how to define *film noir*, in that some see it as a distinctive film genre in its own right, while for others *noir* is simply an umbrella term which encompasses films of diverse genres, such as the thriller, the melodrama, the gangster film and even the Western, that share a number of underlying, core characteristics.[1] For the purpose of this discussion, what clearly distinguishes *film noir* from films of an escapist persuasion is the challenge that such films present to the optimistic, life-affirming and 'magical' spirit of traditional Hollywood cinema. In the 1920s and 1930s Hollywood was accustomed to producing musicals and romantic comedies with their utopian and optimistic sentiments, through which audiences were given the opportunity to 'escape' the social problems of the day. By the 1940s, however, the output of films in American cinema was increasingly, and conspicuously, characterized by a markedly less contrived and artificial ethos, to the point of denoting a significant break from the 'enforced optimism'[2] and 'frothy romanticism at which Hollywood used to be so adept'.[3] It is within this landscape that *film noir* arose.

While this departure was especially acute in Hollywood, the trend was also discernible in Europe. In the Depression-hit Weimar Republic in the 1930s, for instance, although there was undoubtedly a 'constant desire' through films 'to be entertained, to escape to far-away ages, to distant countries or to a better future',[4] there also emerged such bleak and socially realistic films as Fritz Lang's *M* (1933), which concerns the quest for a psychopathic serial killer around the streets of Berlin. At the end of the

1940s and by the early 1950s cynicism and gloom could be said to *typify* the films being produced, especially in Hollywood, as indicated by the tendency of the lighting in films to grow darker, the characters to become more corrupt and the narratives more fatalistic and hopeless.[5] Cinema audiences bore witness to 'haunted visions of doomed men and women for whom love is replaced by blind passion and sexual obsession, which often erupts into violence and cold-blooded murder.'[6] In depicting on the screen a world of 'dark, slick city streets', of 'crime and corruption',[7] where claustrophobia, destruction and evil prevail, Nino Frank and other French film critics – who had missed American films during the Second World War – subsequently gave birth to the term *film noir* in 1946 to refer to this unprecedented trend in contemporary culture.

It is conspicuous from the outset that a parallel can be drawn between the chaotic and disordered world delineated in such *films noirs* and some of the core themes of Christian theology. Whereas escapist cinema may be seen to constitute a theologically uncreative and inadequate site of redemptive possibility, insofar as it can do no more than facilitate a momentary and hollow transformation *from* 'the unevenness and turmoil and fragmentariness'[8] that characterizes human existence, *film noir* entails no such difficulty. Rather, in contrast to the superficiality – even the inauthenticity – of escapism, *film noir* may be seen to engage in a highly focused and theologically constructive fashion with the estranged, disaffected, despairing and fragmentary quality of human existence *from which* – and, indeed, as I will demonstrate in detail, *within and through which* - redemption can ever be a possibility. Without going so far as to suggest that *films noirs* are produced with a conscious and deliberate theological agenda in mind – indeed, it would be fallacious to suppose that *noir* was anything more than 'an innocent, unconscious cinematic reaction to the popular culture of its time'[9] – there is no doubt that *films noirs* do bear witness, whether consciously or unconsciously from the point of view of their creators, to a plethora of religious themes and insights within the context of which redemption can be seen to play a vital and pivotal role in Christian theology.

Redemption realized: traditional theological themes in *film noir*

The basis to *film noir*'s redemptive sensibility can be traced back to the teaching of St Paul, according to whom the present, imperfect world-order can be accounted for by reference to original sin. In Romans 5, Paul explains, 'Therefore as sin came into the world through one man and death through sin . . . so death spread to all men because all men sinned . . . death reigned from Adam to Moses . . . one man's trespass led to condemnation for all men . . .'[10] Adam's sin and subsequent spiritual death have thus been inherited by all humans from generation to generation. Indeed, as Augustine points out, 'for by [Adam and Eve] so great a sin was committed, that by it the human nature was altered for the worse, and was transmitted to their posterity, liable to sin and subject to death'.[11] Even though future generations were unborn and thus did not directly participate in Adam's sin, Augustine holds that all human beings are present in the loins of Adam, and so, to quote Henry Chadwick, the entire human race, 'before ever committing any separate sins of their own, before even entering the world, were guilty sinners and as such were under just sentence of death'.[12] Human history, in short, amounts to the story of a continual degradation, from which, in Augustine's words, 'no can can escape without the toll of toils and tears and fears'.[13]

Significantly, the world delineated in *film noir* bears witness to the corrupt and depraved analysis of the human condition adduced by Augustine: though physically alive, humanity is, by nature, spiritually dead and in slavery to sin.[14] Indeed, it is apparent that the principal characters in *films noirs* are men and women who habitually do not – indeed, cannot – lead safe, 'ordinary' lives in a secure world. In *White Heat* (1949), for instance, James Cagney plays a gang leader, Cody Jarrett, who is 'unbalanced, violent and unpredictable', and even 'a mystery to his own gang'.[15] Moreover, as Thomson attests, 'there is not a reliable or healthy human relationship in the film', but characters are instead 'restlessly vicious and untrustworthy', and predilected towards disaster and death, which comes as 'the only release from psychopathy and grotesque hopes of success'.[16] In many *films noirs* the protagonist is plunged into the hazards and dangers of the *noir* world as a consequence of some meeting or event which is often accidental and the result of chance.[17] In *Kiss Me Deadly* (1955), the protagonist, Mike Hammer (Ralph Meeker), searches for the killers of a beautiful woman he only briefly met – having picked her up in his car upon finding her running down the middle of a road – and becomes caught up in 'a typically *noir* web of corruption and deceit'.[18] In the course of the film he is rendered unconscious several times, kidnapped and even pushed over a cliff. Most of the characters are not what they seem, as deception, lies and cheating are commonplace, and 'all are capable of any extremes, even murder, to achieve their aims'.[19]

According to Martin Luther, moreover, the Fall represents a descent from a human to a sub-human level, such that each individual human being is so enmeshed in, and corrupted by, sin that he or she is constitutionally incapable of forming reliable, and sound, ethical judgements.[20] Consequently, it is significant that an aura of moral ambiguity characteristically pervades the narratives of *films noirs*, as illustrated by Howard Hawks's *The Big Sleep* (1946) which, based on the novel by Raymond Chandler, presents a series of interconnected mysteries in which private eye Philip Marlowe (Humphrey Bogart) becomes embroiled. The film begins with an investigation into blackmail, but is at times frustrating and even impossible for the audience to follow due to the ambiguities and double-crossing of the characters, and the numerous twists and turns and absence of resolution in the plot. While filming the sequence in which one of the characters – Owen Taylor, a chauffeur – is pulled out of the water, Humphrey Bogart allegedly asked the film's director who had killed him, who in turn asked the screenwriter, William Faulkner, because he did not know. When Faulkner could not answer the question, Hawks telegraphed Raymond Chandler, who reportedly replied, 'How should I know? You figure it out.'[21] Such an absence of resolution and clarity in the film's narrative does not, however, impair the essence of the film for, as David Thomson points out, the audience will be conscious when watching it that 'menace and treachery beset this world'[22] – as illustrated by the way 'shadow crowds in on every frame'[23] – such that this is a world in which nothing is clear-cut, and in which it would be unrealistic for everything to be resolved at the end. In the words of Foster Hirsch, indeed, whether or not the story of who killed the Sternwood chauffeur is apocryphal is really beside the point, for it is true in spirit if not in fact: the story of *The Big Sleep* is very hard to follow. Propelled by a series of criss-crosses, double-crosses, betrayals, deceptions, *noir* stories like *The Big Sleep* deliberately try to be knotted and sinuous.[24]

Such is the moral ambiguity of the *noir* universe, further, in keeping with Luther's intrinsic mistrust of human moral decision-making, that fundamental human questions pertaining to innocence and guilt, reward and punishment, are shown to be merely a matter of circumstance and randomness. The 1958 film *I Want to Live!*, for example, features a female protagonist, Barbara Graham (Susan Hayward), who is accused of a murder she could not have committed because she is left-handed. This evidence is disallowed at her appeal because it was already present at her trial, albeit mishandled by her incompetent lawyer.[25] In Tuska's words, the film 'shows how a combination of accidental events combined with a corrupt milieu can destroy a human being'.[26] Further, in Alfred Hitchcock's *The Wrong Man* (1956),[27] a similar miscarriage of justice occurs, in that the character played by Henry Fonda is mistakenly accused of robbing an insurance office.[28] He is set free when the real criminal is caught, but by this time his wife has lost her sanity due to the pressure on the family. In depicting the 'near destruction of a man through a merciless quirk of fate' – namely, a spelling mistake made by the protagonist that is identical to one made by the real criminal, and which implicates him in the crime – and 'the actual destruction of his more fragile wife',[29] the film can be seen to describe 'a cruel and uncaring universe'.[30] Indeed, *film noir* thus displays 'the injustice, and perhaps ultimately the irrationality, of a certain principle operative in life over which men and women have no real control'.[31]

In terms of Augustine's understanding that the destination of humanity, being depraved and prone to sin, is eternal damnation, it is salient that an all-encompassing fatalism lies at the heart of *films noirs*, whereby no matter how hard they may try the characters cannot escape their pasts, nor plan their futures.[32] In such films as *Laura* (1944), *Double Indemnity* (1944) and *The Postman Always Rings Twice* (1946), there is a prevailing sense of 'an irretrievable past, a predetermined fate and an all-enveloping hopelessness'.[33] In the words of the protagonist in the 1946 film, *Detour*, 'Someday, fate or some mysterious force can put the finger on you or me for no reason at all', and 'whichever way you turn, Fate sticks out its foot to trip you'. In *Double Indemnity*, this theme is most notably symbolized by 'the play of shadows on the light-coloured walls'[34] of the home of Phyllis Dietrichson (Barbara Stanwyck), as she descends her staircase to meet insurance salesman Walter Neff (Fred MacMurray). According to Crowther, this image 'foretells their eventual fate',[35] in which they wind up murdering each other. The theme of fatalism also pervades *Out of the Past* (1947), where the protagonist, Jeff Bailey (Robert Mitchum), 'can only take pleasure in reliving a doomed past'[36] because there is no hope for the future. Indeed, according to Schrader, the *noir* protagonist dreads to look ahead, and tries to live for the day – and if that is unsuccessful he has little option but to retreat into the past.[37] This is further exemplified in *Kiss Me Deadly* where the nightmare world in which Mike Hammer becomes enmeshed 'simultaneously mirrors past brutalities while offering a disturbing foretaste of disasters yet to come'.[38] In short, the *noir* world amounts to a chaos world in which the protagonist is destined to journey inexorably on 'a downward path to a miserable death or annihilating despair'.[39]

Although gangster and crime films had existed prior to the development of *film noir* in the 1940s, the difference between the seediness and criminality of such films and the world embodied in *noir* is that the former largely reflected the American Dream, insofar as they depicted young men rising to wealth and fame, albeit by illegal means.[40] Indeed, as John Gabree explains, the 'movie' gangster 'achieves many of the goals – power, money, fame, status – that are held out by society as symbols of success'.[41] He is pictured as vanquishing his enemies and overcoming often incredible odds to come out on top, while managing to retain an energy, dedication and dexterity that, at the very least, 'make us admire him', and 'in some films even love him'.[42] Even if he was eventually defeated – on the grounds that, as the censors wanted to inculcate, 'crime does not pay'[43] – he was nonetheless a figure of vitality and enterprise, arguably offering a certain vicarious satisfaction to disillusioned Depression audiences.[44] In *film noir*, in marked contrast, grim failure underlies most endeavours, with the *noir* protagonist presented as 'resolutely small-scale, unheroic' and 'defeatist',[45] to the effect that *films noirs* could be said to embody the antithesis of the American Dream.

A reinterpretation of Christian thought: post-Enlightenment theology and *noir*

Integral though the concept of original sin, and the concomitant understanding of humanity as wholly depraved and predilected towards failure, is in Christian theology, it is apparent that the period since the Enlightenment has witnessed a shift in emphasis in the way that the concept has been understood. The basis to this development is the transformation in consciousness at the time of the Enlightenment from faith to reason, whereby, in trying to come to terms with the complexities of human existence and purpose, many traditional doctrines – among them original sin, as understood by Augustine and Luther – came to be reinterpreted in the name of historical and scientific objectivity. Indeed, according to Immanuel Kant, the fact that human beings have a propensity towards evil undeniably shows that there must be some state of goodness from which we have 'fallen'. Kant affirms, however, that such a penchant for evil *cannot* be the result of a natural defect since that would destroy the faculty of human moral responsibility. If sin is construed, as in Augustine's terms, as the consequence of original sin, Kant attests that this thereby removes responsibility for evil behaviour from ourselves, and places it instead on our ancestors. Ultimately, for Kant, 'through no cause in the world' can one 'cease to be a freely acting being'.[46] 'Sin' must therefore be understood as the result of a *free* and conscious individual human decision to act against, or violate, what he defines as the moral law of the universe – which dwells in our conscience and which he construes as a reflection of the divine law – and which it is our moral duty and responsibility to emulate.[47]

Hence, rather than having a temporal origin in the progenitors of the human race, original sin has been redefined by Kant as a quality emanating from within each *individual* human being. On this interpretation, humankind is 'fallen', and liable to sin, as a consequence of the fact that although each individual person *actually* exists in an immature and imperfect state, all human beings possess, and have been created with, an innate *capacity* for goodness. According to Friedrich Schleiermacher, further, sin is shaped by our environment and not only our heredity, and is characterized by our human tendency to be overcome by sensuality and worldly desires, the effect of which is to impede our latent potentiality to develop a full *God*-consciousness. Through what amounts, rather, to an evolving *self*-consciousness, we have a *propensity* towards sin. The ultimate manifestation of such a condition is in the form of 'man's' *alienation* from 'the ground of his being', a hypothesis espoused by Paul Tillich. In the second volume of his *Systematic Theology*, Tillich attests that 'creation is good in its essential character', but that, through each individual's alienation from his or her essential condition, 'the state of existence is the state of estrangement'.[48] In his words, 'Existence is estrangement and not reconciliation . . . It is the process in which man becomes a thing and ceases to be a person . . . The existence of the individual is filled with anxiety and threatened by meaninglessness.'[49] Likewise, for Hegel, history itself could be regarded as the history of humankind's alienation, wherein 'man' is in conflict with his nature and estranged from other humans as well as from his own essence and end. Our history on this earth is thereby a chronicle of misery and suffering.[50]

It is thus significant that in *film noir* an especially fertile repository of such recognizably religious reflections and themes pertaining to the alienated and estranged condition of humanity may be discerned. Primarily, as Place and Peterson observe, the cinematography in *film noir* consists of small areas of light which seem to be 'on the verge of being completely overwhelmed by the darkness that threatens them from all sides'.[51] In a style that tends to unsettle and even disorientate the viewer it is common to see 'bizarre, off-angle compositions of figures placed irregularly in the frame', with the result that a world is created which is 'never stable or safe', and which is 'always threatening to change drastically and unexpectedly'.[52] The visual images are often of rain-lashed urban streets, fog-bound runways and empty, echoing city buildings.[53] Even if a scene in the film is set in the daytime it is common to see gangsters, for instance, sitting in buildings where the shades are pulled and the lights are off.[54] Ceiling lights tend to be hung low, and floor lamps are not usually more than five feet high.[55] The faces of the actors are commonly blacked out by shadow, and the central character is, as Schrader attests, commonly standing *in* a shadow.[56]

Further, the aura of estrangement and claustrophobia is generated by the presence of such 'framing devices' as doors, windows, metal bedframes, stairways and shadows to 'separate the character from other characters, from his world, or from his own emotions'.[57] Often, objects may push their way into the foreground of the picture, thereby achieving more focus and power than the characters.[58] Not surprisingly, therefore, when the environment is given a greater weight than the characters, a fatalistic and hopeless mood is generated[59] in which 'there is nothing the protagonist can do; the city will outlast and negate even his best efforts'.[60] The archetypal *noir* picture is probably what Place and Peterson identify as 'the extreme high-angle long shot, an oppressive and fatalistic angle that looks down on its helpless victims to make it look like a rat in a maze'.[61] The world of *film noir* is thus 'made a closed universe', in which each character is 'seen as just another facet of an unheeding environment that will exist unchanged long after his death'.[62] Such a mood is depicted in the 1950 film *Night and the City*, for example, in which 'the forces of darkness press in upon the seedy, amoral world'[63] inhabited by ignoble hustler and wrestling promoter Harry Fabian (Richard Widmark), who 'plunges desperately' during the film 'through a claustrophobic world beset by menacing shadows in a futile attempt to evade his fate'.[64] Due to heavily symbolic and stylized images of London where the film is set, the feeling of claustrophobia is exacerbated 'as shadows lengthen and the unseen forces of darkness impinge upon Harry's small, fearful world'.[65] Indeed, as Crowther points out, he becomes 'a featureless silhouette caught against the dank, backlit walls of the streets and alleyways of this surreal cityscape'.[66]

The pervasiveness of (Christian) alienation motifs in 1970s *film noir*

Rather than as an isolated category of films, however, which reached its apotheosis in the immediate post-Second World War period, it is apparent that the archetypal *film noir* delineation of humankind as liable to sin and error, and living an alienated existence, has been a pervasive attribute of American cinema since the 1970s. Moreover, whereas in the 1940s and early 1950s there is a discernible sense in many *films noirs* that the protagonists are actually caught up in a hostile and menacing world *to which they do not really belong*, in the 1970s the *noir* 'hero' is a much more ambiguous figure, insofar as he is characteristically an alienated and, often, guilt-ridden individual who, in terms of Hegel's identification, may be seen to be both in conflict with his nature and estranged from other human beings as well as from his own essence and end. Indeed, although the classic *noir* hard-boiled detectives Philip Marlowe and Sam Spade were engaged in the corruption and squalor that characterized the city milieu where they lived and worked, they were ultimately uncontaminated by it,[67] appearing instead as no less than honourable and decent men undertaking 'a quest for justice through the ambiguous landscape'[68] of the modern city.

In *The Big Sleep*, the sense of darkness and slumber alluded to in the film's title invokes 'an impenetrable chaos that only the witty and skilled detachment of a Bogart can combat'.[69] Due to his self-protective wit and cynicism, Bogart's Philip Marlowe is able to distance himself from the deception and double-crossing, the complexities and compromises, that constitute the 'underworld' in which he works. Although the solving of the puzzle in such a film as *The Big Sleep* is rendered difficult by the absence of truth and certainty, the protagonist remains courageous, admirable and a man of integrity, with at least one film critic even categorizing Marlowe a 'Chandleresque knight', braving 'the dark evils of the world'.[70] In the 1970s, however, when the revival of *film noir* also witnessed the revival of the hard-boiled detective genre, it is apparent that a very different ethos surrounded the nature and disposition of the detective, and which can be seen to correspond to the recognition within Christian theology that the human individual is essentially *alienated* from 'the ground of his being' and disposed to live in an imperfect and disordered state of existence.

Indeed, in 1973, Robert Altman based his film *The Long Goodbye* on the hard-boiled novel of the same name by Raymond Chandler, featuring Philip Marlowe as the film's protagonist. Yet, Chandler's Marlowe has been completely subverted by Altman, with Elliott Gould, who plays him, appearing as 'a puzzled, passive, deeply abused man, caught in an environment and a moral structure he refuses' – seemingly through a lack of ability as well as indifference – 'to comprehend'.[71] In contrast to Bogart's character, who braves 'the dark evils of the world',[72] Gould portrays the detective as so out of control of his world that there is no possibility of detection but only, at most, of accidental discovery. Indeed, whereas Bogart attempted to discover and investigate regardless of how futile and difficult the attempt may have been, Gould could be said to start from the very inevitability of failure. He does not detect anything actively or passively, in contrast to the conventions of the detective film, but, rather, sets about proving wrong the charge of murder made by the police against his friend, Terry Lennox (Jimmy Bouton). As we learn at the end of the film, Lennox was not only guilty of murdering his wife, but actually used the unsuspecting Marlowe to help him escape to Mexico. In Chandler's novel, Lennox is innocent of the charge. As Gallafent observes, therefore, Altman 'radically re-writes the original in order to stress contemporary rottenness',[73] and 'the moral worthlessness of modern America which the audience is assumed to share'.[74]

Furthermore, Altman's Marlowe is dissociated from the agencies of society, as indicated by the fact that he has no office or staff,[75] while his only relationship to the police is one of 'mutual incomprehension and contempt'.[76] When he is arrested for allegedly withholding information concerning the whereabouts of Terry Lennox, it is significant that the tactics of the policemen, who threaten and physically assault him with a view to securing his co-operation, 'are almost indistinguishable'[77] from those of the gangster, Marty Augustine (Mark Rydell), and his henchmen, who intimidate the unwitting Marlowe into handing over a substantial amount of cash which they believe Lennox gave him before his disappearance. Without doubt, Altman's picture is of a society redolent of, and epitomized by, 'amorality and violence',[78] and where nothing seems to have any value. Drifting through the film without any physical or emotional anchorage in the world,[79] Marlowe is barely coherent even in what he says. In contra-distinction to the Marlowe of the 1940s 'who, through a combin-ation of intelligence, wit and morality, is able to bring a semblance of order to a corrupt, confusing world',[80] in *The Long Goodbye* Marlowe not only understands and solves little, but his wit has degenerated into 'a mumble of unfunny clichés',[81] and his catchphrase 'It's okay with me', which he most notably and repetitively murmurs at the sight of his indifferent, nude and stoned female neighbours practising yoga on the opposite balcony. As well as the language drifting and glancing in incoherent directions, the cinematography lacks focus and consistency. For, as Kolker observes, Altman uproots 'perceptual stability', thereby 'preventing a secured, centered observation of the characters in their surroundings'.[82] Indeed, nearly every shot in the film 'is either a very slow, never completed zoom into or out from the characters observed, or a slow, almost imperceptible, arc around or track across them.'[83] The suggestion, therefore, is that there is always something more to be known, and – in a world of uncertainty and menace – the viewer's own perceptions become 'inscribed into an orderless, almost random series of interchanges and events'.[84]

A development in the hard-boiled detective tradition can also be discerned in the case of Roman Polanski's *Chinatown*, which was produced in 1974. Although it is set in the Los Angeles of 1937, the film's theme of political corruption and power 'would not have seemed strange to a 1974 audience cognisant of the political realities of the Watergate scandal'.[85] In contrast to the ordered and refined world of the Agatha Christie detective, who could 'gain control of complex and dangerous situations through reason and perception',[86] *Chinatown* – which authentically re-captures the tone and atmosphere of the 1930s – presents a corrupt world within which the detective himself is implicated, and he is, even, unwittingly responsible for exacerbating the destruction that prevails.

From the outset, the film's protagonist, Jake Gittes (Jack Nicholson), is shown to be involved in cases of divorce and adultery, which other hard-boiled detectives have conventionally rejected.[87] He also seeks publicity for himself – for example, he spells his name to newspaper reporters while shielding his client, Evelyn Mulwray (Faye Dunaway), from their questions, after she is interviewed by the police in connection with the mysterious death of her husband, the city water commissioner. Even though Gittes perseveres with the investigation into Hollis Mulwray's (Darrell Zwerling) murder after being warned off by thugs – who slit his nose as a deterrent – his motives do not emanate from a desire to seek the truth but, rather, 'worry about losing his reputation as a businessman',[88] as indicated by his declaration to Evelyn, 'I'm not supposed to be the one who's caught with his pants down.' Furthermore, he even 'negotiates contracts for large sums'[89] with both Evelyn and Noah Cross (John Huston) – her father and a strong political figure, who plans to divert the city's water supply for economic gain – despite the fact that there is considerable animosity between the two, which Gittes is prepared to exploit. In short, *Chinatown* presents a corrupt world, where even the individual investigating the corruption is not beyond reproach.

In stark contrast to the world of the classical detective, where there is usually only one, single individual criminal, Gittes stumbles across, and becomes enmeshed in, 'a corrupt *society* in which wealthy and respectable people are linked with gangsters and crooked politicians'.[90] Indeed, what begins as an investigation into marital infidelity soon blossoms into a murder inquiry and the uncovering of a large-scale conspiracy involving big business, politics, the criminal underworld and the entire underlying social and geographical structure of Los Angeles. Unlike the detective of even the corrupt and squalid world of 1940s *film noir* – who would often confront, hear the confession of and sometimes execute the criminal[91] – the protagonist in *Chinatown* finds himself 'confronting a depth of evil and chaos so great that he is unable to control it'.[92] It is therefore ironic that we often witness Gittes making his observations in the investigation from a high position – such as a bluff over the sea, a bank on the Los Angeles river and a roof overlooking an apartment – for 'such a position might suggest that his vision is godlike'.[93] In actuality, rather, he is a naive man who is caught up 'in a dark, violent world beyond his comprehension',[94] as Noah Cross indicates when he warns Gittes at their first meeting, 'You may think you know what you're dealing with, here, but believe me, you don't.' It is a world that is not merely 'indifferent to man's plight', but one that is, in May's words, 'cohesively malignant',[95] and 'deeper and more catastrophic, more enigmatic in its evil, more sudden and inexplicable in its outbreaks of violent chance.'[96]

In a similar vein, Arthur Penn's 1975 film *Night Moves* features a detective who becomes morally and emotionally involved in the quest for truth concerning a series of crimes. In what starts out as an assignment to find the runaway daughter of a faded actress, Harry Moseby (Gene Hackman) becomes embroiled in the world of smuggling and murder, and along the way is forced to question and confront his personal convictions and relationships, which he cannot disentangle from his occupation. May even designates the film a 'metaphysical parable',[97] whereby the protagonist attempts to solve the mysteries he encounters in his investigation while at the same time finding answers to the mysteries at the heart of his private life. However, each time he forces a revelation from the other characters he seems to be a further step behind the truth, as new leads tend to point to new and more complex discoveries. Kolker refers to the detective's subjectivity as being on the point of dissolution, with his investigations filling him with 'almost paralyzing unhappiness' and 'an inability to move in a way that will make things clear and give them order',[98] as is outwardly reflected by his tendency to observe things through screens and windows, rather than directly. Hence, although Penn retains the world Bogart inhabited, with dark streets and labyrinthine plotting, the detective is presented as a figure of contemporary anxiety, with none of his predecessor's wit and bluff or sense of security and self-esteem.[99] Furthermore, sequences in the film are often incomplete and unresolved,[100] thereby pointing to the difficulty, if not the impossibility, of finding answers to questions in an ambiguous and chaotic world. Like other 1970s *films noirs*, including *Chinatown* and *The Long Goodbye*, the film paints a bleak picture of America in which order and justice are absent, 'everyone is implicated, all action is tainted, and "truth" is impossible to discern'.[101]

The notion of the 'hero' as devoid of heroic attributes can, then, be seen to have risen to prominence in the cycle of *noir* films in the 1970s, in a form which accords with the Christian understanding of 'man' as restless, 'fallen', frustrated, disobedient, hostile and alienated in nature.[102] In particular, Gene Hackman's role as surveillance expert Harry Caul in the 1974 film *The Conversation* could be said to epitomize contemporary feelings of estrangement and impotence, in which the effectiveness and potency of the individual is 'physically, emotionally and politically'[103] diminished. Caul undergoes a moral destruction, and becomes subdued by guilt, upon witnessing a murder with his 'hi-tech' surveillance equipment. By the end of the film he becomes the object of surveillance himself, by which time he has become 'a painfully lonely, cynical, paranoid and alienated man',[104] unable to move from the corner of his room where he is sitting. As Kolker observes, the film causes the viewer to question his or her own position of safety in the world, and not only raises questions concerning the morality of spying, and the effects of being spied upon, but about the efficacy, potency and ethics of action itself.[105] It is, in short, a film about paranoia, loss, impotence and despair, in which the film's 'hero' is essentially nothing short of an 'anti-hero'.

Towards a redemptive interpretation of *film noir*

In spite, however, of the *noir* vision of humankind as hopeless and devoid of a secure future, there is nevertheless a significant degree to which, within the Christian tradition, humankind is believed to possess an intrinsic sensibility that *integration* is better than disintegration, and *harmony* is better than cacophony,[106] and which may be seen to have a crucial bearing on the interpretation of such films. Notwithstanding, indeed, that 'the state of existence is the state of estrangement',[107] and that there is a serious dichotomy between the innate propensity for goodness and the actual estrangement of the human condition, at the heart of post-Enlightenment Protestant Christian theology lies the hope that the so-called 'broken' pieces of existence can be *rejoined* and *reintegrated*.[108] At the very least, it is apparent that 'if the question of estrangement is being asked, the answer of reconciliation must at least be possible'.[109] Thus, as Hegel points out, although the Fall bears witness to humankind's 'continuance in misery',[110] we nevertheless have in the Fall narrative an *announcement* and *prediction* of reconciliation. For, once one has experienced despair, Hegel indicates that one is thereby in a position to come to a true consciousness of *life*.[111] Rather than an intrinsically negative process, therefore, which can – and often does – lead to spiritual hardening and death, despair may also be construed as the catalyst and the prerequisite towards awakening, or redeeming, a person to their true and authentic nature.

Indeed, in the second volume of *Either–Or*, Kierkegaard wrote in this regard that 'Every man who has not tasted the bitterness of despair has missed the significance of life.'[112] Although, for Kierkegaard, 'despair is a condition common to all persons',[113] the only way in which one can escape despair, and thereby undergo a redemptive experience, is by first acknowledging and coming to terms with that despair. Redemption is thus inextricably bound up in modern Christian theology with 'the state of estrangement as the main characteristic of existence',[114] and refers to what Tillich identifies as the process of healing and reuniting 'that which is estranged, giving a center to what is split' and 'overcoming the split between God and man, man and his world' and 'man and himself'.[115] Although any victories we achieve in the course of our lives will commonly be 'comparatively small and incomplete',[116] with 'defeats' a regular occurrence – the effects of which may even 'be calamitous'[117] in nature – the suffering and the hardships that we undergo are a necessary, and fundamental, prerequisite of redemptive activity.

Insofar as the dysfunctional and alienated condition of humankind is the starting-point of redemption within the Christian tradition, there is thus a significant sense in which the medium of *film noir*, in bearing witness to and epitomizing this 'fallen' condition, could be said to constitute a potentially rich repository of redemptive significance. A pertinent analogy here lies in the form of the Prologue to the Fourth Gospel, which claims, with respect to the Incarnation, that 'the light shines in the darkness, and the darkness has not overcome it'.[118] Although the darkness is unable to dispel the light, it is, however, significant from a reading of this passage that nor does the *light* completely dispel the *darkness*. For, according to John, although 'the true light that enlightens every man was coming into the world',[119] and even though 'He was in the world, and the world was made through him, *yet the world knew him not.*'[120] Although 'to all who received him, who believed in his name, he gave power to become children of God',[121] when the Logos 'came to his own home', and manifested himself to his people, we learn that 'his own people received him not'.[122] Consequently, although the light shines out in the midst of the darkness, the implication in John's Gospel is that the light, though incandescent, is in no way discernible to everyone.[123] Indeed, while there is a possibility of apprehending the light – Jesus Christ is, after all, designated the Light of the World[124] – in actuality it is the darkness that remains the most fecund and dominant motif. Likewise, although in the *film noir* universe darkness, and the concomitant aura of despair and paranoia, is a fundamental, and defining, characteristic, it is my contention that a glimmer of 'light' analogous to that recorded by the Fourth Evangelist with respect to the Incarnation has the potential to shine within and through the apparent irredeemability of the *noir* cosmos. For if, as the Christian tradition supposes, sin and alienation are the precursors to attaining redemption, the fact that *films noirs* bear witness to, and encapsulate, the Christian understanding of sin and alienation at least raises the possibility that *film noir*, too, is a vehicle capable of engendering an experience of *hope* and a sense of *integration* out of the all-encompassing chaos, disorder and despair.

5

The theological basis of redemption in film noir

Film noir **and redemption through suffering**

Although the world of *films noirs* is unremittingly bleak and pessimistic, with no promise that a better, more coherent and fulfilling future lies ahead, this is not to say that such films are entirely devoid of a redemptive dimension. As with Christianity, indeed, where evil and suffering amount to a precursor to redemptive activity – as epitomized by the inextricable link between Christ's crucifixion and subsequent resurrection – so *film noir* need not be seen as inescapably devoid of redemption. An illustration of how redemption may be discerned in spite of its apparent absence is serviceably illustrated by looking at David Fincher's recent *film noir*, *Seven* (1995), of which the editor of the British film magazine *Empire*, Mark Salisbury, attested at the time of its release in British cinemas in January 1996 that not for twenty years 'has there been a mainstream Hollywood movie as extraordinarily dark, bleak, intense, and as monumentally scary as this'.[1] Set in 'an anonymous' American city 'where it always rains', the film – which concerns a serial killer who slays his victims according to the seven deadly sins – 'creates an overwhelming sense of unease, presenting a world of irredeemable ugliness, a grim, melancholic, depressing and decaying society from which there is no escape'.[2] Yet, in spite of the 'irredeemable ugliness' of the world that *Seven* evokes, it is significant that Somerset (Morgan Freeman), the world-weary detective who has been assigned to apprehend the serial killer, John Doe (Kevin Spacey), explains in voice-over mode at the end of the picture – shortly after discovering in the film's gruesome climax that his junior colleague's pregnant wife is the psychopath's latest victim – 'Ernest Hemingway once wrote, "The world is a fine place, and worth fighting for." I agree with the second part.' Thus, although it may be a largely futile and often hopeless endeavour, there is nevertheless an acknowledgement that, in a world seemingly beyond redemption, the possibility of redemptive grace still exists, where there is a recognition that evil – though pervasive – is not inherently insurmountable.

As part of the investigation into the serial killings, Somerset is drawn to the writings of Aquinas and Milton, at one point quoting from *Paradise Lost*, 'Long is the way and hard that out of Hell leads up to light.' Despite the bleakness of the film's climax, which in some respects makes the path of Mills (Brad Pitt) to redemption far more difficult, in that he shoots Doe, an action which, according to John Wrathall, 'leaves us in no doubt that in doing so he has succumbed to Doe's power, and is now irredeemably damned',[3] at the same time Mills's action carries a potential spark of redemptive significance. Notwithstanding the irony that Fincher chooses to shoot the film's final reel in daylight – such that when the characters 'finally reach the light' for the first time, 'they are still very definitely in Hell'[4] – the passage from *Paradise Lost* at least holds out the possibility that, out of Mills' present hell, a path that 'leads up to light' is not outside his grasp. We do not know what the future actually holds for Mills – the last we see of him is when he is being taken away into custody – but from an *audience perspective* at any rate, although, as Carl Skrade points out, films have the capacity to accentuate and articulate the negative aspects of human existence, they nonetheless serve a positive function by way of enabling one to see and to confront the 'real'. Indeed, in his words, 'Certainly the contemporary film has positive values if it speaks to us in an understandable way about the basic questions we face as persons', such as those pertaining to 'who we are, why we are here, and what it means to live responsibly as men and women in the world today'.[5] As in the case of Christianity, redemption thus proceeds not from an escape from reality but from a more resolute *confrontation* with the truth and the actuality concerning the human condition. At the same time, then, that audiences are being confronted with images of destruction and are given the opportunity through film to 'peer into the depths of the human predicament',[6] film-makers – whether consciously or unconsciously – are also offering audiences what Skrade, writing in 1970, calls 'filmic forms of symbols of renewal'.[7]

David Fincher's next feature, *The Game* (1997), is also imbued with redemptive significance. The film's protagonist, Nicholas Van

Orton (Michael Douglas), a ruthless, workaholic San Francisco business tycoon, is given an enigmatic gift on his forty-eighth birthday from his younger brother Conrad (Sean Penn), in becoming an unwitting participant in an enigmatic and perilous (and at times quite surreal) venture called 'The Game'. The entire fabric of his world is torn apart: he discovers he has been implicated in pornography and drugs, he is nearly drowned, he is shot at, his house is looted, his entire $600 million wealth is plundered and he is poisoned. When he regains consciousness, he finds himself in a graveyard in Mexico, buried alive, at which point, having lost everything – there is no one he feels he can trust, bar, ironically, his ex-wife – he chooses to fight back. Following his 'death', he is, as Philip Strick puts it, 'destined to fall in a Miltonic plunge towards resurrection'.[8] Upon tracking down one of the employees of Consumer Recreation Services – the 'company' behind 'The Game' – he affirms, 'I'm pulling back the curtain; I want to meet the Wizard.' In so doing, he comes to realize just how tenuous and invidious his life has been. He has sacrificed everyone around him for his business interests. Now he has lost those, he is forced to value the lives of those from whom he has been so estranged up to now. He apologises, for instance, to his ex-wife for being such an uncaring husband, and at the end he tentatively embarks on a relationship with one of the Game's participants (Deborah Kara Unger), after acknowledging to Conrad that he has learnt something from – and is, in retrospect, grateful for – this strange, nightmarish and perilous odyssey. He now understands why, towards the beginning of the picture, in asking a former player what 'The Game' is all about, he is told the answer can be found in John 9: 25 – 'whereas once I was blind, now I can see'. His odyssey has been a redemptive odyssey. It is significant that, after discovering his house had been wrecked, he finds a message left for him on a piece of paper, containing a reference to his father's suicide, on *his* forty-eighth birthday: 'Like my father before me, I choose eternal sleep.' Rather than choose 'eternal sleep', however, Nicholas Van Orton opts for 'eternal life'. Out of his plutonian experience comes a willingness to affirm *life*, and to embrace those whom he has hitherto spurned and sacrificed for a lonely, materialistic and self-absorbed existence.

In this light, it is significant that Lesley Stern concentrates upon the often downbeat and tumultuous *noir* films of Martin

Scorsese in her largely personal account of the positive – even 'magical' – properties of cinema. Indeed, Scorsese's *GoodFellas* (1990) is a harsh and brutal dissection of the lives of the people who inhabit the Mafia world in New York City over a twenty-five year period, and yet the experience of watching this film has been designated 'simultaneously fascinating and repellent'.[9] As *Variety* attests, there is 'a giddy sense of exploring a forbidden world'[10] which, in Stern's words, is 'fraught' with both 'wonder and peril'.[11] Stern claims, further, that she finds herself 'transported, entranced by these images' and 'utterly absorbed'.[12] There is thus an apparent sense in which the reason audiences can engage so intimately with the underlying black vision of despair, loneliness and dread that characterizes *films noirs* is not in some way in *spite* of but as a direct *consequence* of their underlying authenticity and realism. Indeed, as Eugenio Zaretti attests, 'because a *noir* protagonist has no exit, no options, and is constrained to do what destiny bids', there is a sense in which audiences can respond to *films noirs* because they authentically encompass 'an element of daily life'.[13] With respect to *GoodFellas*, Keyser points out that 'Scorsese wanted to avoid the mythical dimensions of Coppola's *Godfather* saga and instead capture everyday activities.'[14] Although

> his Cicero clan might take limos to the Copacabana [club] . . . most of the time the family was at the cabstand or local pseudo-Polynesian restaurants like the Bamboo Lounge, playing poker games at smoky social clubs, or guzzling beer-and-a-chaser at Henry Hill's bar, The Suite.[15]

In Erickson's words, then, audiences will always be, at the very least, fascinated by *film noir* because it 'communicates to us about our fears and desires more realistically than any other film formula'.[16] Indeed, it is significant in this respect that, in a discussion relating to his 1973 film, *Mean Streets*, Scorsese himself puts forward a definition of redemption which is bound up with life on the 'mean streets' of Little Italy in his youth, upon which personal experiences the film is based. For, rather than in terms of conventional religious redemption – as ultimately derived from the teachings at 'mass on Sunday mornings'[17] – Scorsese locates redemption within the challenges and confrontations of authentic day-to-day existence, as illustrated in the dilemmas facing the film's characters as they interact and 'deal with other people',[18] as well as with their own inner selves.

Despite, then, its ostensibly negative character, the tone of *film noir* is not inescapably downbeat or devoid of redemption. Such films are, however, very different from the type of film which enables an audience to respond with affection and optimism, in the manner of a fantasy-oriented picture such as *TheWizard of Oz*. For, in contrast to the authentic milieu of *Mean Streets* or *GoodFellas* – in which Scorsese points out that 'we get an insider's look into the actual workings of a family involved in organized crime'[19] – it is apparent that such pictures fabricate images of reality and audiences tend to be required as a prerequisite to suspend disbelief. The effect is thus similar to popular music, in which, as Rob Lapsley points out, it is often the case that 'whatever the ostensibly negative content of the lyrics – whether banal romantic loss or fashionably apocalyptic visions of social breakdown and ecological catastrophe – the tone is upbeat'.[20] A dichotomy is consequently set up between the authenticity of the lyrics, which 'acknowledge the pain of existence and its many causes',[21] and the music which is, conversely, 'celebratory and affirmative'.[22] In the case of 'fantasy' films, in spite of the reality of suffering and pain, audiences are afforded the opportunity to withdraw into a realm apart from the finitude of existence, a so-called 'elsewhere' in which that suffering and pain no longer matters.

Of course, the *'noir'* sequence in Capra's *It's a Wonderful Life* is clearly presented as a threat to the concept of the 'American community',[23] to the effect that *films noirs* and not 'escapist' pictures are seen to be in some sense inimical to human flourishing. However, it is significant that in actual *films noirs* there is no sense in which the small town – as depicted in George Bailey's home of Bedford Falls – is sanctioned 'as a redemptive alternative'[24] to the *noir* city milieu. Indeed, Krutnik observes that there is a substantial sense in which the 'City of Strangers', which characterizes the urban jungle of *film noir*, may in actuality 'hold attractions which are barred from the restricted orbit of small-town America',[25] due to the authentic nature of such a milieu. Ultimately, if the question of redemption is to be raised with respect to *film noir*, it is apparent that it is in terms of the milieu itself – and not by way of an escape from the restrictions and suffering it epitomizes – that such a question needs to be rooted.

In this respect, the process is similar to the experience of witnessing what Allardyce Nicol terms 'an adequate performance of a great tragic drama',[26] in which – although there 'may be no "reconciliation" for the central hero', in the respect that 'Macbeth may go to his death utterly damned and Othello may be forced to take his own life'[27] – we do not 'leave the theatre cast down and in despair'.[28] For, in spite of the sense of waste and emptiness with which the audience may be left upon leaving the auditorium, 'there comes a reconciliation for ourselves'[29] in the form of the opportunity which such a confrontation with tragedy presents for reflecting upon and wrestling with 'the dark and seemingly meaningless elements'[30] of life which are often not addressed in such an authentic fashion. Likewise, the sense in which redemption may be said to function in *film noir* is congruous with the sense within Christianity in which the crucifixion is deemed on the one hand to be the greatest of all evils – insofar as it involves the 'murder' of the divine Son – while on the other it is the occasion of God's salvation. For, although Christ's blood was shed as a result of an ignominious and humiliating death by crucifixion, and is 'menacing and repulsive as a symbol of the suffering occasioned by the world's cruelty',[31] the resurrection causes this symbol to be reversed, such that it becomes potent and salvific, redemptive and life-*giving* instead. Through the suffering that is epitomized by the Cross, therefore, a site of misery and hopelessness has been transformed into a site of comprehensive redemptive significance. With respect to *film noir*, any redemption such films convey may be somewhat obscure and uncertain in form – indeed, it is not the case that people tend to leave a film claiming to be 'saved' – but it is not unreasonable to surmise that occasional, spasmodic glimmers of hope are possible, and, consequently, are a sign that the 'transformation' has begun. The world of such films as *Double Indemnity, The Big Sleep, The Wrong Man* and *Chinatown* will still, therefore, be intrinsically fatalistic and hopeless, but there is an apparent sense in which audiences can come to experience the antithesis of a helpless and impotent response to such films, upon engaging with their fatalistic and oppressive images and narratives.

The analogy of Ecclesiastes

A good analogy of the way in which the images and narratives of *film noir* may be seen to perform a redemptive function is the wisdom literature of the Hebrew Bible, and, in particular, the post-exilic book of Ecclesiastes. Although the concept of redemption is not specific to the wisdom tradition, Ecclesiastes is especially apposite as an analogy of the process operative through *noir* in the respect that, even though the book appears in the canon of the Hebrew Bible, its premise is the unconventional – if not in fact un-Hebraic – notion that there is no more to human existence than the apparent meaninglessness and irrationality that we can observe all around us. Yet, it is evident that the book endeavours authentically to address and wrestle with the place and function of humankind within such an adverse and hostile universe, even managing to conclude that there is a certain hope to be gained within, and from, such an inauthentic existence. Consequently, the recognition that there is a certain positive value to be found in life, in spite of its palpable absence, is, in many respects, analogous to the concept of redemption as it applies to *film noir*.

From the outset, it is apparent that Ecclesiastes radically departs from the positive affirmations of earlier biblical writings, in which Israel is accorded special status over all other nations, and in which God is believed to lie behind the history of Israel, rewarding the righteous and punishing the wicked. Indeed, the mainstream wisdom tradition is characterized by what Soggin terms an affirmation of 'faith in a divine cosmic wisdom which rules and governs the universe with rational and immutable norms'.[32] The book of Proverbs epitomizes this conservative, optimistic and life-affirming essence, in the form of compact, two-member verses which, based upon the work of observation and experience, led the sages to perceive that, for example, 'The rich man's wealth is his stronghold, poverty is the poor man's un-doing.'[33] For it was judged an empirical fact that riches tend to lead to security, while poverty leads, conversely, to *in*-security. Indeed, life was observed to be the supreme good, and reference is often made in Proverbs to the 'path' or 'way' to life, in which the 'wise' person was expected to be able to reach their ultimate destination with confidence that they would arrive there safely, while 'fools', on the other hand, would necessarily *lose* their way.[34]

In stark contrast, however, the author of Ecclesiastes emphasizes from the outset that it is not possible for human beings to fathom and make sense of the 'order' of the universe. For, it is apparent that human history and the phenomena of nature consist of an endless, predetermined cyclical process that excludes novelty and deprives human effort of ultimate significance.[35] In the long term, at least, there is a fundamental sense in which 'all that is repeats itself without essential change',[36] and that only society's bad memory is responsible for causing us to think that anything new or unexpected ever happens. In short, we are at the mercy of forces beyond our control, in which 'What is crooked cannot be made straight, and what is lacking cannot be numbered.'[37] Any effort we make 'seems to make no difference and to have no permanent results'[38] as, ultimately, 'all human values are cancelled out by a man's inevitable and rapidly approaching death',[39] which obliterates both those who are 'righteous' and those who are 'wicked', and those who are wise and those who are foolish, in equal measure. Indeed, in the words of Qoheleth – to whom the superscription of the book attributes its authorship – there is no fundamental distinction, or advantage, between animal and human life, insofar as 'the fate of the sons of men and the fate of beasts is the same . . . all are from the dust, and all turn to dust again'.[40]

Such an apparently comfortless perspective on the universe is clearly analogous to the narratives and images of *films noirs*, in which – as the 1950 film *Night and the City* delineates – human individuals appear to be no more than featureless silhouettes caught up in 'an unheeding environment that will exist unchanged'[41] long after their deaths. Indeed, the sense of futility communicated by Qoheleth, whereby 'all is vanity and a striving after the wind'[42] – to the effect that it is thus 'a sorry business which God has given humankind to occupy itself with'[43] – evidently corresponds to Tuska's assertion that *film noir* is 'a darkling vision of the world, a view from the underside, born of fundamental disillusionment perhaps, but also invariably the result, no matter how timid, of a confrontation with nihilism'.[44] Likewise, Qoheleth's resignation to the fact that we are powerless to mitigate human misery or reverse the cruelty and oppression perpetrated by those who hold power in society[45] is congruous with the impotence embodied in such *films noirs* as *Chinatown*, which bears witness to corruption on both a personal[46] and political scale, and in which the detective who endeavours to solve the mystery unwittingly *exacerbates* the evils in which he becomes embroiled. Ultimately, then, just as in Ecclesiastes Qoheleth affirms that any effort we make is inevitably 'cancelled out'[47] by death and oblivion, so *film noir* exemplifies the 'tenuous quality of existence'.[48] This is epitomized in *The Maltese Falcon* (1931), in which private eye Sam Spade (Ricardo Cortez) explains that a man he was once hired to locate disappeared because he could not come to terms with the caprice and arbitrariness of existence whereby 'nothing ultimately means anything'[49] and 'by which we all live and die'.[50] Despite being a good husband, father, provider and a hard worker, the man realized one day while walking down a street that he was not immune to the tragic consequences of fate, upon being struck – and very nearly killed – by a concrete beam, which had fallen from one of the buildings above. Both Ecclesiastes and *film noir* thus bear witness to the fact that, in the final analysis, any effort humans make 'seems to make no difference'[51] and to have no bearing on our eventual destiny.

As Scott therefore indicates, 'such utterly pessimistic conclusions, if they stood by themselves, would be destructive not only of human values but of the will to live'.[52] Within this context, indeed, it is apparent that Qoheleth 'came to hate life',[53] and to detest 'all my toil in which I had toiled under the sun',[54] and was – on his own admission – driven to 'despair'.[55] However, rather than resign himself to such pessimism and nihilism, it is significant that Qoheleth believes that there is hope to be found in human existence, and which is analogous to the manner in which *film noir* may be construed as a redemptive medium. For, despite his entrenched cynical perspective, Qoheleth affirms that it is when one accepts and acknowledges the fact of death, and the apparent meaninglessness of existence, that it becomes possible to discern that there *is* a positive certainty in life. Indeed, 'far from suggesting *rejection* of life, let alone self-destruction',[56] Qoheleth affirms that *within* the limits of our knowledge, ability and circumstances, and our transitory life-span, once we accept the actuality of death and the finitude of human existence 'without the illusions which the fear of death so easily generates',[57] then the mind can be redeemed and set free from what amounts to 'a major source of crippling activity'.[58] We can subsequently learn to live authentically within the prescribed limitations and boundaries of our existence and, while accepting that we are 'no more the master'[59] of our lives than we are of the day of our death, we can nevertheless *appreciate* and *value* – even enjoy – our 'good fortune if and when it comes'[60] and, even, 'relish the satisfactions and joys of life',[61] even though we know we cannot *depend* on them. There are, then, compensations to be found in life. Indeed, 'a restless dissatisfaction with the present'[62], or a thorough retreat and detachment from life, could be construed as a deprivation of the only 'jewel'[63] that humankind possesses. In short, as Scott identifies, 'the good of life is the living of it',[64] and, as Qoheleth avows, 'if a man live many years, *let him be happy in them all*'[65] – even if that entails no discernible 'residue of achievement and success'.[66]

The metaphysical comedy *Groundhog Day* (1993) provides a good illustration of how compensations may be discerned, in spite of what at first appears to be the absence of anything but hopelessness and despair. The protagonist, Phil Connors (Bill Murray), is a smug, egocentric and arrogant TV weatherman who leaves the city for the small, rural town of Punxatawney, Pennsylvania, to report on its annual Groundhog festival. He is contemptuous of the community and its quaint traditions, and is eager to return to city life as soon as he has completed his assignment. However, due to a storm that he had ironically failed to predict, Phil is unable to leave Punxatawney and, in a bizarre twist of fate, when he wakes up the next morning – and on every subsequent morning – it is Groundhog Day (2 February) all over again. As Richard Corliss puts it, 'he is trapped in time. He wakes up the next day to discover it is still 2 February. The same people he saw on Groundhog Day say the same things; the same unforeseen snowstorm blows into town; Punxatawney is Brigadoon.'[67] Whatever he does to extricate himself from his nightmare – even committing suicide – meets with failure: 'he can't die, he can't escape. *He can only change.*'[68] Yet, Phil consequently learns to respect and even value the lives of others, as he comes to realize that, in knowing the town and its people so intimately, he is in a position to help them. He is able, for instance, to save a boy from falling from a tree, he saves the life of a man choking on a bone in a restaurant, and he attempts to save an old beggar from freezing to death on what is a cold night. According to Corliss, the deeper message of *Groundhog Day* is that most people's lives are like those of Phil Connors: 'a repetition, with the tiniest variations, of ritual pleasures and annoyances. Routine is the metronome marking most of our time on earth. Phil's gift is to see the routine and seize the day.'[69] He may be unable, ultimately, to prevent the old man from dying on that freezing night, but, in the spirit of Ecclesiastes, Phil has attempted to live life to the full, and to have overcome what he initially apprehended as a hellish experience of endless repetition. He is still living in Punxatawney, and among the same community he once despised, but his nightmare has been transformed into something creative, constructive and, ultimately, life-*affirming*.

Likewise, with respect to *film noir*, although its narratives and images delineate a world seemingly devoid of hope, redemption might be said to function by means of an authentic engagement with such an arbitrary and capricious world. Although little of positive value is conveyed through such films, the acknowledgement and recognition on the part of the audience that *films noirs* are an authentic representation of contemporary existence enables an analogous process to operate to Ecclesiastes, wherein Qoheleth proposes that any talk of hope, fulfilment or serenity emanates not from the *solution* of mysteries, or in having the capacity to master our destiny, but in being able to come to terms with the *actual* conditions of our existence. This 'realist' perspective thus lies in contradistinction to the ethos of 'escapist' cinema – and, to an extent, to that of Proverbs – that the root tensions and conflicts in society are, in fact, surmountable, such as in terms of recovering 'the disappearance of good neighbourliness'[70] and 'a purer, better, freer way of life'[71] that, for Frank Capra, epitomized pre-urban society.

Of course, the concomitant danger of such a world-view is that when present existence does not materially or outwardly improve, and that caprice, oppression and chaos continues to characterize contemporary life, then the same sense of dejection and despair that Qoheleth experienced will emerge. For, it is apparent that Qoheleth's initial despair arose because the conventional wisdom understanding that 'the good person, obedient to Yahweh's regulations, would automatically enjoy security, prosperity, and long life'[72] was manifestly contradicted by the experience of the Exile, since how could God's 'chosen people' come to be taken into captivity by a foreign power, so that – as is further exemplified by the predicament of Job – 'neither the God-fearing person nor the blasphemer receives what he or she deserves in this life'?[73] Like Qoheleth, on the other hand, *film noir* does not proffer the idealistic hope that present existence can materially or outwardly improve, or that a better, more coherent world is even attainable. Once again, therefore, redemption can be seen to function in spite of its apparent absence, since it emanates from one's ability to *confront* and come to terms with the intrinsically volatile and fragmentary nature of human existence, rather than in the form of an escape from it.

Wisdom, redemption and Woody Allen

Although the films of Woody Allen do not belong to the category of *film noir*, the degree to which Allen challenges, and takes issue with, the traditionally escapist orientation of Hollywood films could be read as a functional equivalent of *film noir*. In the place of an escapist sensibility, Allen has a propensity for delineating characters who are customarily anxious and neurotic and unable to pull their lives together, such that, as Commins perceives, 'they seem very much like ourselves.'[74] And, in common with the wisdom literature of Qoheleth, it is significant that 'In Woody Allen's world, nothing can be counted on and nothing can be counted out. Life is mystery. It cannot be solved. It is absurd. It does not make sense.'[75] Indeed, Allen tends to picture human existence as comprising a mystery, in which numerous profound questions are raised concerning the meaning of life, evil, suffering and alienation, while it is acknowledged that they can never be solved, and even dispelling any attempt 'to come to a philosophically consistent approach to the human dilemma'.[76] Moreover, as Commins points out, 'not satisfied with undermining every philosophical, religious and psychological attempt to explain the world', Allen subverts even the grounds on which their claims are made'.[77] Hence, although, in *Manhattan* (1979), the Allen character, Isaac Davies, informs his younger partner, Tracy (Mariel Hemingway), that, with respect to her beauty, she is 'God's answer to Job', his films generally take issue with the teaching adduced in the book of Job that there is no room for engaging in rational explanation for the problem of evil and suffering in the world,[78] but that only a humble acceptance and confession of faith before the awesome and ineffable presence of God is valid. In *Love and Death* (1975), for instance, a character responds while looking out at a battlefield strewn with thousands of dead bodies, 'God is testing us', to which the Allen character, Boris, replies, 'If he's going to test us, why doesn't he give us a written?' Ultimately, Allen 'attacks the complacency'[79] of those who espouse what he sees as clichés and empty words 'to explain away awesome tragedy',[80] in the manner of the conventional theodicy model, as upheld by the various religious traditions.

Hence, notwithstanding Allen's reservations about his own picture, *Hannah and her Sisters*, for containing a fairy-tale ending, and to some degree, therefore, conforming to the escapist category of films that I reject as sites of potential redemptive activity, Woody Allen's films may be seen to contain seeds of redemptive significance, in a manner akin to the Qoheleth world-view. For, as with the wisdom literature of the Hebrew Bible, Allen's solution to the problem of evil is not to avoid reality, since in running away from the problems inherent in human existence, such problems will, if anything, be *exacerbated*. His films thus adopt a different kind of attitude to the one espoused in *Stardust Memories* (1980), when the Allen character, Sandy Bates, is a film-maker whose studio advises him that 'too much reality is not what people want' and that 'human suffering doesn't sell tickets in Kansas City'. In contrast, the indication in Allen's films is that people should confront, rather than run away from, the hard facts of reality. Otherwise, as Isaac perceives in *Manhattan*, the concomitant danger with failing to face up to the challenges and realities of life can be seen with respect to the lives of the people in New York City who, as he puts it, are 'constantly creating these real unnecessary, neurotic problems for themselves because it keeps them from dealing with more unsolvable, terrifying problems about the universe'. Indeed, as Gary Commins in-dicates, the suggestion is that if people become preoccupied with false, neurotic and inauthentic concerns then 'they will never come to face the truly important crises of life', and will thereby come to 'live without integrity or courage'.[81]

In contrast to the problems inherent in escapist films, as Allen demonstrates with respect to Cecilia's unfulfilled existence in *The Purple Rose of Cairo*, wherein the 'heavenly' images that sustain her amount to an inauthentic, even 'hellish', existence, Allen in *Play it Again, Sam* (1972) could be said to subvert the conventions of the fantasy-oriented picture to illustrate how an authentic confrontation with reality is able to facilitate an experience of redemption. The neuroses and feelings of sexual inadequacy of his character, Allan Felix, result in a psychological dependency on his idol, Humphrey Bogart, with whom Felix is in dialogue throughout the film. At first, he can only identify with Bogart's toughness and independent spirit, qualities he cannot hope to emulate successfully. In due course, however, he comes to *see through* Bogart's external confidence to what amounts to his more vulnerable inner nature, and realizes that he, like his hero, is 'short enough and ugly enough' to survive by himself. As Girgus thus attests, 'learning to live with himself rather than by imitating false models, Felix really confronts aspects of his character that are hidden . . . sources of strength'.[82] Consequently, at the end of the picture, we observe Felix walking 'off into the fog to find his destiny', and avowing 'his readiness to stand alone'.[83] In contrast, then, to the somewhat ambiguous fantasy of *The Purple Rose of Cairo*, in *Play it Again, Sam* Allen suggests avenues for a new mode of understanding the self, whereby, as Commins puts it, we can come to see 'images of strength through weakness, glory through humility, and self-love through self-sacrifice'.[84] Moreover, the reason such a process operates is precisely because it does *not* involve our being swept off our collective feet and being taken out of this world, but rather involves the act of being freed to be ourselves. Ultimately, therefore, whereas Cecilia never sees past the illusion, and 'waits passively to be saved',[85] such that there is, for her, no distinction between the realms of reality and fantasy, Allan Felix is able to see through the illusory tough exterior of Bogart, and is thereby empowered to change his life and to undergo a liberating, and ultimately redemptive, experience.

Woody Allen has no illusions, however, about the complexity of the process, and of the ease with which one might undergo a redemptive experience. Although glimmers of redemption may be said to be present in his films, they are of an altogether tentative form. For example, at the end of *Manhattan*, Isaac Davies comes to a realization that, although he had rejected his seventeen-year-old partner for a woman closer to his own age, his relationship with Tracy had, in retrospect, come closer than any other love he has experienced to being the most authentic and meaningful one for him, and he regrets breaking up with her. Although she is about to leave for London to pursue an acting career which he had earlier encouraged, and he fails to dissuade her from going, he finally heeds her plea to allow her to be free. In Commins's words, 'The changing expressions on his face leave the viewer in some doubt as to whether he really accepts her liberation . . . But then a smile passes across his face for just a moment. He seems to.'[86] Although there is no clear-cut resolution, it is apparent that he has come to learn much about himself and his own ability to engage in interpersonal relationships, to the point that, although he remains silent when face-to-face with Tracy in this end-scene, there is a sense in which he has also undergone an invaluable life-lesson by this confrontation with his somewhat deluded – and, to a point, selfish – nature, a self-discovery which, to quote Girgus, has 'made him pregnant with possibility'.[87] Indeed, the selfishness he exhibits in trying to prevent Tracy from leaving is followed by an acknowledgement – albeit a tentative one – on his part that he needs to grant her the opportunity to achieve her own identity and to fulfil her own potential, the very advice he had previously espoused in order to convince her to go to London. The conclusion of *Manhattan*, which is in a fundamental sense far removed from the archetypal Hollywood 'happy ending', may thus be read as a sign that 'liberation is somehow possible in Allen's world, perhaps only because nothing can be counted on or counted out, not even the lack of an exit'.[88]

A connection can thus be made between Allen's films and the argument espoused by Thomas Merton that 'it is only when the apparent absurdity of life is faced in all truth that faith really becomes possible'.[89] This then ties in with the fact that in the Old Testament wisdom literature – and particularly in Ecclesiastes – redemption could be said to emanate 'from being faithful to one's experience and one's reflection on that experience'.[90] Redemption, if it happens at all, derives from human experience itself, within and through its evil, suffering and apparent meaninglessness. Although there may be no ultimate resolutions or 'happy endings' as such in his work, it is this fundamentally authentic quality that makes Allen's films especially amenable to a redemptive interpretation. Hence, with respect to *The Purple Rose of Cairo*, in spite of the film's delineation of the dangers bound up with escapist cinema, it is by means of Allen's ability to convey and expose what he terms 'the difference between fantasy and reality' and 'how seductive fantasy is' that we are able to acknowledge, in the final analysis, how 'we must live with reality', regardless of 'how painful that can be'.[91]

It is most apposite, therefore, that, in *Crimes and Misdemeanors* (1989), the Allen character, Cliff Stern, is designated as naive for failing to accept as credible what amounts in the plot to a true story concerning how a person can come to feel no remorse for committing a murder and who thus feels no sense of 'existential responsibility for his actions',[92] preferring instead to hear a story with a 'neat ending' in which the guilty are punished for their crimes. To the narrator, Judah Rosenthal (Martin Landau), Stern's failure to comprehend how such a 'tragic' ending can actually happen is a testimony to the fact that, to quote Rosenthal, 'you see too many movies', and that 'if you want a happy ending, you . . . should go see a Hollywood movie'. Rather, in creating films which bear witness to 'contemporary moral ambiguity and uncertainty', in which 'there is no resolution' and 'no ultimate reconstitution of moral meaning and structure',[93] Allen's films, in marked contrast to conventional Hollywood escapism, may be seen to expose all such conventional forms of unity for the illusions they are. In a world, then, which, as Qoheleth acknowledges, is characterised by evil and suffering, and not by 'happy endings', the potential only exists for humans to live out an authentic existence if they manage to *avoid* retreating from, or neglecting, the fundamentally ambiguous – even, at times, antipathetic – nature of human life and to endeavour, instead, to face up to the challenges and realities of existence, in which, as Rosenthal's story testifies, the guilty often go unpunished, and come to feel no contrition for, their actions.

6

Film protagonists as exemplars of redemptive possibility

While a process of redemption analogous to that found in Christianity is at least potentially operative through the narratives and images of *film noir*, it is however apparent, from a Christian perspective, that a confrontation with human suffering, with inauthenticity and with the apparent meaninglessness of existence, is not *by itself* sufficient to generate an experience of redemption. In spite of analogous threads so far discussed, one distinctive feature sets Christian redemption apart from redemption in *film noir* – namely, the figure of Christ as the agent of redemption. Indeed, while redemption can only function provided there has been an authentic human confrontation with the alienated, fragmentary and estranged nature of human existence, redemption is meaningless from a Christian perspective without due consideration of the role played in the redemptive process by Jesus Christ, as humankind's redeemer. If *film noir* is therefore to constitute a site of redemptive activity that is analogous to the process at work in Christianity then there has to be a sense in which a *redeemer-figure* – a functional equivalent of Christ – performs an integral function in the redemptive process. Indeed, while the images and narratives of *films noirs* may enable the audience members to begin a process of redemption, by inviting them authentically to confront and wrestle with the truth and the actuality of the human predicament, to be completed such a redemptive process needs to be supplemented and qualified by the specific function of a *redeemer-figure*, without which the process could be said to lack both focus and intelligibility.

Traditionally, therefore, Christ is seen in the Christian tradition as the ultimate, and exclusive, redemptive figure, in that he is believed to have come into this world by the grace of God to bring about the salvation of sinful humanity by means of his sacrificial death upon the Cross. In this respect, there is no possibility or hope of redemption outside the boundaries of the Christian faith, or at the very least unless the specific presence and activity of Jesus Christ is in some way integral to the redemptive process. According to Martin Luther, indeed, 'man' cannot achieve salvation by any means other than through faith in God's grace and justice, as disclosed through Christ.[1] On this basis, *film noir* would seem a very bizarre candidate for redemptive activity. Within Christian theology, however, there has been an increased tendency among many theologians, especially over recent centuries, to change the orientation and scope of the concept of redemption from one which construes Christ as the ultimate, and exclusive, redemptive figure to one which accords a more prominent emphasis to the role of the *human individual* in the redemptive process. Redemption may be inextricably bound up with the person of Christ, but those whose lives have been variously touched and transformed by Christ's redemptive work, and who have subsequently sought to model their lives after him, are categorized, in effect, as *Christ-figures*. The New Testament, for example, challenges all Christians to become followers, or models, of Jesus Christ, as indicated by St Paul's exhortation in his first epistle to the Christian community at Corinth to 'Be imitators of me, as I am of Christ.'[2] In the light of this somewhat anthropocentric dimension to the redemptive process, which has widened out the definition of who or what actually constitutes a redemptive figure, I will demonstrate in this chapter how *film noir* has a particularly good claim to be interpreted as a site of redemptive activity involving the clear presence of what may be said to amount to functional equivalents of Christ.

The Christian basis of the filmic redeemer/ Christ-figure

Whereas Augustine perceived the whole of human history to be the story of a continual degradation as a consequence of original sin, a number of Christian theologians, particularly since the Enlightenment, have been influenced by an anthropological dimension to the redemptive process. The theology of the second-century thinker Irenaeus has been especially crucial in this regard. According to Irenaeus, the sin of Adam and Eve did not result in the forfeiture of perfection and in any hope of its restoration by anything other than external, supernatural means, in the form of the redemption wrought by Jesus Christ on behalf of the sins of humanity. Rather, human beings must have been created in an imperfect state and, having been endowed with free will, are capable of *self*-improvement, and of *themselves* becoming 'children of God'. In Irenaeus' words, 'Man was a child; and his mind was not yet fully mature . . . How then will any man be a God, if he has not first been made a man? How can any be perfect when he has only lately been made a man?'³ As Augustine's contemporary, Pelagius, attested in the early fifth century, since Jesus, in the Sermon on the Mount, orders human beings to *perfect* themselves, perfection must then be within their power. This is clearly in contradistinction to Augustine's claim that, without the intervention of Christ, humankind is 'a race condemned', and destined to live for eternity in 'that dreadful abyss of ignorance from which all error flows'.⁴ Ultimately, for Pelagius, we must be capable of progressing to better and better states until heaven on earth is ultimately achieved. If, in marked contrast, it was not possible to reach perfection because something in human nature blocks it, then, argued Pelagius, God would be a sadistic divinity, ordering us to do what we cannot help but fail to do. According to Pelagius, we sin by a *voluntary* imitation of Adam's sin, 'corrupted indeed by external environment and by successive wrong choices that weaken the will's resolution, but never by a fault inherent in the "nature" with which we are born into the world'.⁵ Hence, according to Clement of Alexandria, a new born baby could not have fallen under Adam's curse insofar as he or she has not actually done anything wrong. Only our *personal* misdeeds render us liable to sin.

Consequently, in the Enlightenment, 'there was a widespread suspicion of any notion that help was available from *beyond* the human mind'.⁶ What was ultimately needed was a change in human beings rather than 'the placating of any supernatural authorities'⁷ if redemption was to be operative. This essentially *anthropological* approach to redemption was, moreover, an important step at a time when the traditional understanding of sin as a hereditary transmission from generation to generation was becoming increasingly untenable in the light of contemporary scientific discoveries. As a corollary of Charles Darwin's theory of evolution, indeed, as expounded in *The Origin of Species*, the creation of species, including humankind, was shown to have required no divine 'plan' but had originated, rather, by virtue of the continual 'struggle for life' between individuals and varieties of the same species. In Darwin's words,

> Can we doubt (remembering that many more individuals are born than can possibly survive) that individuals having any advantage, however slight, over others, would have the best chance of surviving and of procreating their kind? . . . This preservation of favourable individual differences and variations, and the destruction of those which are injurious, I have called Natural Selection, or the Survival of the Fittest.[8]

Evolution therefore called into question the existence of Adam and Eve as two fully human beings created at the start of time, and, as a corollary, of the need for redemption from original sin. Since it has taken human beings millions of years to reach our present stage of development from what is commonly supposed in modern evolutionary theory to be our origin in Ramapithecus, 'an ape-like creature who lived between fourteen million and three million years ago',[9] it is wholly unintelligible to suppose that a fully formed human being came into existence on the sixth day of creation, and in whose transgression the entire human race was subsequently implicated.

In the light of these insuperable difficulties with the traditional understanding of sin and redemption, it is significant that, in the Enlightenment, there was generally a shift in emphasis away from the – albeit fundamental – role played by God and Christ in the redemptive process, and a concomitant tendency to concentrate more on the manner in which each individual human being has the capacity to undergo redemption *within themselves*, with Jesus as the primal historical *model* of such a process. While Lutheran and Calvinist Protestants continued to focus on a scripturally based discussion of the nature and character of God, to the effect that redemption was believed to rest exclusively within God's juris-diction, other Protestant groups, such as the Methodists, Quakers and Pentecostalists, directed attention more onto the nature and character of the human individual in the redemptive process. For modern liberal theologians, indeed, rather than being in need of redemption through Jesus Christ there is a key sense in which each individual person is believed to be capable of attaining his or her *own* redemption, by consciously and authentically responding to the innate potential for goodness that is intrinsic to each person. Immanuel Kant, for example, held that redemption lies in our imitation of Jesus' praxis, or moral example, and that it is our moral duty to elevate ourselves to his example of moral perfection.[10] In *Religion within the Limits of Reason Alone*, Kant points out,

> We can certainly hope to partake in the appropriation of [Christ's] atoning merit, and so of salvation, only by qualifying for it through our own efforts to fulfil every human duty – and this obedience must be the effect of our own action and not . . . of a foreign influence in the presence of whom we are passive.[11]

The moral individual thus determines what he or she does, and bears the responsibility for his or her own actions. Redemption is therefore an *inward* experience, whereby, as Kant puts it, within the heart of each individual person the new moral person in us suffers vicariously for the old 'sinner'. Although there are clear parallels with Anselm's satisfaction theory of atonement, insofar as one needs to make a satisfaction for the guilt that he or she has incurred – such that, in Livingston's words, 'The new man in us is our Redeemer who accepts the punishment of the old man's sins as a vicarious punishment'[12] – Kant nevertheless *interiorized* Anselm's theory, interpreting it as a largely *symbolic* activity, and thereby stripping it of the somewhat offensive and morally abhorrent notion of an innocent human being bearing the guilt for somebody *else's* sins.

For Kierkegaard, moreover, only an 'extreme individualism' and a 'subjective introspection'[13] would enable a human being to make 'that personal leap of faith from melancholic guilt, fear and despair'[14] to something which resembles an experience of redemption. For Kierkegaard, sin – which was 'the fundamental fact of man's spiritual and moral position'[15] – could only be overcome by 'the transformation of the whole life of a man',[16] and could be reached only *subjectively*, 'in the conflicts of personal experience'.[17] Although redemption cannot be seen in isolation from a living faith in Jesus Christ, and requires for its operation a decisive act of faith, 'a leap or spring into a new relationship with God'[18] – such that it is in the individual person's decision *vis-à-vis* God, the Wholly Other, that redemption from sin is possible – it is nonetheless possible to see in Kierkegaard's theology a certain existentialist strand of thought which, in Vidler's words, 'left God out of the picture and saw the human person as ultimately alone in his freedom and in his obligation to decide what he was going to do with his freedom'.[19] Such thinking also permeates the thought of other post-Enlightenment Christian theologians, for whom, like Friedrich Schleiermacher, everything in Christianity is bound up with the redemption accomplished by Jesus Christ, but in which the starting-point is the individual Christian's *experience* of Christ's redemptive work. As Livingston points out, with respect to Schleiermacher's theology, 'God cannot be known as an independent object, out there somewhere, but only in relation to our own self-consciousness.'[20] Although, for Schleiermacher, the process of redemption cannot be dissociated 'from the person of Jesus Christ by means of his self-communication to man of his unique God-consciousness',[21] the redemptive process necessarily involves an essential *human* response to Christ's activity. Indeed, without 'a vital human receptivity'[22] to the redemption accomplished by Christ, we would be unable to overcome our sensuality and worldly desires and our propensity to sin, or to order our earthly lives in such a way that pain and melancholy ultimately give way to pleasure and a state of equilibrium.[23]

   This anthropological dimension to the Christian understanding of redemption has one of its most cogent, and recent, formulations in the theology of John Hick, according to whom the term must be thought of 'in terms of the actual quality of human existence'.[24] Indeed, whereas salvation used to be thought of in Christian theology 'as a juridical and metaphysical idea',[25] whereby since 'Christ had died for us on the cross . . . so now God could justly forgive and accept us'[26], Hick recognizes that 'it is very hard today to make sense of so morally alien an idea.'[27] In its place, Hick proposes that 'the meaning of our present earthly life'[28] can be seen to lie in the struggle in which all humans are engaged with the problem of evil. Although it has traditionally been supposed that redemption entails suddenly being 'made perfect' or being 'magically protected'[29] from the evil and suffering that prevails on earth, Hick argues that redemption requires the process of confronting and seeking to thwart the problem of evil *within human existence*. Indeed, if humans are to have a chance of 'becoming more of what their innate potentiality for growth promises',[30] then the 'divine hand must be stayed from interference'[31] in human affairs. Moral responsibility and personal growth are, then, only possible in a world where human beings have to face the challenges and adversities of human existence, and so of becoming more fully human and 'fulfilling the God-given potentialities of their nature'.[32]

The model, or exemplar, of this person-making process is Jesus Christ, in that, although his crucifixion represents a supreme act of evil, an unjust and fearfully painful death – indeed, it constitutes the 'murder' of the Son of God – the spirit in which Jesus accepted his suffering on the Cross was not one of enmity, of meeting evil with 'an answering evil of hatred',[33] but one rather of *selfless acceptance*. This attitude of Jesus has, as Hick attests, 'been in the pattern of the Christian response to suffering ever since'.[34] For, although evil is not in itself a good, and does not by itself become good, its existence can nevertheless be *used for* good, in the respect that it can give men and women a chance to perform *positive* acts. Amid hardship, for instance, Hick points out that people 'have found strength of character' and 'in crises have become competent to help others'.[35] Ultimately, a world without evils would be a world in which we 'could show no forgiveness, no compassion' and 'no self-sacrifice'.[36] While Hick indicates that God 'desired' his Son to undergo his death on the Cross 'for the sake of mankind',[37] such that there is an atonement-dimension to Christ's redemptive activity, Hick is nonetheless resolutely clear that humankind's attainment of redemption is a strictly *personal* and *human* endeavour and responsibility.

Ultimately, therefore, the modern interpretation of redemption has a substantially human-centred, and even subjective, orientation, its tendency being towards *anthropocentrism*. Whether construed in terms of Schleiermacher's talk of 'God-consciousness', Kierkegaard's 'paradoxical faith beyond reason' or Hick's 'person-making' theodicy, the traditional tendency to lay total responsibility for the redemptive process on Jesus Christ has been de-emphasized within modern liberal theology, with the focus residing not on the Messiah's saving of humankind through the shedding of his blood on the Cross but on the role played by human beings themselves as they endeavour to reach perfection *within themselves*, by following the moral and spiritual example set by Christ. Within the context of this more anthropological approach to redemption, there is a significant degree to which *film noir* may feasibly be construed as a fertile site of redemptive activity. While the influence of Jesus Christ is neither explicit nor implicit – indeed, it is non-existent – in *films noirs*, and while among many orthodox Christians today redemption 'is so uniquely Christian that it is hardly worth one's effort to look for instances of it'[38] outside of the Christian faith, there is an intrinsic sense in which an *analogous* process is in operation. For, the *noir* protagonist may be interpreted as a *functional equivalent of Christ*, who performs the Christ-like role of undertaking a process of redemption from sin, guilt and alienation, the benefits of which may be passed on and imparted to other human beings.

Discussing the World Council of Churches' Commission on World Mission and Evangelism, which addressed the theme of 'Salvation today' in preparation for its 1972 meeting, Thomas Wieser has written that, in contradistinction to the (ever-diminishing) affirmation within the Christian faith that 'outside the Church there is no salvation',[39] a number of Christian churches have come to concede that 'the universal significance of salvation in Christ becomes manifest in many situations', and that the Church 'can at best be *one* of the groups manifesting salvation today'.[40] The specific context of Wieser's argument, and the WCC Commission which prompted it, is whether or not non-Christian religious traditions – such as Hinduism, Buddhism, Islam and Judaism – have the capacity to offer salvation, but it does not seem too wide of the mark to propose, especially in an age in which the media can be seen to be all-pervasive, that the medium of film, while functioning outside traditionally demarcated boundaries of religious activity, may in actuality prove to comprise an equally fecund repository of religious significance. Although within the film's (fictional) space the *noir* protagonist may be little more than 'a rat in a maze', who, in the manner of Harry Fabian in *Night and the City*, 'plunges desperately through a claustrophobic world beset by menacing shadows in a futile attempt to evade his fate',[41] the *noir* 'redeemer', I will evince, has the potential to enable the *film audience*, in a manner akin to the influence of the person of Christ upon the *Christian community*, to confront their human inadequacies and weaknesses and to undergo a subsequent personal and/or moral development, without the need for 'any direct encounter with God' or the 'placating of any supernatural authorities'.[42]

Film as a site of Christological significance

It is thus significant that, as Peter Malone attests, although film-makers may not be committed to belief in the person of Christ, many of them – whether consciously or unconsciously – use Christ-figures in their work.[43] Indeed, 'Diverse cultures around the world have absorbed the Gospels into their consciousness and into their imagination and language',[44] with the result that it is not uncommon to find in the medium of film the person of Christ used as a metaphor, a symbol or as an image of certain values which the film-makers wish to explore. In Gaye Ortiz's words, 'many film heroes are in fact Christ figures, who experience the kinds of things Christ did or who personify the righteous, loving, self-sacrificing Christ'[45] of the Christian tradition. The qualification needs to be made, however, that of the films which either feature Jesus Christ as the central figure – in cinematic versions of biblical stories, for instance – or which feature characters who may be interpreted as functional equivalents of Christ, it is not the case that, in all such representations, the Christ-figure bears any affiliation – implicit or explicit – with the quintessentially alienated and dysfunctional nature of the *noir* protagonist.

Indeed, while a substantial number of contemporary film characters bear witness to, and may be seen to embody, discernibly Christian characteristics and motifs pertaining to redemption, he or she is, on the whole, closer in nature to the kind of figure portrayed in many of the pre-Enlightenment formulations of Christology within the Christian church, wherein, as the fourth-century Christian apologist Apollinaris of Laodicea espoused, 'Christ is not a human being'[46] but is no more than *like* a human being, since, by virtue of his divine status as the Son of God, it is inconceivable for such a figure to possess a human nature, let alone ordinary human flesh. Hence, while redeemer-figures may abound in popular film, there are marked differences regarding the manner in which they need to be interpreted and understood, with many such figures corresponding more to categories and genres of film of an escapist and wish-fulfilment sensibility than to the intrinsically human and estranged milieu of *film noir*.

'High' forms of Christology

According to Apollinaris, since only God can save the world then, if Christ is our Saviour, he must be a completely *divine* figure. In effect, since the human mind is prone to sin, it is unthinkable that the Logos 'should be affected by physical conditions of any sort or that he should share in human emotion or human ignorance'.[47] Although one may be inclined to speak of the body of Christ in human terms, it is more properly to be understood, according to Apollinaris, as belonging to the *divine* life, which has simply been *conferred* on the body. In his words, 'Christ is not a human being but is *like* a human being, since he is not coessential with humanity in his highest part.'[48] In spite of the post-Enlightenment tendency within Christian theology to interpret the person of Christ as an intrinsically *human* figure who, as Kant attested, is the exemplar or model of human moral conduct and behaviour, it tends to be the case that, as Alan Richardson has pointed out, 'Many people to-day are Apollinarian'[49] in their Christology, whether they are conscious of it or not. It is often, indeed, understood to be the *orthodox* Christian interpretation of the person of Christ, and is borne out in such commonplace Christian affirmations as 'Jesus is God' and when one says that in the person of Christ we see God living out a human life for the purpose of our redemption.

In the light of this emphasis upon the divine nature of Christ, at the expense of the human, it is significant that Don Cupitt argued in *The Sea of Faith* that

> From its Protestant background American popular culture has inherited a craving for supernatural redeemer-figures, beings who descend to earth and live incognito until the moment when they are called upon to reveal their true identity and use their superhuman powers in the cause of truth, justice and the American Way.[50]

The plethora of such characters in films is a testimony to the substantial degree to which superhuman and essentially divine figures perform an integral function in contemporary Western culture, in a manner which might be compared to the emphasis accorded by such theologians as Apollinaris to Christ's divine nature. As Lee Mason has indicated with specific reference to superhero comic books, from which a number of such cinematic figures originate, the superhero-figure in popular culture is elevated beyond the context of society 'into an essentially fantastical world of possibly archetypal conflicts'.[51] 'Superman', for instance – the subject of four motion pictures between 1978 and 1987 – first appeared in *Action Comics* in 1938 as an ostensibly human newspaper reporter 'who, when a crisis threatened, ripped off his dull suit to reveal the bright attire of an alien being of incalculable power dedicated to saving lives and fighting crime'.[52]

In their book, *The American Monomyth*, Robert Jewett and John Shelton Lawrence detect in American popular culture the repeated myth of a community in a harmonious paradise which is threatened by some evil – usually cosmic in its consequences – which normal human institutions and agencies are incapable of overcoming. In such situations, 'a selfless superhero emerges to . . . carry out the redemptive task'.[53] The redeemer-figure thereby delivers a decisive victory over the forces of evil and restores 'the community to its paradisal condition'.[54] The analogy with the Apollinarian Christology is especially potent when it is considered that the superhero does not work within society's law enforcement structures, such as the police and the judiciary, but relies, rather, on his *own* (superior) power and intelligence. The superhuman protagonists in popular film amount, effectively, to self-reliant individuals who possess the capacity to stand aloof from society, to operate according to their own code of honour and thereby achieve the requisite victory.

Steven Spielberg's 'Indiana Jones' is capable of overcoming the seemingly most impossible odds to achieve victory over those who would seek to thwart the path of justice and righteousness. What is not questioned in *Raiders of the Lost Ark* (1981), for instance, is that Indiana Jones (Harrison Ford) is the embodiment of good, and, even, the necessary agent of morality in an otherwise all-too-human world, where the absence of such certainty and sense of virtue is a pervasive, even defining, characteristic. In a similar vein, messianic connotations are clearly discernible in *Star Wars* (1977), insofar as the protagonist, Luke Skywalker (Mark Hamill), is a simple farmboy who becomes a disciple of the last of the Jedi Knights, Obi Wan Kenobi (Alec Guinness), who fought to defend the 'Force'. Kenobi's death then completes the Christ-link since it is at the hands of a cosmic rebel, Darth Vader (David Prowse) – who has been likened to Judas in the Christian tradition[55] – and with whom Skywalker engages in an apocalyptic confrontation at the end. In a manner analogous to Jesus' bestowing the Holy Spirit, or Paraklete, on his disciples – 'Peace be with you'[56] – as testified in John's Gospel, Luke Skywalker places his blessing – 'The Force be with you' – on Hans Solo (Harrison Ford) at the end of *Star Wars*. Hence, just as Christ informs his disciples that the Spirit of Truth will fulfil the function of Jesus once he has ascended and is no longer in the physical presence of his followers – thereby consoling and comforting future Christians once he has materially 'gone away'[57] – the intergalactic, effectively supernatural, battle between Darth Vader and Luke Skywalker will be waged not by the Christ-figure himself but by future generations of disciples and converts. The messianic influence of the Christ-figure can therefore be seen to spread, with his divine attributes inherited by individuals who are also engaged in a distinctly *super*-human struggle.

Furthermore, Clint Eastwood's character in *Pale Rider* (1985) may be interpreted as a messianic character, or Christ-figure, who arrives in a small mining community to dispense judgement when the community falls victim to a powerful strip-mining company that wishes to drive the people from the land. As a young girl reads aloud from a passage in the Book of Revelation, which speaks of 'a pale horse' and its rider, whose 'name was Death',[58] who were 'given power over a fourth of the earth, to kill with sword and with famine and with pestilence',[59] a stranger appears from out of nowhere, riding on a pale horse. As Robert Banks points out, he gives no indication as to where he has come from, the suggestion being that he is a supernatural figure or agent of some sort.[60] He is not reluctant to use force against the mining baron and his operations, and, indeed, the end-battle has been likened by Conrad Ostwalt to Armageddon, after which the 'righteous' community is left to establish its own utopia.[61] Although Eastwood's character remains somewhat ambiguous – we do not even learn his name – there is a discernible Christian connection inasmuch as he turns up during a fight wearing a dog collar, and is accorded the name 'the Preacher' by the community. He exclaims 'God damn' when defeating his opponents, and 'Jesus' when he comes out unscathed from a gunfight with five men. According to Banks, these names seem to be as much identifications as to which powers are at work in him as they are profane exclamations.[62]

Moreover, even among films which are *specifically* about the person of Christ, the traditional emphasis is also on Christ's divinity, in which – in a form which the divine and supernatural natures of the redeemer-figures in films such as *Star Wars* could be said to emulate – 'everything combines to suggest inhuman agency'.[63] In George Stevens's *The Greatest Story ever Told* (1965), for example, the focus is on the divine Jesus of Apollinarian thought, even to the extent that, as James Wall has observed, Jesus (Max von Sydow) is presented as an 'ethereal' figure, and 'above the common squabbles'[64] that beset finite, human beings. Indeed, the early religious epics about the life of Christ were predilected to portray the Messiah as 'a golden-haired, "Jesus meek and mild"'[65] stereotypical character, whose disciples were effectively 'mere puppets who blindly followed a man'[66] as a consequence of his exalted, even magisterial, status as the Son of God. In respect of his absolute and thoroughgoing divinity, the blind are therefore made to see, the lame to walk and the deaf to hear,[67] Lazarus is made to rise from his tomb, water is turned into wine, five barley loaves and two fish are more than sufficient to feed a crowd of five thousand people, and Jesus is to be resurrected and glorified on the third day – all without any need for rational explanation or empirical authentication. Virtually every Hollywood treatment of the life of Christ has, indeed, taken such an approach, with 'inspirational readings of scripture', and 'swelling music' used to complement the 'grandiose spectacle'.[68] In short, then, it is apparent that among both films which specifically delineate the person of Christ and films whose protagonists may be read as in some sense Christ-figures, it is the Apollinarian portrait of Jesus that holds particular resonance. As Babington and Evans put it, 'the greatest constraint on the Hollywood Christ narrative is its requirement at least formally to accept Christ's divinity'.[69]

The need for a human (low) Christology

In order, however, for the person of Christ to constitute an *exemplar* or *paradigm* of redemptive activity in the way that the Christian tradition believes is fundamental to his nature and essence, it is clear that the Apollinarian emphasis on Christ's divinity is in need of a substantial revision. For, as Bruce David Forbes observes, 'traditional Christian doctrine about Jesus Christ

as both fully human and fully divine requires inclusion of the
human side of the equation in order for the crucifixion to serve as
atoning work'.[70] Indeed, without an adequate emphasis on the
authentically human nature of the person of Christ, which is liable
to result from an over-emphasis on his divinity, the extent to
which the person of Christ constitutes a redemptive figure is
actually placed in serious jeopardy. In short, contrary to the
Apollinarian understanding that Christ is the redeemer simply by
virtue of his divine essence, the inherently human aspect of his
personality is absolutely essential to the redemptive process.
Consequently, according to Christian teaching in this regard,
Adam's sin and subsequent spiritual death have been inherited by
all humans from generation to generation,[71] to the effect that God
was not present in any other human being until Jesus' entry into
the world. As the Antiochene Christological picture, as adduced
by Theodore of Mopsuestia in the fourth century, attests, since the
soul is the centre of our consciousness, the soul is therefore that
part of human nature which is in need of redemption, and – by
logical inference – for redemption to be operative a *human* soul is
necessarily required. Provided that Christ's human nature is in no
way compromised, Jesus Christ is thus able to perform the
function of humankind's redeemer, by having undergone what it
means to be fully human, the epitome of which is his death upon
the Cross.

Hence, while not denying that Jesus was the Son of God,
Theodore argued that it is Jesus' completely *human* nature 'in
whom humanity's common destiny is both summed up and
determined'[72] that enables Jesus to be construed as a redemptive
figure. Although Christ is believed to have conquered decisively all
hostile powers that impair human life, this has only been achieved
at the cost of considerable *human* suffering.[73] Rather than as a
fearless and invincible figure, therefore, he 'has been beaten
down'[74] and 'has descended into the utter depths of weakness',[75]
trembling with human fear and anxiety. In short, Christ has
performed the role of the 'Second Adam', by reversing Adam's
original disobedience, and as a consequence of which – and *only*
as a consequence of which – we are able to share in his saving
power.

In bearing witness to an Apollinarian Christology, a film such as
The Greatest Story ever Told therefore poses substantial problems,

and these are mirrored in the criticism that the film has received. *The Greatest Story* may have been made in the grand, Hollywood epic-spectacular style, with widescreen photography, a massive set, elaborate costumes and choreography, an ever-swelling musical score and no apparent limit on costs,[76] but, in Lloyd Baugh's words, the film was actually a failure 'both in transmitting faithfully the content and meaning of the Gospel narrative and in representing adequately the person and significance of Jesus the Christ'.[77] As Baugh puts it,

> In Stevens' mind, the awesome salvific event of Jesus the Christ, the narrative of universal human redemption through the extraordinary intervention of the incarnate Son of God, clearly the greatest story ever told and a story in which he, as a devout Christian, sincerely believed, required a vast, cosmic, universal, timeless framework.[78]

Furthermore, the Jesus of Stevens's film speaks in phrases from the King James Version of the Bible, which has the effect of placing Jesus in a category apart from all the other characters in the film, 'who use colloquial vocabulary and speak in everyday tones and cadences'.[79] The film repeatedly affirms its protagonist's identity as 'the Divine One', from the words of the Prologue to the Fourth Gospel which are invoked at the beginning, to the 'Hallelujah' chorus at both the raising of Lazarus and, at the end, as the finale accompanying Christ's resurrection and ascension. In reducing Jesus' humanity in this way, the pivotal human and incarnational dimension to his character is effectively lost, resulting in a Jesus who is divine and transcendent, yet far from an archetypal human being, or a model, or exemplar, of redemptive possibility. Consequently, as well as being a commercial disaster – the film's budget spiralled from around $10 million to $25 million,[80] and it made an overall loss of $18 million[81] – *The Greatest Story ever Told* may also be seen to constitute 'a colossal failure'[82] on theological grounds.

The cinematic portrayal of Christ as an authentically human figure

Jesus Christ may thus be seen to constitute for Christians the ultimate, and supreme, redemptive figure inasmuch as he constitutes an exemplar of humanity – he has gone before us as an example and pioneer – and we are thereby able to share in the benefits of his salvation. Indeed, as Peter Malone indicates, 'In times of doubt and disillusionment, the redeemer-figure offers some notion of meaning, reconciliation and atonement.'[83] Even among non-believers, Malone attests that human beings throughout the course of history 'have been able to draw on the experience of Jesus as a metaphor or as a symbol of the suffering which does not turn in on itself in despair or bitterness but is offered to others for support, courage or endurance'.[84] It can, at the very least, reveal to us something of our potential as human beings, and provide directions as to how one can lead one's life. As regards the cinematic presentation of the person of Christ, it is thus significant that, in contradistinction to the ethereal and divine interpretation of Jesus as delineated in a film such as George Stevens's *The Greatest Story ever Told*, recent Christ-films have, on the whole, portrayed Jesus as a thoroughly human character, like the *noir* protagonist, struggling to come to terms with his humanity.

Such a representation is, for example, reflected in Nicholas Ray's *King of Kings* (1961), which is inclined to concentrate more on the human nature of Jesus (Jeffrey Hunter), rather than on his divinity. According to Edward O'Connor, moreover, 'Not once in this film is Christ shown claiming divinity, and some scenes are so constructed that he seems to be disclaiming it.'[85] Only two minor miracles are represented in the picture, and even then they are performed in silence, while all that Ray allows the viewer to see is Jesus' shadow. The person healed is not even touched by Jesus. There is no raising of Lazarus, cleansing of lepers or feeding of the five thousand. Even the one exorcism that Jesus carries out is seriously downplayed, in that the demoniac literally stumbles into Jesus' arms. His preaching is limited to the Sermon on the Mount, and it is notable in this scene that Jesus refers to himself on more than one occasion not as the Son of *God* but as the Son of *Man*.

A clear parallel can be drawn, furthermore, between Ray's interpretation of the person of Christ and some of the prot-agonists – who amount effectively to functional equivalents of the human figure of Jesus of Nazareth – in his other, ostensibly secular films. Humphrey Bogart in *In a Lonely Place* (1950), for instance, plays a character who takes the side of the underdog, as a washed-up actor who comes to be victimized by his enemies, thereby developing discernibly Christian motifs on the subject of Christ's betrayal, humiliation and suffering. In both of these films – the one specifically religious in theme, the other implicitly religious – as well as in Ray's 1951 picture *On Dangerous Ground*, Babington and Evans observe that 'there is a moment where the male protagonist must make a decision about the direction to be taken for the rest of his life'.[86] In *Rebel without a Cause* (1955), moreover, it is apposite that 'this moment of renewal actually takes. place against an Easter background'.[87] Ultimately, then, although on the one hand we observe Ray's Jesus as a figure endeavouring to 'construct the heroic identity that will lead him to fulfil his destiny'[88] as the divine Son of God, on the other we see in the person of Christ signs of an authentically human struggle to come to terms, and to engage, with his basic *humanity*, further testimony to which is disclosed in Ray's 'secular' Christ-like protagonists.

The epitome of an Antiochene Christology: *The Last Temptation Of Christ*

Martin Scorsese's emphasis on the humanity of Jesus even goes one stage further than Ray's picture, as his *Last Temptation of Christ* (1988) testifies, to the extent in fact that Scorsese's Jesus (Willem Dafoe) is an especially apposite prototype of the *film noir* protagonist. On its release in 1988, the film received a storm of protest from a variety of evangelical groups, which was, according to Roy Kinnard and Tim Davis, 'far more widespread and volatile than any previous criticism directed against a Hollywood religious film'.[89] The US Catholic Bishops' Conference even called for a nationwide boycott of the film, 'the first such boycott the conference had ever recommended'.[90] Many of those who protested against the film had not actually seen it, however. Among these was Franco Zeffirelli, who had made a film about Jesus for television back in 1977, *Jesus of Nazareth*, and who condemned Scorsese's film at the 1988 Venice Film Festival for being a 'truly terrible and totally deranged'[91] piece of work. Ironically, however, the Christology of *Last Temptation* is far more theologically acceptable than most filmic representations of the person of Christ. According to Michael Morris, in a review of Scorsese's picture in the October 1988 edition of *American Film*,

One notices how free it is of the ponderous solemnity that so typifies the genre. Gone are the endless choirs of angels singing in the soundtrack. Gone are the awestruck audiences surrounding Christ. Gone is the starchiness that tends to mummify the actor playing the lead role.[92]

In its place is a more human and personal representation of Jesus who, appropriately for a figure who is a model or exemplar of redemptive possibility, is, to quote Lloyd Baugh, 'more in touch with issues that trouble . . . humanity'.[93]

Whereas in Ray's film, the scene when Jesus delivers the Sermon on the Mount is visually sublime, 'with Jesus looking down on a huge multitude-filled valley, its epic scale underwritten by the improbably huge audience',[94] Scorsese's picture locates both Jesus and his audience on the same physical level. And, in the place of what Babington and Evans identify as Ray's smooth, structural mobility, we have in *The Last Temptation* Scorsese's use of jagged editing, fast pans and 'the camera's pretence at failure to predict Jesus's sudden movements leading to rapid reframing'.[95] What is more, although the Jesus of *King of Kings* is questioned by the crowd, he nevertheless responds to their questions with an 'almost metronomic authority'.[96] Scorsese's Jesus, on the other hand, *exudes* doubt and uncertainty in the manner of the *noir* protagonist, seeming at times to plead for approval from his audience. Whereas the Sermon on the Mount in Ray's film concludes with the Lord's Prayer, in *The Last Temptation* the Sermon is a confused and uncertain event in Jesus' ministry, in which 'the crowd rushes off in vengeful disarray', before he has even finished speaking, having 'fundamentally misunderstood'[97] his teaching. This ambiguous delineation is further exemplified by Scorsese's use of music on the film soundtrack, not to underscore inspirationally 'the truths of Christianity, as in the traditional usage of the Ray sequence' but to signify, rather, an escalating sense of 'clamour and chaos'.[98]

Ultimately, therefore, it is apparent that *The Last Temptation* takes issue with the Alexandrian portrait of Jesus that, as Scorsese points out, he was taught at his Roman Catholic school in his youth, whereby the figure of Jesus effectively glowed in the dark and carried his celestial choir around with him everywhere.[99] Scorsese's Jesus has an unambiguously human essence, even to the degree that he is unsure as to whether he is merely an ordinary mortal as opposed to a divine incarnation and whether his vocation is to start a family rather than, in line with popular messianic expectations of the first century, to save a nation, reform a religion or forge a *new* path to salvation. In Keyser's words, in this respect,

> His path to Golgotha is rocky and uneven, and his time on the cross unsettled and confused . . . His Christ wavered between roles, as saviour and loving husband, as Messiah and worldly patriarch, as military deliverer and Prince of Peace, as mystical visionary and disturbed carpenter, as priestly king and as humble homesteader.[100]

In stark contrast, then, to traditional Christ films, 'Scorsese's Jesus offers the viewer little escape from his tormented consciousness',[101] to the point that he is essentially 'fragmented' and 'almost schizophrenic' in nature,[102] talking in a 'fragmented, personal voice, adrift and uncontextualised', and 'speaking incoherently of the external forces that possess him'.[103]

However, this emphasis on Jesus' humanity is necessary for, 'if Christ is solely God', then 'temptation is meaningless, resistance is easy, struggle is absent' and the film – and, by inference, the ontological purpose of the incarnation and redemption – 'loses its *raison d'être*'.[104] Indeed, what comes to the fore in Scorsese's *noir*-orientated picture is that 'Christ triumphs on the Cross not simply because as God he can do no less but because as man he faces down his demons'.[105] *The Last Temptation* does not deny Christ's divinity, but, in contradistinction to the traditional Christ epic, it stresses the *unity* between the divine and human natures such that, as an example and pioneer, Christ can fulfil the function of redeemer through having already undergone what it means to be fully human. In theological terms, Scorsese's picture thus fits comfortably into the Antiochene Christological formulation, in which, as Theodore believed, both the divine and human natures subsist, and are juxtaposed in, the same *prosopon*, or person, of Christ. Although both natures are *capable* of separate existence, Theodore assigns a 'hypostasis' – an objective, real existence – to each of the two natures, without playing down Christ's human nature at the expense of his divinity.

In one critical respect, Theodore's Christology is much more conservative than Scorsese's interpretation of Jesus, insofar as

Theodore believed that Jesus never wavered in his response to God since he possessed the 'co-operating grace' of the Logos from the very beginning, which 'corresponded with His own determination'[106] that good was always to be sought and evil avoided, whereas Scorsese's Jesus is a weak, dithering individual, 'beset by voices he cannot still calling him to a vocation he does not want'.[107] One must be cautious, therefore, of assuming out of hand that Scorsese's representation of Jesus is, without qualification, completely theologically sound, and thereby draw the logical corollary that the *noir* protagonist is, equally, an innately orthodox and fundamentally Christ-like figure. There are, however, enough discernible, and judicious, *parallels* between the Christian understanding of the person of Christ and Scorsese's *noir*-orientated protagonist to warrant an affiliation. Indeed, although *The Last Temptation* concludes with Jesus fully accepting his divinity and embracing his messianic calling, as prefigured by his ability earlier on in his ministry to cure the sick, raise Lazarus from the dead and to turn water into wine at a wedding feast, this only occurs *after* he has been tempted off the Cross to live and die as an ordinary human being.

Hence, although Jesus' divine nature may ensure that he is able to transcend the possibility of being tempted, as a complete human being Jesus is nonetheless capable of yielding to temptation, as the film somewhat provocatively testifies. And, despite departing in many respects from the Christian gospel – the basis to Scorsese's Jesus is, after all, Nikos Kazantzakis's novel *The Last Temptation of Christ* – there is a clear biblical foundation to the picture. The authentically human facet of Jesus does, of course, concur with much of the New Testament record, where the human nature of Jesus is clearly delineated. The Fourth Gospel, for instance, presents Jesus as an emotional individual, insofar as we learn that 'Jesus wept'[108] and was 'deeply moved in spirit and troubled'[109] at the death of Lazarus, and the Gospel of Mark portrays Jesus as being prone to anger,[110] as well as being, at one point, 'beside himself'.[111] Despite pacific tendencies, moreover, Jesus is capable of uttering inflammatory words,[112] he overturns 'the tables of the money-changers and the seats of those who sold pigeons'[113] in the temple for turning 'a house of prayer'[114] into 'a den of robbers'[115], and he even curses a fig tree because it fails to provide him with any fruit.[116]

By laying stress on Jesus' humanity in this authentic – and scripturally consonant – fashion, Scorsese may thus be seen to be inviting audiences to respond to Christ as an *exemplar*, which the traditional over-emphasis on his divinity actually precludes. He is a salvific figure – and, indeed, the Christ – precisely *because* of his human weaknesses and struggles. The picture may ostensibly concern an individual who lived in Palestine some two thousand years ago, but the intrinsically *human* dimension of Jesus' struggle necessarily has import for a contemporary audience for whom, as in the case of Jesus, redemption is no sudden and easily attainable activity but the product of an often painful and protracted confrontation with one's basic human condition. At the very least, in an age which, to quote William Telford, 'has demystified its saints, removed its icons from their pedestals, and demoted its heroes, it is fitting that the more realistic and introspective Christ of the 1990s, as brought to us by Scorsese, should share our human capacity for doubt as well as faith' and 'for scepticism as well as hope'.[117]

In Scorsese's delineation of an authentically human character who undergoes a redemptive experience with his finite human condition, the audience's ability to identify with the figure of Jesus may therefore be seen to constitute a site of potential redemptive activity in the spirit of the Antiochene understanding that, since he constitutes 'one of us', *we* are able to share in the redemption that Christ has accomplished. Consequently, the *challenge* of Scorsese's picture is therefore not merely to be able to follow and to make sense of *Jesus'* temptation and struggle, but, as Jonathan Rosenbaum puts it, for the audience to be able 'to identify with it, masochistically as well as narcissistically'.[118] Indeed, just as Christ's life is a persistent conflict and the occasion for considerable self-questioning and, even, neurosis, before his eventual redemption, the film may be seen to 'stage this same conflict and victory in the spectator',[119] wherein the figure of Jesus becomes, in effect, the paradigm, or model, of that experience. It would not be inappropriate, therefore, to categorize *The Last Temptation* as a film redolent in comprehensive redemptive significance and, even, as Rosenbaum attests, as ultimately capable of bringing 'the question of faith alive in a way that few religious films have attempted'.[120]

Redeemer-figures and the role of the film audience

Of course, in order for one to claim that the audience of a film is in a position to undergo an experience of redemption by following the model, or exemplar, that is set by cinematic presentations of Christ, one must assume that the film audience is at least potentially *receptive* to a religious experience. As I have illustrated, a film is open to multiple readings. A religious interpretation of film constitutes just one of many possible interpretations, and one which has traditionally been shirked by film and religious theorists alike. While the way in which an audience interacts with a film requires, in the final analysis, an empirical investigation into audience behaviour, as far as the *religious* reading of a film is concerned an empirical test is fraught with difficulties. While it is theoretically possible for someone to claim, having watched a film, that they have been in some sense 'redeemed' as a consequence of following on screen the achievements and endeavours of the film protagonist – with the result that their own personal life has been transformed in a manner analogous to a person's having been redeemed by a religious conversion, such as through attending a church service or receiving the religious and moral instruction of a 'guru' or church official – the activity of redemption is not actually such a straightforward and observable process.

It is possible to testify that a film is 'good' or 'bad', whether its quota of romance, action, suspense, special effects or acting has amounted to a worthwhile cinematic or video experience, but a *redemptive* experience is not something that is so readily amenable to analysis or quantification. Since an experience of redemption must involve some sort of transformation of existence, encompassing a confrontation with the sin and alienation which the Christian tradition supposes is our basic human condition, it is unlikely that such a radical and profound activity could emanate from the mere watching of a single film over a two-hour period, no matter how magical or overwhelming the experience. Nor would such a transformation be easily measurable on any empirical scale. Unlike cathartic pleasures, or escapism, redemption would seem not to be located in a dark movie house, where the opportunity to suspend disbelief is sometimes irresistible, but, rather, it requires an authentic encounter with one's very humanity, and the transgressions and weaknesses that form an intrinsic part of human existence.

While it is thus difficult to gauge the degree to which the audience interaction with a film character constitutes a potential redemptive experience, it is striking from many of the reviews and criticism that *film noir* has received from film authors and theorists that, for all the bleakness, chaos and volatility that such films delineate, it is *noir*'s emphasizing of precisely these themes that warrants a religious reading. Without necessarily being explicit about the religious dimension of *film noir*, a number of film reviewers and writers have borne witness to the religious dimension of such films, finding in *noir*, and its protagonists, analogues and surrogates which, upon reflection, match with, and correspond to, those of the audience's own predicaments and quandaries, which traditional religious traditions also address. Instead of delineating illusory people who have never existed, in the spirit of many of the characters in films of an escapist sensibility, there is a significant degree to which, to paraphrase H. A. Williams's words as regards the characters who appear in poems, plays and novels, the *noir* protagonists 'are us. They are everyman.'[121] Indeed, the *noir* protagonist can only really be known by us to the extent to which the feelings and the predicaments he[122] undergoes are *apprehended* by us as our own. When we therefore meet the characters in film, there is a sense in which 'it is ourselves we meet, even if hitherto we have been unaware of our potential'[123] for sharing any characteristics with such characters, in that they may be seen to exist in a different geographical space, in a separate social or historical context, to have different work and family responsibilities from us, and to find themselves in particular physical or moral circumstances which we have had the fortune, or misfortune, not to have experienced directly.

At the very least, in Ostwalt's words, there is evidence to suggest that 'a good portion of the millions of people who watch movies are affected or changed in some way and that films can exert influence on attitudes, beliefs, and behaviors'.[124] Indeed, in-tellectually elusive though the process may be, if a film was simply perceived as the idiosyncratic vision of its director or producer, it would be difficult to make sense of why *film noir* has the propensity to stimulate such powerful feeling in its audience. If the film audience was not in some sense a part of the film 'text', we would be unable to share the experiences of the film protagonist, and it is doubtful that *films noirs* in particular could have engendered such a high level of response and criticism from film viewers and critics, and enabled *noir* motifs to permeate so much of contemporary cinema, more than fifty years after the term was first appropriated by Nino Frank. Although redemption is an activity that defies strict quantification and measurement, I aim to demonstrate that it is possible to read *noir* protagonists as possible exemplars of redemptive activity, which, in a manner akin to religious faith, entails an often introspective, wholly personal and, at times, painful and protracted experience, facilitated by a complex interaction and exchange between the film 'text' and its audience.

Commonly espoused examples of human Christ-figures in film

That such a process is at least theoretically possible is indicated by the fact that contemporary cinema's predilection to delineate an authentically human Jesus – and thus to portray a figure capable of imparting the possibility of redemption – is mirrored in much of contemporary 'secular' film, where, aside from the plethora of divine and superheroic Christ-figures in the *Star Wars* vein, functional equivalents of human Christ-figures may be seen to abound. In this regard, it is significant that Joel Martin begins his introduction to *Screening the Sacred: Religion, Myth, and Ideology in Popular American Film* by referring to a college associate of his who, after watching Sylvester Stallone's performance as a poor, disenfranchised Italian-American boxer in *Rocky* (1976), was inspired to 'want to get into the best shape possible.'[125] In Martin's words, 'He started jogging and pumping iron; he lost weight and became a respectable athlete',[126] whereas hitherto he was not known for his discipline and drive, but, rather, as someone who frequently drank, played poker and listened to rock and roll. Consequently, 'Jack' 'was not merely entertained for a couple of hours. The event changed his life for a significant period of time – he participated in no less than a conversion experience.'[127] The scenario is analogous to Martha Nussbaum's claim that when audiences attended Greek drama it 'was not to go to a distraction or a fantasy, in the course of which one suspended one's anxious practical questions',[128] but was, rather, a way of engaging in a process of inquiry and reflection. A film may be unable to provide an audience with 'readymade solutions'[129] to personal and social anxieties and concerns, but films do have the potential to 'articulate specific problems and longings'[130] that may pertain to an audience, even managing to help imagine *alternatives* and sometimes *remedies* to the problems at hand.

In this respect, it is pertinent that, in a number of contemporary films, the (human) protagonist may be seen to fulfil a function not incongruous with that of Jesus Christ in the Antiochene tradition. For example, in Marsh and Ortiz's *Explorations in Theology and Film*, Ian Maher's chapter examines the religious theme of liberation in Penny Marshall's *Awakenings* (1990), at one point formulating a connection between the figure of Dr Malcolm Sayer (Robin Williams) – a New York doctor in the 1960s who manages to bring back to consciousness, albeit for a relatively short time, a number of comatose patients, who were victims of the sleeping sickness epidemic encephalitis of the 1920s – and the person of Christ. According to Maher, 'liberation' is concerned with overcoming that which prevents a person from becoming fully human, and – in terms of liberation theology – of 'rescuing all human life from darkness and despair'.[131] In the film, Sayer, based on the real-life neurologist Oliver Sacks, is willing to take on the oppressive and bureaucratic structures at Bainbridge Hospital in the Bronx for the benefit of his helpless patients, with little or no regard for the potential risks to his own reputation or to his future career prospects. Even after the patients have reverted to their comatose condition, when the effects of the drugs used to sustain them have worn out, a conspicuous change has taken place through the care, compassion and love that the patients were shown, and where there had previously been no hope. Liberation has been achieved since the value and worth of each individual human person has been recognized, and each patient has been accorded the dignity each human being deserves, in contra-distinction to the previous implicit assumption by the hospital authorities that the patients were beyond hope of improvement. As far as the audience of the film is concerned, while it is apparent that the effects of liberation can easily be lost, Sayer's work nonetheless illustrates that, to quote Maher, 'awakening moments break through in life in all sorts of unexpected places',[132] and – while often no more than transitory in form – can help us to rethink our attitudes in a manner analogous to his ability to transform the perspectives of the hospital authorities. The qualified nature of his success can, at the very least, enable audiences to rethink their attitudes to the status and humanity of other human beings, and to provide what Maher calls 'signposts to a better way'.[133]

In Peter Weir's *Dead Poets Society* (1989), further, the ability of one individual to enable other human beings to redeem, and transform, their lives is epitomized in the figure of John Keating (Robin Williams), an unorthodox teacher of English in a public school in Vermont in the late 1950s. Welton Academy is a stifling environment. One of the first scenes is of the school's stern trigonometry teacher setting his pupils a heavy quantity of difficult homework, followed by that of the equally strict and conformist classics master regimenting the rote learning of Latin verbs. Academic excellence is the overarching philosophy of the school, where nothing but the highest, most uncompromising pursuit of scholastic distinction is accepted. However, in the words of Brie and Torevell, 'Into this cauldron of conformity steps John Keating who immediately disorientates his students by taking them outside the confines of the classroom for what is essentially an initiation into the world of the "Free Thinker."'[134] Keating becomes the boys' spiritual leader – even advising them to address him as 'Captain' – as he inspires his pupils to follow a path of self-fulfilment and to encounter themselves as individual human beings against the forces of conformity and insti-tutionalization, which have the potential to impede human growth and development. He appeals to them to 'suck the marrow out of life' and *carpe diem*, to 'seize the day', and so make their lives 'extraordinary'. As Brie and Torevell suggest, Keating could therefore be seen to constitute a 'saviour figure', especially in that none of the boys featured has an understanding father in whom they can confide their innermost thoughts. Keating's appeal to self-improvement and edification may even be said to correspond to the biblical injunction to live life to the full, rooted in an embrace of the God-given goodness of creation, and specifically to Jesus' proclamation, as recorded in John 10: 10, that 'I came that they may have life, *and have it abundantly.*'[135]

As in the case of Jesus Christ, however, *Dead Poets Society* demonstrates that the consequence of living with compromises within a social context is that there will, sometimes, have to be *sacrifices*. When Keating's exhortation to 'seize the day' conflicts with the conservative and reactionary disposition of the school, one of the pupils, Neil Perry (Robert Sean Leonard), is driven to suicide, since his ambitions to become an actor, as encouraged by Keating, who recognizes his creative potential, run contrary to his father's wishes that he receive a more conservative education in order that he may pursue a career in medicine. Having been influenced – indeed, transformed – by Keating, and having learned to pursue a life of dignity, truthfulness, freedom and authenticity, there is an intrinsic sense in which Neil's death possesses great redemptive significance: though tragic, it demonstrates that, once achieved, the relinquishment of authentic human personhood is too high a price. In a symbolic gesture, Neil places a crown of victory on his head – which he had worn earlier that evening in the school play as Puck in *A Midsummer Night's Dream* – and slowly descends the stairs of his father's house, effectively emulating Christ's path on the Via Dolorosa, the Way of the Cross, to Calvary, before shooting himself in the study with his father's gun. According to Brie and Torevell, 'The redemptive quality of this scene is not too difficult for the viewer to experience. Throughout the episode, the dark ritual tone suggests that this death, although tragic, has much to teach the world.'[136] Although it is impossible to predict how each individual viewer will 'read' this film, it is significant that Brie and Torevell propose one interpretation of *Dead Poets Society* which assumes that the audience members can themselves gain from Neil's redemptive act, since it constitutes 'a symbolic and cathartic event which can save the world from spiralling further into misunderstandings'.[137] Beyond the film's fictional space, indeed, Keating's influence – which has the capacity to transform and redeem the lives of his pupils – can be imparted in turn to the audience members, in that Neil by 'seizing the day', 'has shown decisively that it is possible to be true to one's self',[138] even when the price of that realization, and of that authentic experience, is physical death.

While the central characters in such films as *Rocky*, *Awakenings* and *Dead Poets Society* offer discernible, albeit miscellaneous, examples of such *human*-orientated Christ-figures, it is, however, in the category of *film noir* that the closest approximations in cinematic art to the person of Christ as expounded by the Antiochene tradition can be located. Indeed, while Rocky Balboa, Malcolm Sayer and John Keating are all, in some respects, *Christ-like*, and are much closer to the person of Christ than the more-than-human redeemer-figures of Indiana Jones and Eastwood's Preacher, they are not fully fledged Christ-figures. Clearly, it is not the case that all film protagonists are 'Christ-like' simply by virtue of being intrinsically human in nature, and performing acts that accord with various tenets of Christ's life and work. Rather, for the film protagonist to be in any fundamental sense Christ-like, and to be capable of imparting the possibility of redemption, there must be a specific confrontation with evil and suffering, and with the human propensity towards sin – the absolute and non-negotiable prerequisite of redemption in the Christian tradition. Dr Malcolm Sayer in *Awakenings* arguably comes closer than John Keating to such an authentically human confrontation in that he manages to awaken the minds and perspectives of those around him as a consequence of his unrelenting *challenge* to the *status quo*, even managing in the process to overcome his own inability to engage in personal relationships with other individuals, as illustrated by his confession early on in the film that he is 'not very good with people'. However, although these figures may awaken human consciousness, and provide models of behaviour and activity with which film audiences may engage, it is apparent that such figures are not *categorically redemptive*-figures, even if in offering models of *liberation* from bureaucracy (Sayer) and from rigid institution-alization (Keating), there are discernible correlations with Christ's redemptive activity.

Indeed, according to Louise Sweet, in her review of *Awakenings* for the *Monthly Film Bulletin*, the character of Malcolm Sayer is no more than 'a pixie-ish liberator in the *Dead Poets Society* mould . . . who stumbles, Mr Magoo-like, on the cure'.[139] *Awakenings* is a very sentimentalized film, Sweet continues, with an optimistic 1960s tone, and ultimately life-affirming message.[140] In order to construe Sayer as a more authentically redemptive figure, the film would have needed to capture more of the range of insight, in a two-way healing and learning process, that passed between doctor and patient.[141] In the case of Keating, furthermore, while there is something redemptive about his exhortation to 'seize the day', there is also something inescapably naive about such an appeal. His motivations might be pure, but, as Brie and Torevell acknowledge, there is also something immature and unwise about them. His failure to foresee the potentially destructive effects of his teaching, as epitomized in Neil's suicide, is an instance of this. In failing to change the conservative ethos of Welton Academy from the ground up – such as by encouraging the authorities at the school to legitimize and endorse his unorthodox methods, or, at the very least, by seeking to integrate his radical and un-conventional approach to education within the school's general curriculum – there is a certain inevitability about Keating's eventual removal from his post, and of the bitter conflict between his boys and their parents and the school authorities that prevails at the film's conclusion. As Richard Combs pertinently remarks, how Keating 'came to be, or survives as, a teacher in academies like Welton is a mystery, subverting them it seems without com-promise, conflict or contradiction, as easily as he encourages his students to rebellion without disturbing anything'.[142]

While Keating remains a sympathetic figure, the audience may be inclined to feel by the end that, rather than an *agent* or *model* of redemptive activity, Keating is unable to be perceived as a redemptive figure since he has not himself come face to face with his own limitations and fallibilities as a human being, a confronta-tion which is a necessary prerequisite of redemption. Indeed, 'Keating remains as purely liberating a force as the school is patently a repressive one, and out of this manufactured scheme the film can only produce the manufactured tragedy of Neil Perry and his frustrated acting ambitions to bring things to a head'.[143] In *film noir*, on the other hand, there is a conspicuous emphasis on the striving towards redemption *on the part of the redeemer,* often at the expense of his own life, and certainly one that is inherently painful and protracted in its accomplishment. The world of *film noir* is thus markedly different from the somewhat manufactured sensibility of *Dead Poets Society*, whose theme of tragedy-liberation 'has been obvious, and obviously specious, every painstaking, tactful step of the way'.[144] Only in the more authentic figure of the *noir* protagonist, as I shall illustrate in detail, do we have a truly viable model or exemplar of redemption *for other human beings*, since the protagonist has undergone a personal process of redemption and can thereby provide a model as to how that activity can be achieved, in turn, by others.

The film noir protagonist as agent of redemption

In effect, the more authentically human the film protagonist, the more authentic and fertile the possibility of redemptive activity. As with the crucifixion of Christ, if it was not for the suffering and pain that the redeemer undergoes, there could be no concomitant *redemption* on the part of the film audience. As Rudolf Bultmann puts it, the Christian believer is able to 'make the Cross of Christ'[145] his or her own, and undergo crucifixion with Christ, thereby 'crucifying the affections and lusts of the flesh' and 'enjoying a freedom, albeit a struggling freedom from sin'.[146] Likewise, the film protagonist – who may, of course, have absolutely no influence upon a member of the film audience in the same way that Christ's crucifixion and resurrection will not be deemed to be life-transforming by every single human being, religious or otherwise – may provoke the spectator into undergoing an analogous experience of *redemption through suffering*. In the spirit of Scorsese's thoroughly human Christ, it is the Christ-figure's ability to suffer and undergo an authentically human experience that renders such a figure a prime *model* of redemptive activity. Since the dark, cynical and oppressive milieu of *film noir* epitomizes the human condition, and, as I have demonstrated with the analogy of Qoheleth, is thereby a fertile site of redemptive activity, there is a fundamental sense in which the film audience has the potential to undergo an experience of redemption *vis-à-vis* such characteristically alienated and estranged – even disturbed – individuals.

In particular, it is significant that in the 1930s and 1940s film audiences began to be influenced and inspired by what Neil Hurley identifies as 'rebels' and 'pain-heroes', in the form of the characters played by actors such as James Cagney, Paul Muni, John Garfield, Humphrey Bogart and Alan Ladd, 'even though they were on the other side of the law or died for violating society's code'.[147] Indeed, as Hurley puts it, 'How often we identified with gangsters, criminals, gun molls, and prostitutes in Hollywood films'.[148] It is therefore no coincidence from the point of view of this present discussion both that the above actors have played some of *film noir*'s most renowned and distinguished protagonists – Cagney was Cody Jarrett in *White Heat* and Garfield played Frank Chambers in *The Postman Always Rings Twice* to name but two examples – and that, according to Hurley, their characters share certain similar characteristics with the person of Christ, in the respect that Christ also died *as a criminal*.[149] Hurley thus feels it is reasonable to accord such rebellious and crime-orientated individuals an analogous religious aura or dimension. Hurley's argument is in need of a certain qualification – in the Christian tradition Jesus was put to death not so much because he was a criminal but because he was *perceived* as a threat to the Jewish law and religion, while Garfield and Cagney's characters *are* corrupt and, indeed, guilty of murder – but Hurley is nonetheless correct in his implicit supposition that it is the intrinsically flawed, fallible and, above all, *human* nature of the *noir* protagonist that renders a correlation with the Christian tradition, and with the person of Christ, so compelling.

From an audience perspective, indeed, while the *film noir* protagonist is an often tempestuous, sinful and, indeed, criminal figure, there is an intrinsic sense in which only a tainted individual can, meaningfully and authentically, speak to, and be in a position to address the needs of, a tainted and sinful humanity. Since, as the Christian tradition supposes, humankind possesses an innate sensibility that integration is better than disintegration and that harmony is better than cacophony, we require a model or exemplar to enable us to rejoin and reintegrate the 'broken' pieces of human existence – a function performed in the Christian faith by Jesus Christ – and it is here that the *noir* protagonist plays a crucial role. While the *noir* protagonist may die at the end of the film, as in the case of Cody Jarrett in *White Heat*, without imparting much in the way of a concrete model as to how we should orientate and live our lives, such figures do, nevertheless, confront and wrestle with the key questions, dilemmas and predicaments that lie at the heart of the human condition, from which redemption is sought. Indeed, *film noir* may be seen to bear witness to a plethora of dysfunctional, estranged and often violent protagonists who perform the Christ-like role of facilitating a process of redemption from the sin, guilt and alienation in which both they and – insofar as they represent universal and rudimentary human concerns – the *film audience* may be said to be embroiled.

As Paul Plouffe demonstrates in his thesis on 'The American hero in *Film Noir*',[150] the concept of the hero has, since ancient times, 'embodied the collective wish of the race'.[151] With respect to *film noir*, then, it is significant – from the point of view of the audience – that the 'heroes' in *noir* are 'everyman' characters, with whom the audience can readily seek identification. In contrast to the gangster pictures of the 1930s, crime in *film noir* is the province of everyone, with no one, seemingly, immune from its attraction and infection.[152] In *Double Indemnity*, Walter Neff (Fred MacMurray) is an insurance agent, who turns to murder and fraud when spurred on by a seductive woman. In *The Woman in the Window* (1944), the protagonist, who becomes involved with a woman after killing her jealous lover, is a middle-aged psychology professor. In *Scarlet Street* (1945), a shy clerk becomes involved with a prostitute, whom he later kills. And, in *Somewhere in the Night* (1946), the 'hero' is an amnesiac ex-serviceman whose search for his own identity leads him to believe he is a murderer. In wrestling with the age-old struggle between guilt and innocence, damnation and salvation as it affects *everyday* characters, Plouffe identifies that there is consequently a purgative process at work in *films noirs*.[153] For, as Tellotte puts it, 'in trying to articulate our personal and cultural anxieties', *film noir* works out a 'cure, offering a better sense of ourselves, or at least a clearer notion of who we are individually and socially'.[154] In this regard, it is significant that Erickson explicitly notes that *film noir* offers 'some of the most fascinating insights the cinema has provided'[155] on the theme of redemption.

Although not all of his pictures may strictly belong to the category of *film noir*, the films of Alfred Hitchcock may be seen to wrestle with the theme of redemption through suffering as it affects 'everyman' characters. In *The Paradine Case* (1947), a lawyer, Anthony Keane (Gregory Peck), becomes attracted to the murderous Mrs Paradine (Alida Valli) precisely *because* of her association with evil and sexual transgression.[156] Yet, this obsession with evil becomes the vehicle of the protagonist's own redemption, in the respect that it effectuates his subsequent humiliation in court, and which thereby 'chastens the insouciant, chameleonic – even, perhaps, satanic – style of lying that Keane as a professional lawyer had perfected',[157] and renders him less willing to deceive his faithful wife. Through engaging with evil and corruption, therefore, redemption from such a state of adversity is able to take effect. Rather than as an abstract process, however, which has no import beyond the scope of his films, there is a profound sense in which Hitchcock is showing his audience that their lives – no matter how ordinary and commonplace – are not immune from the operation of redemption. For, according to Rohmer and Chabrol, Hitchcock is a Roman Catholic auteur whose films may be read as allegories of universal sin and the fall of humankind,[158] which is the basis upon which the process of redemption functions.

In *North by Northwest* (1959), the Everyman motif exists in the form of advertising executive Roger Thornhill (Cary Grant), who is gradually stripped of his securities upon becoming accidentally caught up in an espionage plot involving foreign agents and the Central Intelligence Agency. Underlying the surface of this extraordinary – if somewhat implausible – narrative, we witness Thornhill's gradual transformation from 'a self-centered, mother-dominated, twice-divorced irresponsible man who refuses all commitment',[159] whom we see at the start of the film conning a man out of a taxicab, into a hero by the end, who is prepared to sacrifice himself for, and make a commitment to, another person, in the form of Eve Kendall (Eva Marie Saint), whose life he had unwittingly placed in jeopardy. Neil Hurley identifies in this regard the presence of the 'primordial' process of redemption that pervades 'the most commonplace lives' and alters their direction.[160] In probing beneath the often 'deceptively innocent surfaces of the world',[161] *North by Northwest* could thus be read as an examination of 'how all mankind participates in original sin'[162] and is forced to seek its own redemption, upon being confronted – as in the case of Thornhill – with the nature of one's self. It is significant in this regard that Paul Giles identifies in the films of Alfred Hitchcock signs of

> that old Catholic paradox whereby the rank black sinner, the person who is horribly aware of the awful potential of damnation, can be closer to redemptive grace than the honest citizen who has never troubled himself about anything beyond his or her own domestic affairs.[163]

The *noir*-orientated protagonist is thus able to facilitate the audience members in their striving towards redemption without the predilection of either traditional Christianity – or the traditional Christ-film epic – to see redemption in terms of celestial beings and supernatural phenomena. Rather, the *human* attainment of redemption is able to operate on a *human* level and, due to the 'everyman' status of the *noir* protagonist, does not require audiences to take on board the baggage of a specific religious tradition, to which they may not subscribe, or phenomena they do not accept as real, in our predominantly scientific and secularized society. Indeed, it is the *noir* protagonist's intrinsic feasibility and authenticity, even when – or, perhaps, especially when – that entails the delineation of human existence lived out at its most *sub*human, at its most brutal, oppressive and capricious, that makes a redemptive reading so pertinent. A case in point, here, is John Schlesinger's *Midnight Cowboy* (1969), which documents the underbelly of New York City life in the late 1960s, and the lives of two of its disenfranchised inhabitants – one, Enrico 'Ratso' Rizzo (Dustin Hoffman), a diseased con man, and the other, Joe Buck (Jon Voight), a profoundly naive street hustler who is at first hoodwinked by Rizzo into parting with his (paltry) income, before later befriending him. Whereas Neil Hurley begins his analysis of this film by suggesting that the 'average moviegoer' will be prompted to ask 'What can issue from the sewer existence of nighttime Times Square, with its parasitic and pathological denizens',[164] he then, conspicuously, attests that Schlesinger

> succeeds in winning us over to the fact that human affection, honest and unpretensious, can flourish even on barren, metropolitan sidewalks. The final scene of Rizzo's quiet demise in the arms of his Texan friend on the bus to Miami is not without . . . theological significance.[165]

For, in what Hurley acknowledges is 'some twisted, obscure' and 'antisocial, *but nonetheless providential way*',[166] the friendship struck up between the two dysfunctional souls in the face of suffering and death is a form of redemptive grace, which – in the light of Hurley's assumption about the way audience perspectives are transformed during the course of the film – has the capacity to provoke and to stimulate us into re-evaluating the way in which we make sense of and confront the sinful, oppressive and fragmentary nature of human experience. The root of Christ's teaching, after all, is that of *love*, the practical demonstration of which is in terms of love for one's neighbour, and this is mirrored in Joe Buck's willingness to take care of a man unto his death *in spite of* his having earlier been exploited by him, financially and emotionally, for his naiveté and vulnerability. Hence, Joe Buck may be seen to comprise a functional equivalent of Christ insofar as he performs the Christ-like role of redeeming a man from his sin, 'which is the ultimate root of all disruption of friendship, and of all injustice and oppression',[167] and going so far as to enable him, in his dying moments, 'to live in communion with him'.[168] It is thus significant that, in a manner akin to liberation theology, it is by means of entering into what it means to be less than human, as epitomized by Christ's undignified death at the hands of a sinful humanity, and from the starting-point of what Gustavo Gutierrez calls 'the man who is not a man'[169] that the Christian tradition understands redemption to be a possibility. Indeed, without an adequate understanding of poverty, and of the oppressive and destructive forces that render human life somewhat less than human, there can be no liberation, or redemption, from suffering and affliction. Rizzo and Joe Buck's attempt to overcome their suffering by making a new life for themselves, by setting forth for Miami, even in the face of continuing poverty and, in the case of Rizzo, of imminent death, is, though pitiable and hopeless on one level, on another, more fundamental level a supreme and authentic attempt to *overcome* and to *make amends for* the hopelessness and the failures of the past, and, in a sense, to *purge* themselves symbolically of their sins and of their past misdemeanours.

7
Redemption through the cinema of Martin Scorsese

A general introduction to the films of Scorsese

It is in the cinema of Martin Scorsese that it is possible to discern one of the most fully realized and accomplished explorations in popular film of the Christian model of redemption through suffering. Indeed, as Rosalie Savage indicates, using *film noir* stylistics in many of his films, Scorsese probes deeply 'into his characters' inner states of mind, often revealing lonely, outcast, and/or psychotic individuals whose dysfunctional nature ultimately requires redemption'.[1] Through the use of such quintessential *noir* motifs as paranoia, alienation and despair, Scorsese's films may be seen to bear witness to the Christian model of redemption through protagonists who may be read as functional equivalents of Christ, in the respect that – in line with an Antiochene Christology – any redemption that is attained has an intrinsically human dimension, and is achieved at the cost of immense physical and psychological suffering. While the Christological themes at the heart of his pictures may, for some interpreters, be somewhat implicit in nature, it is nonetheless apparent that the links with the human nature of Jesus that Scorsese himself delineated in his 1988 adaptation of Kazantzakis's *The Last Temptation of Christ*, are considerable. In such pictures as *Mean Streets* (1973), *Taxi Driver* (1976), *Raging Bull* (1980), *After Hours* (1985), *The Color of Money* (1986), *Cape Fear* (1991) and *Casino* (1995), Scorsese reveals a myriad of authentically human individuals who, in their idiosyncratic and diverse ways, characteristically experience, and find themselves forced to wrestle with, the innately human encounter with what Les Keyser categorizes as 'doubts and despair, psychotic action and rage, guilt and the quest for expiation and salvation'.[2]

That there is an intrinsically religious orientation to Scorsese's work is attested by David Jasper in an otherwise critical analysis of the religious propensity of Hollywood cinema, which he designates as 'an art of illusion'[3] that deliberately, and solely for commercial benefit, absorbs 'all vision into its own, offering the viewer a commodity which can be consumed without fear of significant change or disturbance'.[4] In marked contrast, Jasper likens Scorsese to the gospel writers, insofar as he is 'a teller of a simple story with a driven and often ambiguous central character embedded in a tradition, and with a defined point of view (which is the invitation to the theologian) frequently erupting into violence and confusion.'[5] This religious perspective is no contrived or artificial ingredient, however, in Scorsese's cinema, nor does a religious interpretation merely amount to one possible reading of an otherwise 'secular' body of films. Rather, as Friedman puts it, 'As much as the Italian immigrant culture he was born into or the movies he grew up on, it was the Roman Catholic Church'[6] that shaped and has helped define the life and career of Martin Scorsese. Although he is now a lapsed Roman Catholic – he last went to confession in 1965[7] – Mary Pat Kelly has referred to Scorsese as a 'priest of the imagination',[8] who wants his films to be experienced by audiences on a *spiritual* level. In an interview in 1988, for instance, Scorsese indicated that he has 'never gotten over the ritual of Catholicism',[9] and, in a discussion of the influence of the Catholic Church on his life and work, published in 1987, Scorsese has acknowledged that, although he once embraced the priesthood as the surest means of salvation, 'wanting that vocation, selfishly, so that I'd be saved . . . I wound up finding a vocation in making movies with the same kind of passion'.[10]

Despite his orientation towards Roman Catholicism, however, and what Savage identifies as 'his obsessions with guilt, penance, Christ's suffering, and humanity's redemption',[11] it is palpable that Scorsese does not presuppose that his characters will be redeemed through traditional religious rites, meditations, prayers and rituals, intrinsic – even exclusive – to salvation though they may be from an orthodox Roman Catholic perspective. Rather, as Kelly explicates, in Scorsese's youth

> every soul was a cosmic battleground on which the forces of God and the devil contend. It did not matter whether that soul belonged to you or to a failed hood, a street-corner kid, a driven musician, a

prizefighter, housewife, prostitute, or taxi driver; in the drama of salvation each one was as important as the Pope himself.[12]

Roman Catholicism is, indeed, a *sacramental* religion, which holds the conviction that 'such earthly realities as fire and water, light and darkness, bread and wine, oil and sexual love are metaphors for God',[13] and that, like the bread at the Eucharist, humankind – in all its variety and diversity – is the channel through which God's grace and redemption can be shared with all creation.[14] It need not be too wide of the mark, therefore, to conjecture that underlying Scorsese's films is a sound Catholic teleology, wherein 'the assassin's bullet can convey the judgement of God, a taxi driver can unleash divine retribution, and a boxer can bear witness to Christ's suffering'.[15] Scorsese's protagonists characteristically wrestle with feelings of sin, guilt, fear and, even though it may not always be possible so to do, undergo an experience of redemption and thereby aim to lead a moral life in what amounts to a defective and fallen world. By means of penances, and through purging their souls of their sins and transgressions, they aim – often without the words to articulate and voice their inner struggles – to undergo an inextricably Christian process of redemption, and to confront the question posed by Scorsese himself in a 1987 interview: 'How do you live a spiritual life, how do you live a good life, when the system is just the opposite? . . . There's got to be a way to do it in modern life . . .'[16]

For Scorsese's *noir* protagonists, it is frequently the case that violence and physical pain are the only means by which redemption from a state of oppression, estrangement and suffering can be achieved. Although Scorsese has often been criticized for the intense and unremitting level of violence and bloodshed that imbues his films,[17] there is a fundamental degree to which, as Savage observes, 'this violence serves an important, redemptive thematic function'.[18] Michael Bliss, for example, has referred to Scorsese as a 'poet of violence'[19] in the respect that he endeavours to explore the inner, psychological minds of characters who have a proclivity towards expressing themselves through violence *while at the same time* disclosing how, as a consequence, this violence has the capacity to function as a cleansing and purgative process.[20] Indeed, due to the dichotomy between the ideal of spiritual purity, harmony and integration, as laid out in Christian teaching, and the actuality of a dysfunctional, sinful and often squalid world in which his protagonists are enmeshed, violence could be said to comprise a *redemptive* force, which acts, albeit paradoxically, as a *cohesive* agent that, to quote Bliss, 'reintegrates the aberrant individual'.[21] While, on a superficial reading, this may be seen to constitute an atypical, or deviant, interpretation of what is a fundamentally Christian activity, it is apparent that Scorsese's delineation of an oppressive *noir* world 'in which doomed characters strive for atonement and inevitably receive salvation through violence'[22] has, in actuality, an inextricably Christian, indeed biblical, foundation. Indeed, the concept of atonement both in Judaism – at least before the destruction of the Temple in 70 CE – and in Christianity may be seen to involve 'an act of immense violence',[23] insofar as the Jewish system of animal sacrifice on the Day of Atonement, in which Israel's High Priest offered blood sacrifices, or 'sin offerings', to effect a reconciliation between God and his errant people,[24] and the figure of Jesus Christ suffering on the Cross are profoundly violent events, involving bloodletting and, ultimately, physical death.

(a) Redemption through *Mean Streets*

There need be no fundamental disparity, therefore, between the Christian concept of redemption and a film such as Scorsese's *Mean Streets* (1973), whose theme of redemption through violence and suffering in many respects emanates from Scorsese's own childhood in New York's Little Italy, where, as he recounts,

> I grew up in the tenements . . . Most mornings on the way to school, I'd see bums fighting each other with broken bottles. Blood all over the ground. I had to step around the blood and the bottles – and I'm just eight years old. Or I'd be sitting in the derelicts' bar across the way . . . We'd watch guys get up and struggle over to another table and start hallucinating and beating up someone.[25]

In an interview for *Time* magazine in November 1973, Scorsese categorized *Mean Streets* as a 'religious statement',[26] which asks whether or not one can be a saint in the contemporary world, where, on the 'mean streets' of Little Italy, at any rate, violence and suffering is the norm. Indeed, the fragmented Italian–American society delineated in *Mean Streets* could be said to epitomize the concept of the world as 'fallen' and enmeshed in sin. As Friedman puts it, 'the fallen world, so often hazily metaphorical, is grittily palpable' in the film's 'lurid nightscape', which, appropriately 'illumined by the red of neon signs and gaudy nightclub interiors', resembles a 'latter-day inferno . . . a nightmare world of smoky rooms and shadowy streets'.[27] The local bar, 'Tony's', in particular, is always shown 'bathed in an orange-red light',[28] thus evoking connotations with the fire of hell, and is evocatively represented by Scorsese 'as a sinful, sexual cesspool'.[29] Most symbolic of all is the dichotomy between spiritual and material, sacred and profane landscapes that feature in the film, such that, in Paul Giles's words, at one point 'the fire of a cooking hamburger turns into a memento of Satan's eternal grill',[30] while the radiant and luminous lights of Little Italy's pornographic and sex shops constitute 'a demonic inversion of the bright lights of a Catholic church service'[31] that we are shown at the beginning of the picture.

Within this urban jungle, however, Scorsese delineates as his central character a small-time hood named Charlie (Harvey Keitel) whose desire for advancement within the New York Mafia, for whom he 'runs numbers' and acts as a loan shark, clashes somewhat incongruously with what amounts to an intense Catholic guilt and a sense of unworthiness at having failed to live up to the demands of a spiritual life. Although Charlie knows that in order to succeed in Mafia society he must appease his Mafia boss uncle, Giovanni (Cesare Danova), he simultaneously 'fears divine retribution for doing so'.[32] While his conscience directs him to emulate Christ's ideals of brotherhood, this conflicts with his material desire to run an ageing restaurant, implicitly promised him by his uncle, whose incumbent proprietor is unable to keep up his protection payments to the Mafia. Much as he fears hell and wants his sins to be cleansed, Kelly observes that 'the "Our Fathers" and "Hail Marys" he receives as penance seem insufficient to save a soul exposed to the temptations of the street'.[33] Indeed, despite trying to live a life that, as Scorsese indicates, 'is philosophically tied in with Roman Catholic teaching',[34] by way of 'offering up penances, suffering for the atonement of his own sins, dealing with the sins of pride and selfishness'[35] and endeavouring to love one's enemy, Charlie simply cannot reconcile such high spiritual demands and ideals with living in a gangster environment. As he confesses at one point in the film, 'Priest gives me the usual ten Hail Marys, ten Our Fathers and whatever. Now, you know that next week I'm going to come back and he will just give me another ten Hail Marys and another ten Our Fathers . . .'

As a consequence of this fundamental conflict between the demands of the Church and the realities of the streets, there is a discernible sense in which *Mean Streets* bears witness to a secularization of the struggle for redemption, wherein the need and demand for redemption from sin is no less imperative, but in which the instrument and agency through which redemption is imparted is transferred and reappropriated from the Church to the streets themselves. In line with the Roman Catholic emphasis on salvation through works, Charlie asks for a sign powerful enough for him to purge his guilt, and subsequently uses his irresponsible, reckless and untrustworthy cousin, Johnny Boy (Robert De Niro) as his penance, and becomes intent on saving *him* as the vehicle of his own redemption. As Savage points out, Christ did not simply 'speak eloquently of the Kingdom of God but *acted* to save the world from eternal damnation through his crucifixion and resurrection',[36] and Francis of Assisi did not merely give sermons on the need to adopt a poor, simplistic lifestyle, but undertook social *acts* of brotherhood and charity. In an analogous fashion, for Charlie to redeem himself, by redeeming Johnny Boy from his transgressions, he must *act*. While this Roman Catholic understanding of salvation through works differs somewhat from the Protestant interpretation of redemption as a much more individualistic process – whereby, since the Enlightenment in particular, each individual human being is believed to be capable of attaining his or her own redemption by following the model or exemplar of behaviour set by Christ – Scorsese's film nevertheless performs a comparable function, insofar as it is only by seeking to correct his mistakes and to be amenable to reform that redemption is a possibility for Scorsese's protagonist. In an article on *Mean Streets* in the winter 1973 edition of *Sight and Sound*, David Denby explains that the fate of these two men is inextricably intertwined: 'Charlie, the Mulberry Street Jesus, needs that lying, cheating punk Johnny Boy for personal absolution just as Johnny Boy needs Charlie to keep himself alive'.[37] Johnny Boy, in effect, is the cross that Charlie must bear, and, as a corollary, 'the greater Johnny's faults, the greater Charlie's sacrifice'.[38]

Since Johnny owes Michael (Richard Romanus), a neighbourhood loan shark, more money than he can ever repay, the fact that Charlie has vouched for him, and has made Johnny's debt his own responsibility, results in the scenario whereby, in line with an orthodox Christian interpretation of the atonement, the debt – now Charlie's as much as Johnny's – will finally be paid in blood. The film's bloody and violent denouement, in which both men are involved in a climactic car crash while attempting to flee Michael's wrath, invokes images of a vengeful Yahweh in the Old Testament carrying out retribution against a transgressing people. For Charlie, this moment epitomizes his hitherto implicit acknowledgement that without a painful penance or sacrifice one cannot hope to be redeemed, in a manner analogous to the model or exemplar of Christ on the Cross through whose pain and suffering the redemption of humanity can be secured. In Charlie's case, it is Johnny Boy's sin that is the prerequisite to his own ability to undergo a process of salvation, as symbolized by the physical pain he experiences from having been shot in the palm of his hand by Michael, the event which triggered the car wreck. As with Christ, the incision in his hand is Charlie's stigmata, and could be said to signify a message of hope rather than of despair. While Scorsese is ambiguous about whether or not Charlie has successfully redeemed his own tortured soul, the theme of redemption through suffering is nonetheless symbolized in the fact that the car hits a fire hydrant which then erupts in a fountain of cleansing water, which could be said to *bathe* Charlie as he stands before the palpable carnage of what he has done, and for which he must take responsibility. Both Charlie and his penance, Johnny Boy, survive the collision, and there is a sign that the process of redemption has at least been opened up for Charlie through his confrontation with sin and with his struggle for harmony and integration. Charlie confesses just before the experience of the car wreck and shooting from which he struggles to extricate himself, 'I guess you could say things haven't gone so well tonight. But I'm trying . . . I'm trying.'

The role of the film audience

While an audience may, of course, respond to the film, and to the experience of redemption through suffering that Charlie undergoes, in a multiplicity of ways, *Mean Streets* has, significantly, elicited a response from audiences that concurs with Scorsese's affirmation that the film is a predominantly 'anthropological or sociological tract',[39] and an attempt to delineate on screen not a fictional world, of how redemption through suffering *might* occur, but 'an attempt to put myself and my old friends on the screen, to show how we lived' and to convey 'what life was like in Little Italy'.[40] While demonstrating that the traditional agency of redemption is the Christian Church, Scorsese's film points both to the potency and, in many respects, the autonomy of the Roman Catholic Church to administer and to dispense penances, and to indicate how redemption may be accomplished, and the *inadequacy* of the Church as the sole means and avenue by which an individual human being can come to be redeemed. In his words, 'It's very easy to discipline oneself to go to mass on Sunday mornings. That's not redemption for me: it's how you live, how you deal with other people, whether it be in the streets, at home or in an office.'[41] John Berger, indeed, in an article on the power of the medium of cinema for *Sight and Sound*, published in June 1991, attests that, in the instant in which Charlie confesses that, although 'things haven't gone so well, tonight . . . I'm trying', he 'becomes the repentant child in all of us and a soul in Dante's Hell',[42] suggesting that Scorsese has achieved for the hell of New York much the same effect as Dante, 'whose vision of the Inferno was modelled after the cities he knew in his time'.[43]

As with his 1995 picture, *Casino*, which delineates the greed, allure and the ultimate disintegration of the Mafia world of Las Vegas in the 1970s, where some of these themes are played with no less explicitly, Scorsese could be said to be *challenging* his audience 'to face up to the lure of evil, the deep fascination of Lucifer and the fallen angels that Milton understood'[44] from a contemporary, twentieth-century perspective. Even when the characters in his films are, seemingly, 'genetically incapable of doing anything straight',[45] Scorsese presses the point that 'Very often the people I portray can't help but be in that way of life. Yes, they're bad and they're doing bad things. And we condemn those aspects of them. But they're also human beings.'[46] Although it may be easy, even effortless in some instances, to criticize them for their evil and perverse proclivities, Scorsese is nonetheless emphatic that, whether one acknowledges it or not, his characters reflect 'the frailty of being human', to the point, indeed, that, in his words, 'I want to push audiences' emotional empathy with certain types of characters who are normally considered villains.'[47] Scorsese's protagonists may be 'anti-heroes', whose 'own vicissitudes', as David John Graham puts it, 'are all too apparent',[48] yet for them the chance of undergoing an experience of redemption amidst and through the empirical reality of violence and suffering is a pertinent, indeed vital, possibility.

Although *Mean Streets* bears witness to a number of discernibly, even explicitly, Roman Catholic motifs on redemption, it is, then, the *universality* and innately *human* dimension to the film that makes a theological reading so pertinent. While Scorsese's Catholic heritage has clearly influenced, and may be seen to underpin, his film-making career, it is not a corollary of this position that audiences who are not accustomed to, or conversant with, his particular religious sensibility are necessarily unable to apprehend Scorsese's cinema as a site of prodigious redemptive activity. Indeed, since *Mean Streets*, Scorsese has collaborated on (to date) four occasions with Paul Schrader, a screenwriter, director and former film critic and scholar – whose 'Notes on *Film Noir*', published in 1971, amounts to one of the most influential works on the subject – whose own religious upbringing was Dutch Calvinist, while in 1997 Scorsese further demonstrated his versatility in making *Kundun*, a chronicle of the early life of the fourteenth Dalai Lama, and the conflict between religion and society not on the 'mean streets' of New York's Little Italy but in the Chinese occupation of Tibet.

Ultimately, inasmuch as they correspond to the *film noir* delineation of humankind as enmeshed in sin and as *alienated* and *estranged* in essence from what, for Tillich, is 'the ground of our being', Scorsese's protagonists may be seen to comprise 'everyman' figures, in whose conflicts and struggles may be seen to lie a paradigm of the universal human condition. In the majority of cases, there is no overt religious dimension to such figures. With the exception of *Mean Streets*, *The Last Temptation of Christ* and *Kundun*, Scorsese's protagonists, upon initial encounter at any rate, are substantially oblivious to and unacquainted with religious – let alone specifically Roman Catholic – tensions and solicitudes. In the spirit, however, of David Jasper's affirmation that films in general 'are often most interesting to the theological enterprise when they are being least theological',[49] there is an intrinsic sense in which Scorsese's *noir* protagonists may be seen to be performing a religious function not because they purport to emulate the religious life, ideals and teachings of Jesus Christ, but because, as authentically human individuals who are engaged in an innately human struggle, such figures may be seen to bear witness to the inextricably human nature and orientation of *Christ's* redemptive work. The discussion that follows of three of Scorsese's other pictures, *Taxi Driver*, *Raging Bull* and *Cape Fear*, will, I hope, serve further to illustrate and elucidate this process.

(b) Redemption through *Taxi Driver*

In effect, while *films noirs* in general may be seen to comprise a significant site of redemptive activity, it is in the films of Martin Scorsese that one is able to find one of the most fertile and thoroughgoing examples in contemporary cinema of the theme of redemption through the experience of sin, alienation and suffering. The strength of this claim is especially pertinent when it is considered that Scorsese's 1976 picture, *Taxi Driver*, delineates a much bleaker and more intensive vision of the human condition as estranged and in need of redemption than was ever disclosed in classic 1940s *films noirs*. Indeed, Travis Bickle (Robert De Niro), Scorsese's 'everyman' protagonist in *Taxi Driver*, even designates himself 'God's lonely man', and is identified at the beginning of the picture as a Vietnam veteran who feels alienated from what he perceives as the 'filth' and sordidness of the streets of New York City, where he spends his days and nights driving a taxicab. Travis refers to his environment as 'sick' and 'venal', for the streets in which he plies his trade are, in his words, 'where all the animals come out at night – whores, skunks, pussies, buggers, queens, fairies, dopers, junkies'. And yet, his detestation of what he observes is in no sense an objective or dispassionate analysis of the decay of contemporary urban America. Rather, paradoxically, Travis 'drifts through a city he hates but cannot abandon, entering and even participating in the sexual exploitation rife in some of the meanest streets used as the setting of a feature film'.[50]

Travis spends the time when he is not driving his taxicab at pornographic movie theatres, in a café which is populated by pimps and drug addicts, or alone in his squalid apartment. Despite his revulsion at what he sees, we nevertheless observe Travis drifting through Broadway and Forty Second Street night after night, not so much because he is in search of a fare but because he is strangely – perversely, even – fascinated by what he sees, and which he is driven to meticulously record in his diary every day. Although no rational analysis will judiciously account for his behaviour, the overwhelming impression is that Travis is so much a part of his environment that he is incapable of leading a life that is distinct from the codes and vices of the nightmarish and perilous world of the modern American city. Indeed, as Hirsch indicates, the city is such a potent dramatic presence that it not only reflects Travis's 'terrifying disconnectedness and ferocity'[51] but also acts as a *catalyst* for it.[52]

From a theological perspective, Travis's predicament may be seen to accord with the Christian understanding of hell. Although, since the Enlightenment, no other 'traditional Christian doctrine has been so widely abandoned',[53] at least in its most literalistic formulation as a physical place of eternal punishment and everlasting torment 'where there will be weeping and gnashing of teeth',[54] over recent centuries in particular the doctrine has come to be interpreted not as an actual material site used by God to punish the wicked but as a metaphor for *spiritual* misery. In Milton's *Paradise Lost*, for instance, Satan attests, in book IV, 'Which way I flee is Hell; myself am Hell',[55] and according to Jerry Walls in a recent study of *Hell: The Logic of Damnation*, published in 1992, hell, rather than a remote, other-worldly location is said to stand in clear continuity with our *present experience* in this world,[56] where it denotes an experience of complete isolation.[57] In Walls's words, 'On this picture, the damned are like prisoners in solitary confinement, whose misery is compounded by the fact that they must bear it utterly alone', wherein each so-called 'damned person is an isolated unit of misery' who 'makes up his own individual world of self-inflicted suffering'.[58] Travis Bickle could be said to epitomize this 'state of spiritual, emotional, and mental misery.'[59] After all, sin, suffering, insomnia, paranoia and homicidal–suicidal impulses may be seen to abound in Travis's world, in which Savage talks of his being banished 'to the hell of his isolation'[60] in an existence that is essentially devoid of authentic human interaction. In particular, in the opening scene, while the credits are rolling, Lesley Stern observes that,

> It is dark. There is a clash of symbols, and the film begins. From centre screen steam gushes, swirling like light out of a manhole, polluted light, glitteringly opaque . . . The bumper of a yellow checker cab moves in slow motion through the steam, coloured neon lights are refracted by the rain, the urban landscape is rendered almost abstract, overcrowded, electric . . .[61]

Stern attests that 'the steam rising out of manholes hints at a rotting universe beneath the streets, a decay that is barely contained',[62] and which, according to Marie Connolly, 'is reminiscent of the yellow smoke and fog of T. S. Eliot's *Wasteland*', while 'the smoke, red filters, and greenish distortions of light make the city look like Dante's *Inferno*'.[63] In short, this picture of New York City with images of steaming sewers, rainslicked streets and glaring neon lights, has led some critics to categorize *Taxi Driver* as constituting 'a vision of hell on earth',[64] in which, to further the symbolism, we see Travis's eyes at one point tinted red.[65]

As in Christian theology, however, where, as Walls attests, the doctrine of hell cannot be dissociated from the Christian scheme of salvation – insofar as 'Its main thrust is a message of how we can be saved from our sins and receive eternal life'[66] – so Travis may be seen to be a saviour-figure who endeavours to redeem himself and others within a *noir* landscape. Indeed, though a deeply flawed human individual, Travis's alienated and dysfunctional conditon may be seen to provide the impetus for a redemptive mission to purify what he construes as the morally depraved city streets and to cleanse their inhabitants of their sins. In effect, so all-encompassing and pervasive is the contamination that Travis both observes and in which he is enmeshed that he is even predilected to categorize his redemptive mission in terms of a divine and essentially messianic vocation, in which he becomes God's agent. Initially, he writes in his diary, 'May 10th. Thank God for the rain which has helped wash away the garbage and the trash off the sidewalks', but soon he *becomes* the rain, the agent of cleansing and purification. Hence, what begins as a generalized detestation of 'filth' becomes a fixation on an objective to *confront* and to *stand up against* the sin and depravity that has pervaded the city, thereby casting himself as both 'scourge and redeemer'.[67] In Travis's own words, 'Here's a man who would not take it anymore, a man who stood up against the scum, the cunts, the dogs, the filth, the shit, *here is someone who stood up*.' Travis's alienation thus becomes, in *Taxi Driver*, 'a holy calling'.[68] Indeed, according to Scorsese, 'Travis really has the best of intentions', and, in a manner akin to St Paul, 'believes he's doing right', wanting 'to clean up life, clean up the mind, clean up the soul'.[69] Like the saints in the Christian tradition, Scorsese holds that Travis possesses a certain 'energy'[70] and sense of moral righteousness, whereby 'he sees something ugly or dirty and he has to clean it up', such that, as far as he is concerned, 'he is doing good work'.[71]

The concept of redemption from sin and suffering is particularly apparent in *Taxi Driver* with respect to the particular means by which Travis undertakes his redemptive mission. For, what in particular provokes Travis into action is his encounter with a twelve-year-old prostitute, Iris (Jodie Foster), on the Lower East Side, which for him personifies and epitomizes all that is wrong with the city. He endeavours to rescue Iris from her life on the streets and so enable her to return 'home' to her parents. From the time she sought to escape the clutches of her pimp, 'Sport' (Harvey Keitel), by climbing inside his taxicab, Travis is obsessed with the idea that his mission is to save Iris, in spite of her subsequent inability to remember her attempted flight. In Travis's words, 'Don't you remember any of it? Well that's alright, I'm gonna get you out of here.' Notwithstanding the violent, indeed homicidal, form that his mission takes – whereby he invests 'Sport' 'with all the perilous powers of pollution', and designates him 'as a target to be erased, washed away' and 'eliminated'[72] – it is apparent that Travis sees his mission 'as an act of pious salvation'.[73] As an analogy, Friedman indicates that for various characters in Greek mythology, 'a stopover in hell'[74] is a prerequisite for the accomplishment of their respective redemptive missions, in the respect that 'Heracles makes off with Cerberus, the watchdog of hell; and Orpheus almost rescues his wife Eurydice from the kingdom of the dead. Travis, already in Hell, must brave its nether regions to rescue Iris.'[75] Indeed, in delivering Iris to her parents, Travis believes he is going a significant way towards cleaning up the degenerate city.

As with Christianity, furthermore, sacrifice is intrinsic to the redemptive process in *Taxi Driver*. The carnage at the end of the picture, in which we witness Travis murdering 'Sport' and his associates and attempting his own suicide, could be said to constitute a baptismal, cleansing bloodbath which shows the extent to which Travis is prepared to sacrifice himself on behalf of the endangered Iris and the sinful world in which she has become enmeshed. The end shots of the massacre, which are depicted from an overhead point of view and which scan Travis's path of destruction, are, for Scorsese, essentially 'a reexamination of the elements of the sacrifice . . . a ritualistic, religious experience like the Mass'.[76] Likewise, as Friedman attests, the final, apocalyptic shootout could be interpreted as 'a purgative ritual'.[77] In effect, therefore, even the means by which Travis carries out his re-demptive mission is congruous with the more conventional form of redemption in Christianity. For, notwithstanding Keyser's observation that Travis 'embraces guns and blood' in 'the place of liturgy and sacraments',[78] it is apparent that Christ's redemptive activity was achieved by means of his suffering and violent death on the Cross. As the Letter to the Hebrews indicates, it is through Christ's blood that redemption from sin is ultimately secured.[79] Travis's self-sacrifice is likewise required if his redemptive mission is to be fully accomplished. Indeed, whereas through Christ's sacrifice, Christ redeemed the sins of the world – to the effect that, to quote Ambrose of Milan, 'He condemned sin in order to nail our sins to the Cross'[80] – there is a sense in which, through Travis's self-sacrifice, Travis had hoped to cleanse the streets of New York City of its sins. Only by engaging with, and confronting, the 'filth' that has suffused the city can Travis's redemptive mission be fulfilled, in a manner analogous to – albeit ontologically different from – Jesus' becoming incarnate and bearing the sins of humanity in order to fulfil *his* redemptive mission.[81]

At the very least, it is apparent, with respect to the end of the picture, that we no longer observe Travis as a pathologically alienated and lonely individual, who circuits the 'mean streets' of New York City with a view to annihilating the sin and vice in which he too is embroiled, but as someone who 'now chats easily' with his taxi driver colleagues 'on a street corner in the film's coda'.[82] Through his redemptive action, therefore, there is a sense in which Travis has managed to redeem *himself*, in the respect that

by facing up to and confronting the factors which have precipitated his alienation he has succeeded, at least to some extent, in
extricating himself from his plight. Furthermore, the anonymous
and outcast Travis is subsequently accorded an 'heroic' status, in
that he is proclaimed a 'hero' by the press and by Iris's parents,
who thank him by letter for rescuing their daughter. In this respect, Savage indicates that, according to some interpreters, 'Travis
the Savior has been *resurrected*'.[83] As with traditional Christian
teaching, therefore, in which Christ's resurrection constitutes its
pivotal message, it is apparent that the transformation and
reorientation of Travis's estranged condition may be seen to
constitute a site of related – if not actually identical – redemptive
activity. Ultimately, indeed, there are substantial grounds for
seeing in *Taxi Driver* a potent illustration of the redemption of the
individual from a state of sin and alienation, which corresponds to
significant integral elements of Christian teaching.

The role of the film audience

In the case of Christianity, however, there is a further dimension
to the redemption accomplished by Christ which Scorsese's
protagonist needs to attain if a judicious comparison is to be made
between Travis Bickle and the person of Christ. For, notwithstanding the personal redemptive experience that Travis undergoes
in *Taxi Driver*, which may be read as analogous to Christ's
redemptive activity, the *raison d'être* of Christ's redemptive work is
that, as a consequence of his atoning death on the Cross, redemption may be *imparted* and *accomplished* in turn by those who
hear and have responded to the Christian message of salvation.
While it is clearly possible to believe in the redemption wrought by
Christ 'as an event wholly unique to him and entailing no
consequences for the rest of humanity',[84] unless there is a universal
dimension to his redemptive activity it is hard to see what purpose
the concept serves. According to the Creeds, for instance, the incarnation took place 'For us men and for our salvation',[85] and if it was
not for this *universal* dimension it is hard to see why the crucifixion
and resurrection of Christ should retain any contemporary
significance aside from purely historical interest. In effect, although
Travis Bickle may have undergone a prodigious redemptive activity
in *Taxi Driver*, if the film is to constitute an analogous site of
Christological – and, as a corollary, of redemptive – activity to that

found in Christianity then there must be a degree to which Travis not only suffers and is himself redeemed, but is *himself* an *agent* and a *bearer* of redemption, the benefits and the impact of which may be felt and experienced in the lives of others.

While, at first, the limits of such a process would seem to be restricted to the lives of the other characters within the film's (fictional) space – Travis redeems Iris from a life of prostitution, for instance – there is a degree to which *Taxi Driver* can come to adopt a much wider and more universal function in that the religious themes and symbols utilized in the film possess a substantial connotative and symbolic power with which the film audience can engage, the result of which may be interpreted as a potentially *redemptive* experience. Indeed, in an article on *Taxi Driver* in the summer 1976 edition of *Sight and Sound*, Colin Westerbeck attests that the film manages to offer its audience 'provocation',[86] insofar as it succeeds in tapping 'into people's emotions at a deeper level than movies are usually able to reach',[87] to the point of inspiring 'passionate, sometimes even crazed responses'.[88] Significantly, the inspiration for the film for the screenwriter, Paul Schrader was his own experience of a time in 1973 when he was predominantly living in his car in Los Angeles, drinking heavily and frequenting pornographic theatres. It occurred to him, after he landed in hospital with an ulcer, that he had not properly spoken to anyone in two or three weeks, and that he felt like a taxi driver, 'floating around in this metal coffin in the city, seemingly in the middle of people, but *absolutely, totally alone*'.[89] Hence, as Friedman attests in this regard, rather than a study of one paranoid, aberrant individual, there is a clear sense in which *Taxi Driver* has a *commonality* to it.[90] Schrader, indeed, has quoted Thomas Wolfe's idea that loneliness is 'the central and inevitable fact of human existence',[91] such that, in Friedman's words, Travis could thus be construed as 'the supreme exemplar of a universal affiliation'.[92]

More important, therefore, than whether *Taxi Driver* is a film about religious experience as it pertains to its protagonist, Travis Bickle, and to Iris, whom he redeems from a life of vice, is, as Westerbeck argues, 'the question of whether [it] become[s] a religious experience *for us*'.[93] Rather than entailing a purely abstract and detached audience relationship, Scorsese himself recounts that

> People related to the film very strongly in terms of loneliness. I never realized what that image on the poster did for the film – a shot of De Niro walking down the street with the line, 'In every city there's one man.' And we [Scorsese and Paul Schrader] had thought that audiences would reject the film, feeling that it was too unpleasant and no one would want to see it![94]

The universal and all-encompassing appeal of the film is implicitly recognized in an article in the *New York Times* upon the film's release in 1976 which, referring to the composition of the audience of one of *Taxi Driver*'s first screenings, pointed out that it ranged 'from rather tough-looking teenagers to overdressed dowagers, from middle-class couples out on a date to, I would guess, taxi drivers sneaking a few hours away from the job'.[95] Referring to this observation, Westerbeck assesses that the audience therefore 'seems, in point of fact', to comprise 'very much the same wide cross-section of New York's population that appears in the movie itself'.[96] Moreover, even amongst audiences who are not New Yorkers, and who may be seeing the film for the first time, say, more than two decades later, Westerbeck, writing in a London-based publication, suggests that even though Travis's life may initially fascinate us merely because 'it is beyond our ken and we have no other access to it',[97] the most remarkable experience is the one suffered not by Travis Bickle 'but by us'.[98] Not only does he posit *Taxi Driver* as a site of potential religious experience, but he construes it as a religious experience of 'the most binding and fanatical kind', amounting indeed to 'a conversion'.[99] Consequently, therefore, having gone to the cinema 'to see an exposé of someone else's life, we come away having got something even better: an apology for our own lives'.[100]

(c) Redemption through *Raging Bull*

While *Taxi Driver* clearly constitutes a prodigious site of redemptive significance, Scorsese himself has explicitly spoken of his 1980 picture, *Raging Bull*, as a profoundly redemptive 'text' *vis-à-vis* the film audience. As with Travis Bickle, the film's protagonist, the boxer Jake La Motta (Robert De Niro), may be an unsympathetic – even a loathsome – character, with emphasis placed on the sordid and unrespectable nature of his domestic life, but, in a comparable fashion, it is La Motta's very inadequacies and imperfections that enable the film to be perceived as a site of comprehensive redemptive significance, in line with an Antiochene Christology. Like Travis, La Motta is presented by Scorsese as an inarticulate character, who is so alienated from, and essentially unconscious of, his own feelings and emotions that he is at war with himself. The more he tries to communicate, the more he faces his inarticulateness. Consequently, whatever he feels – 'rage, guilt, even lust'[101] – he finds that the only way he can express himself is through violence, both in the ring and at home, where he hits his wife, Vickie (Cathy Moriarty), over what he suspects is her infidelity, and manager-brother, Joey (Joe Pesci), as if they were opponents in the ring. Significantly, Scorsese has explicitly identified La Motta as an 'Everyman' figure: the protagonist could just as easily be someone in the audience who can empathize with La Motta's estranged condition. In Scorsese's words, 'You could take anyone . . . the ring becomes an allegory of whatever you do in life.'[102] That *Raging Bull* amounts to more than a film about an unsympathetic former middleweight champion, and comes closer to an allegory of the human condition, is further exemplified by Veronica Geng's argument that the film can be linked to the Christian concept of the Fall and to a prelapsarian universe, in which 'the whole human race took a dive with Original Sin', to the effect that 'La Motta's fall' is one such 'version of *the* Fall'.[103]

In line, however, with the Christian model of redemption through suffering, it is apparent that, despite being a largely inarticulate and 'barely civilized human beast',[104] La Motta is, to some extent, conscious of the unfavourable things he has done and actually sees his defeats in the ring as a kind of punishment. In Friedman's words, indeed, La Motta is such a guilt-ridden individual that he 'atones for his sin by absorbing vicious punishment in the ring'.[105] In this respect, rather than attribute the gradual decline of his fighting ability to 'the natural processes of aging',[106] there is a sense in which La Motta sees the inevitable deterioration of his prowess as the penalty for his transgressions, such that he comes to relish 'the brutal punishment he receives . . . as welcome retribution for the guilt he is continually experiencing'.[107] As with the fourteen Stations of the Cross, then, the screenwriter, Paul Schrader, has indicated that *Raging Bull* may be apprehended as an examination of the theme of 'redemption through physical pain',[108] with one torment following on from another. Indeed, the boxing ring has even been construed as 'a metaphorical recreation of the crucifixion',[109] with the confines of the ring representing the combatants' last avenue for salvation.[110]

Towards the end of the picture, La Motta is sent to prison in Miami after he is arrested for soliciting minors and his failure to raise the $10,000 in bribes required to get the case dropped. By this time, it is evident that he has destroyed everything and everyone important to him, not least his wife and brother from whom he is estranged, such that he consequently hits rockbottom. In his cell, he 'pummels his head against the walls' and 'hammers the bars with his fists, as if protesting violently against the physical condition in which he finds himself entrapped',[111] to the effect that, as Giles points out, 'the prison cell operates as an extension of La Motta's own loathsome carcass from which he yearns to escape'.[112] Despite his despair, however, there is a sense in which the violence he inflicts upon himself in the cell constitutes a spark of redemption. For, as manifested by his cry of despair, 'I am not an animal', Kelly indicates that La Motta thereby 'faces himself and, somehow, redemption begins. The sign of salvation is small – he embraces his brother – but the moment is unforgettable. A man recognizes his own soul.'[113] By means of his suffering, therefore, La Motta is 'brought to an understanding of the essential nature of his own human limitations',[114] and manages to embrace his brother, Joey, with an unprecedented tenderness and affection, which provides a distinct counterpoint to their hitherto tumultuous relationship, wherein verbal obscenities and physical violence were the archetypal means of communication. From a destructive – and essentially self-destructive – existence, then, La Motta manages to make peace with life and undergo what amounts to a redemptive experience.

It is particularly significant that, as demonstrated at the end of the picture, the essentially inarticulate La Motta should resort in his retirement to reciting words for a living. In his recitation on stage at the Barbizon–Plaza nightclub from the works of Shakespeare, Tennessee Williams and a scene from *On the Waterfront* (1954), it is apparent that what constituted La Motta's biggest drawback has now been transposed into a prime, if not actually defining, characteristic of his existence. As Friedman thus indicates, 'it is not too much to suggest that Jake is redeemed via his hard-won ability to translate the body language of the boxer into the verbal language of the actor'.[115] In particular, Scorsese points out that, as we see La Motta rehearsing his lines in the dressing room, 'you feel him finally coming to some sort of peace with himself in front of that mirror',[116] to the effect that this scene could also be said to testify to his redemption. In order to underline the extent of La Motta's redemptive experience, furthermore, this end-scene concludes with the appearance on screen of a quotation from John's Gospel, in which the blind man cured by Jesus attests that 'All I know is this: once I was blind and now I can see.'[117] In a manner akin to that of the blind man, La Motta may be said to have undergone an awakening, or redemption, from his state of *spiritual* blindness. Like the blind man, indeed, La Motta may be perceived to be a hopeless case, but in the respect that, as Kierkegaard has acknowledged, despair is also the prerequisite of redemption, then there is a substantial sense in which the gravity of La Motta's sins and the apparent hopelessness of his estranged condition have the potential to engender a prodigious redemptive experience. *Raging Bull* may, therefore, be a story told in terms of – often extreme – physical violence, but it may also be seen at the same time to encompass significant Christian themes and to constitute what Veronica Geng identifies as 'a tremendously powerful biography of a soul' and of an individual's 'violent *spiritual* desire'.[118]

The role of the film audience

Ultimately, then, in what Friedman designates 'Scorsese's vestigially Catholic moral calculus', there is a substantial sense in which, as with *Taxi Driver* and in common with a Christian reading, 'the presence of sin' in *Raging Bull* 'evokes the possibility of redemption'.[119] As with Travis Bickle, and in accordance with the authentically human Jesus portrayed by Scorsese in *The Last Temptation of Christ*, it is in the delineation of an intrinsically human character who undergoes a redemptive experience through a personal encounter with his basic human condition that the *audience's* identification with La Motta may also be seen to constitute a site of potential redemptive activity. Indeed, it is significant that Scorsese has indicated that he hopes the audience of *Raging Bull* can, like him, learn from La Motta's attainment of redemption. Prior to making the picture, Scorsese acknowledges that his personal life was falling apart, in that his second marriage was breaking up and he was in a state of poor health and depression. In his words,

> I started to physically fall apart. Towards the end of the summer of '78 during the week I would spend two or three days in my bed unable to function . . . It got to the point where I couldn't work any more and then around Labour Day of 1978 I had to be hospitalized . . . I couldn't function. I didn't know what was happening to me. Basically I was dying. I was bleeding internally and all over . . . It was like a nightmare.[120]

Yet, as he attests, at this point *Raging Bull* offered a way out of his creative and personal impasse and became a means of *redemption*. As a consequence of the self-destructiveness which had landed him in hospital, Scorsese was in a crucial sense 'ripe for the epiphany that bound himself to La Motta',[121] precisely because he had 'gone through a similar experience'.[122] In his words, 'I had found the hook – the self-destructiveness, the destruction of people around you . . . I *was* Jake La Motta.'[123] Scorsese's identification with his protagonist was so intensive, indeed, that, as he reflects, 'I just knew that he survived and he survived with knowledge',[124] to the point that 'he became at peace with himself and the people around him'.[125] As a corollary, Scorsese has expressed the hope that by forcing *viewers* into the ring and bloodying their noses[126] as they follow La Motta down, 'see him graze at the bottom' and 'then see the beginning of a trajectory up to some kind of salvation',[127] they might be able to *confront* La Motta and identify with his need for purification, expiation and vindication.[128] Just as the challenge of *Last Temptation* is not simply to be able to follow and to make sense of *Jesus'* temptation and struggle but for the audience to be able 'to identify with it, masochistically as well as narcissistically'[129] so Scorsese has attested with respect to filming *Raging Bull* that 'I wanted to do the fight scenes as if the *viewers* were the fighter, and their impressions were the fighter's – of what he would think or feel, or what he would hear',[130] to the effect that they, too, could undergo an ultimately redemptive and purgative process through sharing the experience of 'being pounded all the time'.[131]

(d) Redemption through *Cape Fear*

Pertinent though *Mean Streets, Taxi Driver* and *Raging Bull* are, however, as sites of potential redemptive activity, it is in many respects the 1991 picture *Cape Fear* that constitutes not only Scorsese's but one of *the* most explicitly religious films to have been produced in contemporary American cinema, with a serious treatise on redemption underlying its origins as a mainstream Hollywood thriller. Although the film was essentially 'a project concocted for mass appeal and commercial profit',[132] the film, in contradistinction to the more usually escapist orientations of the thriller and horror genre, is an intensely religious picture, whose characters, themes, images and narrative all contribute to the dispensation and transmission of an innately redemptive sensibility. Moreover, as in the case of the protagonists in *Mean Streets, Taxi Driver, Raging Bull* and *Last Temptation*, whose authentically human characteristics enable them to be apprehended as especially fecund models or exemplars of redemptive possibility, so the family in *Cape Fear* may be seen to bear witness to the Antiochene tradition's emphasis on the intrinsically human – often painful and protracted – dimension to redemption, the benefits of which experience may be passed on and imparted in turn to other human beings. The 'everyman' dimension to the family may, indeed, be said to account for Pam Cook's testimony, in an article on *Cape Fear* in the April 1992 edition of *Sight and Sound*, that the experiences of the characters in Scorsese's picture mirror our own as we wait and are held in suspense to discover their fate. In Cook's words, 'We shift anxiously in our seats as we are drawn into games of disguise and pursuit which postpone the final resolution. And we revel squeamishly in scenes of ritualistic punishment and death.'[133] Ultimately, the reason we can engage so intimately with the protagonists is that, unlike the traditionally escapist Hollywood film, whose images of spectacular and idealistic worlds and delineation of exemplary protagonists may often be seen to have had an adverse effect upon audiences for whom life 'doesn't work that way',[134] in the case of *Cape Fear* it would not be a misrepresentation to posit that we, the film audience, *are* the protagonists.

Indeed, rather than merely a presentation on screen of a wholly contrived and fictitious American family, who possess no fundamental import or resonance beyond the film's 'illusory' space, the family in *Cape Fear* may be seen to epitomize the universal human condition. This is especially borne out when the film is set against the 1962 version of *Cape Fear*, directed by J. Lee Thompson, whose characters and themes Scorsese has inverted.[135] In the original picture, the Bowdens are presented as a model family who are confronted with evil from without, in the form of ex-convict Max Cady (Robert Mitchum), against whom Sam Bowden (Gregory Peck) once testified in a rape trial. Cady is presented as a psychotic brute, completely unjustified in his revenge against Sam and what is presented as the traditional nuclear family. Although, as the Christian tradition supposes, sin and alienation are, in many respects, intrinsic to human life and experience, the problem with the 1962 film is that, in the words of Jenny Diski in the February 1992 edition of *Sight and Sound*, 'The Bowden family is untouched by suffering, and as nice as the apple pie Peg Bowden [Polly Bergen] undoubtedly makes for Sam and their cutely precious daughter, Nancy [Lori Martin].'[136] There are no discernible tensions or antagonisms at the heart of the family until the moment in which, as Diski puts it,

> Robert Mitchum, barrel-chested, heavy-lidded and BAD, takes the keys out of amiable, dull, puppet-wooden Gregory Peck's ignition and reminds him who he is. It's simple. You know where you are; the bad guy's come along, and the family – THE FAMILY – is under threat.[137]

In short, Cady is 'simply a figure of evil invading from outside the idyllic all-American family and derailing its daily routine'.[138] This clear-cut dichotomy between 'good' and 'evil' actually pervaded the original script for the 1991 version of *Cape Fear*, which was due to be directed by Steven Spielberg.[139] As Scorsese points out, however, 'It was more black and white than I could accept', as exemplified by a scene in which the 'model' family was shown sitting around the piano and singing together in harmony.

In Scorsese's more authentic – and indubitably religious – picture, in marked contrast, it is the Bowdens' dysfunctional and 'fallen' nature that acts as the catalyst which mobilizes the film's themes. In a manner consonant with Schleiermacher's assessment that each individual human being exists in an immature and imperfect state, and has a concomitant propensity towards sin, Sam Bowden (Nick Nolte) is a public defender who had, fourteen years earlier, buried evidence pertaining to his client, Max Cady (Robert De Niro), who had raped and battered a sixteen-year-old girl. The report attested to his victim's promiscuity which, if disclosed, could have given him at least a lighter sentence. Cady consequently seeks restitution and revenge for Sam's crime by terrorizing the Bowden family, in which – as the film's editor, Thelma Schoonmaker, points out – '*Everyone* is guilty.'[140] Indeed, Scorsese's focus is, to a large extent, on what amounts to a dysfunctional, sinful family, whose members are essentially estranged from one another. Sam has committed various in-fidelities in the past – and is presently involved in a clandestine affair with Lori (Illeana Douglas), a law clerk in his office – and this contributes to a substantial degree to the dysfunctional nature of the family in the present. His wife, Leigh (Jessica Lange), is unwilling and unable to forget about his adultery, and seizes every opportunity to remind him of his misdemeanours. She is a graphic artist who is so self-absorbed in her work and unhappy in her marriage that she neglects their fifteen-year-old daughter, Danielle (Juliette Lewis). As Savage points out, her 'sin' is thus in failing to fulfil her duties as mother.[141] And, Danielle sins in her failure to acknowledge her sexually charged liaison with Cady at one point in the picture, and in running away from, and literally shutting the door on, her parents' fighting. Ultimately, indeed, all the 'family members sin when they fail to communicate with each other and confront their transgressions'.[142]

Upon a superficial reading, *Cape Fear* would seem to be qualitatively different from *Taxi Driver* and *Raging Bull* in the respect that Travis Bickle and Jake La Motta endeavour to redeem, respectively, a corrupted world fallen from grace and their own sinful and guilt-ridden existence, while Max Cady's steadfast mission is not to save but to *destroy* the Bowden family. As with Scorsese's other protagonists, however, what may be construed as a violent and destructive undertaking is, in actuality, the prerequisite of a prodigious *redemptive* experience. Indeed, some may argue that Max Cady functions as an avenging angel whose mission is to redeem the Bowden family from their guilt and transgressions, by forcing them – especially through the use of extreme violence – to acknowledge and confront their sins. Certainly, Cady conceives of his mission in religious terms. When we see him at the beginning of the picture walking out of prison, after serving his fourteen-year sentence, it is apparent that 'an ominous boiling sky'[143] lies overhead, which, as Lesley Stern perceives, corresponds to the 'ominous world, boiling with retribution'[144] that Cady wills into being. On his back is a tattoo of a cartoon figure holding a gun in one hand and a Bible in the other, as well as an image of the scales of truth and justice hanging off either side of a cross. Imprinted over his arms and chest are several biblical quotations, including 'Vengeance is mine', 'My time is at hand' and 'Time the Avenger', with references inscribed next to the quotations like footnotes. Cady thus amounts, effectively, to a functional personification of the 'Word made flesh', and, indeed, to quote Stern, 'in a macabre travesty of the Judaeo-Christian law, he is the Flesh made Wordy'.[145] From the outset, then, it is clear that Cady is obsessed with judgement, and may be seen to function as a Christ-figure – albeit in a twisted sense – as he metaphorically weighs the scales on Judgement Day, which for the Bowdens is imminent. His desire for revenge against the family causes him, indeed, 'to literally embody the letter of the law as the Word of an Avenging God',[146] and as, in Scorsese's words, 'an instrument of God carrying out his revenge'.[147]

As a consequence of their transgressions, the members of the Bowden family are thus vulnerable to Cady's incursion into their lives. Indeed, there is a sense in which Cady has actually been created by Sam as a consequence of what Scorsese refers to as 'his moral mistake'.[148] The inextricable connection between Sam and Max Cady is illustrated in the case of Cady's brutal assault on Lori, with whom Sam is engaged in an extramarital relationship. For, as Friedman indicates, 'it is Sam's sexual bad faith' and 'transgression' that 'links Bowden the adulterer to Cady the rapist', with Cady's attack on Lori constituting 'a macabre (sub)version of her relationship with Bowden'.[149] Since Sam stands Lori up one evening, she thereby 'provides an easy mark for Cady who savages her precisely because she is sexually involved'[150] with Sam. When, towards the beginning of the picture, Sam and Lori are shown playing racquetball together, the camera is slammed around, and their panting, sweaty bodies could be read as an intimation of their sexual relationship. Cady's rape of Lori is largely analogous to this event in terms of its speed, noise and violence, to the effect that Savage draws a parallel between Sam and Max, arguing that they should both be construed as 'monsters'.[151] This doubling between the two also occurs when Sam watches Cady being strip-searched by the police through a one-way mirror and when Cady is being beaten up by Sam's hired thugs. In both cases, despite him being out of sight, Cady is intuitively aware that Sam is watching him. Ultimately, regardless of what Sam does, or the extent to which he endeavours to get rid of Cady – whether through arranging for him to be beaten to a pulp, setting a trap for him inside his house, or, as at first, trying to remove him with the assistance of the police – Cady's permeation into Sam's family is relentless and unstoppable. No matter how far Sam runs, he can never escape his nemesis, who will not – indeed, cannot, due to their inseparability – depart until, or unless, Sam confronts, and is punished for, his transgressions.

The traditional role of heroes and villains – which forms the basis of the 1962 version of *Cape Fear* – is thus subverted in Scorsese's picture, with 'heroes and anti-heroes, redeemers and destroyers' becoming 'almost inseparable within the same character'.[152] Significantly, the family come to some form of acknowledgement of Cady's function as redeemer, as opposed to that of unmitigated destroyer, after Sam is instructed at one point by Cady to 'Check out the Bible, councillor. The book between Esther and Psalms.' Upon finding out that he is referring to the book of Job, Sam learns that the character, Job, was a seemingly righteous, God-fearing man, whose faith was put to the test by God in a wager with Satan – one of the attenders in the heavenly court – whereby God deprives Job of his family, his livestock and his reputation, and he is afflicted with an atrocious form of skin disease.[153] Although Cady's offensive against the Bowdens in *Cape Fear* is not identical in form to God's devastation of Job's secure existence, the family may be seen to take Job's place, in that – although by no means morally blameless – they are forced by Cady to question and confront, like Job, the values and assumptions which they had hitherto taken for granted, and, in the case of the Bowdens, the transgressions they have failed to face up to, and take responsibility for. Consequently, just as Job was, at first, bewildered as to why God should want to subject his own handiwork to such ruinous effect,[154] the Bowdens do not at first consider themselves deserving of Cady's malevolent incursion into their lives. While Job eventually comes to acknowledge that God's wisdom is not akin to human wisdom, such that there may actually be a rationale for suffering – albeit one which humankind is not in a position to apprehend – the Bowdens come to realize that, unwelcome and even irrational though Max Cady's malignant presence may be, there may, in actuality, be a profound purpose and design behind the suffering and affliction to which they are being subjected. As Leigh confesses upon seeing Sam reading from the book of Job, 'I'd like to know just how strong we are, or how weak. But I guess the only way we're going to find that out is just by going through this.'

In the case of *Cape Fear*, the rationale behind the family's inexorable persecution by Cady is that out of their suffering they may be able to undergo a process of redemption. Indeed, in Cady's words to Danielle,

> Every man carries a circle of hell around his head like a halo. Your Daddy too . . . Every man has to go through hell to reach his Paradise. You know what Paradise is? . . . Salvation. Because your daddy's not happy. Your mommy's not happy. And, you know what, you're not happy, are you?

A parallel can thus be drawn between the family's recognition of their need to suffer and the sense in which Job's immense suffering points not to Yahweh's weakness or lack of care, but actually entails the means by which the process of redemption can operate. For, although Job may be required to suffer in this life, some theologians have read into the book of Job the possibility that, as a consequence of his affliction, redemption is impending in the form of a life after death, in the respect that if Job matters to God 'then God will miss Job if he allows him to collapse into nothingness'.[155] Indeed, it has been suggested in this regard that it is a prerequisite of the problem of evil that the suffering individual, in this case Job, will necessarily enter into a redemptive state where he will be recompensed for his suffering in this life.[156] According to John Hick, for instance, as a consequence of suffering one is thereby able to participate in what he terms the 'justifying good' and so be 'able to see their own past sufferings as having been worthwhile'.[157] For both Job and the family in *Cape Fear*, therefore, it is apparent that out of suffering and destruction come the possibility and hope of redemption.

In the case of the Bowdens, however, rather than wait until a future life, the process of redemption actually occurs in the present, in the apocalyptic showdown at the end of the picture on the family houseboat on the murky waters of Cape Fear, wherein Cady literally forces the family to acknowledge and confess their sins. He thereby fulfils his earlier promise to Sam that 'You might say I'm here to save you', as well as his pledge to Danielle that the purpose of his coercive mission does not stem exclusively from a desire for retribution against her father, and a wish to see him destroyed, since 'I don't hate him at all. Oh, no. I pray for him. I'm here to help him. I mean we all make mistakes . . . But at least we try to admit it . . . But, your daddy, he don't.' Hence, as Stern points out, Cady both personifies revenge and functions as an instrument of salvation.[158] On the one hand, Cady assumes the role of judge and transforms the haven of the family houseboat into a makeshift courtroom, and sets about trying and convicting Sam of the crime of burying the report, some fourteen years earlier, which could have saved him from serving such a substantial prison sentence:

> MAX: I'm Virgil, councillor, and I'm guiding you to the gates of Hell. We are now in the Ninth Circle. The Circle of traitors. Traitors to country. Traitors to fellow man. Traitors to God. You, sir, are charged with betraying the principles of all three. Can you please quote for me the American Bar Association's Rules of Professional Conduct canon seven?
>
> SAM: A lawyer shall represent his client . . .
>
> MAX: . . . shall *jealously* represent his client within the bounds of the law. And I find you *guilty*, councillor. Guilty of betraying your fellow man. Guilty of betraying your country. Guilty of abrogating your oath. Guilty of judging me and selling me out. And with the power invested in me by the Kingdom of God, I sentence you to the Ninth Circle of Hell. Now, you will learn about loss. Loss of freedom. Loss of humanity . . .

On the other hand, however, Kelly interprets Cady's vendetta against Sam as signifying, 'I'm the best thing that's ever happened to you',[159] and

> Yes, I'm going to kill you. You will be dead. But in the process, I will have divested you of all the things that would have prevented you from getting into heaven. *Therefore I am your salvation.* Because I'm going to

take everything away from you, and you just might make it through the Pearly Gates, by the time I'm done with you.[160]

In actuality, however, Cady does not succeed in annihilating the family, who manage – albeit at the cost of much suffering – to survive the ordeal. One interpretation of the end of the film, in which the Bowdens manage to abandon their wrecked houseboat and swim through the murky waters to a desolate river island, is that, having burned in the metaphorical 'fire of their trans-gressions', they have now undergone a resurrection 'from the ashes of this baptismal fire of water', and are 'reborn' while 'they huddle in the mud', a site which represents 'new life and primordial beginnings'.[161] Indeed, Leigh has been redeemed in that she atones for having hitherto neglected her daughter by protecting Danielle from being raped by Cady: she pleads with him to 'do whatever you have planned *to me* – just not to her'. Danielle's redemption arises from her admission of having concealed a sexually charged liaison with Cady and she helps to protect her family from Cady's violent beating of her father, and rape of her mother, instead of running away from any con-frontation with, and actually siding against, her parents, as had been characteristic of her former conduct. Moreover, Sam has acknowledged and confronted his role in unlawfully sending Cady to gaol. In particular, the sign that Sam's redemption has been achieved is denoted by the blood-stains on his hands, following the ferocious battle with his nemesis, which, according to Scorsese, symbolizes his 'guilt and a sense of a horrible deed he has committed' but which is then 'washed away'[162] by the water. Indeed, there is a sense in which, by washing away 'the blood from the stigmata in the cleansing river',[163] Sam Bowden is at this point symbolically purging himself of his sins.

Consequently, therefore, although of all Scorsese's Christ-figures Cady is the most overt, at least in respect of the abundance of religious tattoos on his body and his self-designation as God's agent, it is the family, and not Cady, who, ultimately, bear witness to the authentically human experience of redemption through suffering, as prefigured by the Antiochene interpretation of Christ. In his own right, indeed, Cady is barely a human being, let alone a Christ-figure – he seems almost supernatural in character, as implied in his disclosure to Sam, 'I spent fourteen years in an eight by nine cell surrounded by people who were less than human. My mission in that time was to become *more* than human.' He is able to enter and depart the family residence undetected, even though Sam has employed a private detective to set a trap for him inside the house, using equipment which, Sam is ironically informed, would be sufficient to prevent the 'Holy Ghost' from 'sneaking in'. Cady can, further, withstand the pain of candle wax and boiling water, as he demonstrates on the houseboat towards the end of the picture, following the Bowdens' desperate attempts to eliminate him. If, however, Cady is interpreted as a kind of psychological manifestation and embodiment of the family's own guilt and transgressions then his function becomes apparent. Cady amounts, in essence, to the instrument or agent of the Bowdens' attainment, or potential attainment, of redemption. The more the family compound and exacerbate their guilt, the more intensive Cady's incursion into their lives becomes, until their eventual confession and redemption.

In this respect, Cady resembles the vengeful God of the Old Testament, trying to redeem his errant people from their transgressions, more than he does the image of God in the New Testament as a loving, merciful figure.[164] In Judges 2: 11–23, for instance, we learn that 'the people of Israel did what was evil in the sight of the Lord . . . and they provoked the Lord to anger'.[165] Consequently, 'he gave them over to plunderers . . . and he sold them into the power of their enemies round about, so they could no longer withstand their enemies'.[166] Yahweh, the passage informs us, did, though, raise up judges for his people, 'who saved them out of the power of those who plundered them'.[167] However, 'whenever the judge died, they turned back and behaved worse than their fathers, going after other gods, serving them and bowing down to them . . . So the anger of the Lord was kindled against Israel',[168] and God again decided to punish them. If Israel was to be redeemed, the people thus had to overcome their sins, often by physical, violent means. Cady's punishment of the Bowdens could be read as analogous to this picture of God in Judges. They are (physically) punished until they finally confess their sins.

The role of the film audience

In short, then, in order for a film protagonist to be apprehended by audiences as a model or exemplar of redemptive possibility, such a figure must, in the spirit of the Antiochene Christological formulation, be a completely and authentically human individual, who, in contradistinction to Hollywood's propensity towards escapism, reflects and embodies the ambiguities and vicissitudes of human existence. The family in *Cape Fear* are thus extremely apposite models of redemption: in contrast to Scorsese's fear that his 1986 picture *The Color of Money* has the capacity to *cheat* and *shortchange* audiences in its delineation of 'easy' emotions, the ending of *Cape Fear* may be seen to expose all such 'conventional instances of unity for the illusions they are'.[169] The 'good' versus 'bad' dichotomy of J. Lee Thompson's original picture has been thoroughly exorcized by Scorsese, and replaced instead by a blurring of such traditional absolutes into more authentic, and concomitantly more ambiguous, shades of grey. What is more, Scorsese can be seen to *implicate* the audience in the moral ambiguity that lies at the very kernel of the picture. In Jenny Diski's words, indeed,

> We know that the right to an adequate defence is a fundamental of civilisation; we also know that Cady is too violent and vicious a creature to be allowed to roam free . . . Bowden is no longer simply a good man upon whom evil is unjustly unleashed. He is a much more modern hero, with a burden of ethical guilt. He faces not only violent retribution, but disbarment by his peers.[170]

In like manner, Cady does not simply trap Danielle in the basement of her school, in the manner of the 1962 film. Rather, he entices her, and she is willing to accept the bait. In a much more authentically human fashion, and in line with a Christian sensibility, Scorsese *denies* the audience 'popular Hollywood's conventional ability (to appear) to give order and meaning to an otherwise chaotic and fragmentary experience of life'.[171]

Although the climactic ending has been criticized by some commentators for being too melodramatic and, unusually for a Scorsese picture, as stretching the boundaries of credibility,[172] Scorsese acknowledges that, while he was 'taking risks'[173] with this part of the film, 'the truth of what a couple might go through emotionally and psychologically is still there, far-fetched as it is'.[174] At no point does Scorsese offer the viewer a straightforward and facile interpretation of redemption, in the manner of the conventional Hollywood 'happy ending', wherein redemption is perceived to be an easily attainable activity. Indeed, Rosalie Savage even posits with regard to the ending of *Cape Fear* that it is, in actuality, open to question as to whether the Bowdens – though redeemed physically from Cady – have truly learned from their sins and past mistakes,[175] and thereby undergone a fully fledged process of redemption. From Danielle's voice-over, for example, we learn that the family 'never spoke about what happened, at least not to each other', for 'to remember his name and what he did would mean letting him in to our dreams'. There is thus an insinuation that the Bowdens have returned to their formerly troubled lives, in which they are prone to reject the need to confront their 'demons' and the troubles of the past,[176] an – albeit short-lived – acknowledgement of which was responsible for securing their redemption in the first instance. Nevertheless, this ambiguity, rather than a sign that redemption is ultimately missing from the film, as Savage suggests, is in a fundamental sense the very *prerequisite* of what amounts in the Christian tradition to a prodigious redemptive activity, to the point of rendering *Cape Fear* especially amenable to a redemptive reading, in line with Christian teaching.

Ultimately, it is Scorsese's representation of his characters' lives as rather contradictory and unstable that is the starting-point of their ability to undergo an experience of redemption. And, as with traditional Christian theology in this respect, even where signs and glimmers of redemption are apparent, the process 'should not be understood to happen suddenly, but gradually and by steps, as . . . the process of improvement and correction advances by different degrees in different individuals'.[177] Rather than as a once-for-all activity, therefore, it is not contradictory to suppose that the process of redemption has merely *begun* in Scorsese's characters, and is in no way *complete*. As Origen maintained, indeed, although all of the suffering we undergo in the course of our lives is intended to teach us a lesson, and must have an end and ultimate resolution, this state of *apocatastasis*, or 'restoration', is not a *sudden* happening, but a process which is '*gradually* effected by stages during the passing of countless ages'.[178] In the case of the Bowdens, therefore, it should be of no surprise that, for a family alienated from within by deception and transgression, future life-situations and challenges will invariably pass before a final or definitive experience of redemption can in any way be attained.

From an audience perspective, the experience of the Bowdens, as understood in the light of Origen's teaching, may thus be seen to constitute an indication or model as to how one's *own* redemption may be achieved. Although, to an extent, Origen's theology would seem to take issue with the strictly this-worldly and present-oriented dimension of realized eschatology, which forms the basis of how redemption may be understood in *film noir*, insofar as he speaks of 'the passing of countless ages'[179] before redemption may finally be accomplished, it is the experience of the individual *in the here and now* that is of fundamental concern to Origen. Indeed, in contrast to the traditional eschatology, in which it is anticipated that the end of this world and of history will witness a divine and dramatic intervention by God, resulting in the resurrection and judgement of all persons and a subsequent destiny to be spent in either 'heaven' or 'hell', Origen attests that redemption can be apprehended by individuals in a more *spiritual* sense, wherein 'men will bring judgement on themselves'[180] by their actions and behaviour in *this* world. Hence, as Brian Daley explains, 'clearly the most important part of the Church's traditional images of the future, for Origen, is what they can tell us, *in a symbolic way*, about the individual Christian's growth towards salvation'.[181]

The 'redeemed' state thus amounts, in effect, to the point at which each individual human being manages to come face to face with their basic human condition and nature, which, from the point of view of the Christian tradition, entails a confrontation with one's propensity towards sin and transgression, and a concomitant openness to reform. From the 'fire' of judgement which is kindled by each individual sinner, and whose 'own vices form its fuel',[182] the estrangement and lack of cohesion that is the 'hell' of our present existence may be seen to precipitate the individual's quest towards redemption. There may, then, be a certain ambiguity at the end of *Cape Fear* as to whether or not the family has undergone anything resembling a redemptive experience, but, in light of the necessarily complex, and protracted, nature of the redemptive process, it is sufficient that Scorsese holds out the possibility that the Bowdens *may be* redeemed for their transgressions and does not suggest – in the spirit of the conventional Hollywood 'happy ending' – that redemption *has been* achieved, without qualification, for the principal characters, with 'good' triumphing unambiguously over 'evil'.

8

Redemption or regression? The escapist ethos of contemporary film

While not providing all of the answers, it is nonetheless apparent that *film noir* and the cinema of Martin Scorsese can at least give certain pointers and indications as to how the creative dialogue between film and Christian theology has the potential to offer new and challenging ways of understanding and interpreting the Christian concept of redemption. Invariably, different interpreters will approach the subject from a different perspective. As Conrad Ostwalt points out, for instance, with reference to the religious orientation of film in general, 'The question is not so much how are films religious, or what religious themes crop up in popular films, or how do films inform or support religious beliefs and vice versa.'[1] Rather, Ostwalt posits that 'the more appropriate question is, how are films and religious imagination related, and how does this relationship help us to understand contemporary society, cultural values, and individual beliefs'.[2] While this broader approach may be seen to run contrary to my examination of the specific theme of redemption *vis-à-vis* the medium of film, it is my underlying premise that redemption is a rudimentary and pervasive human concern, such that it is through a particular examination of redemption, as in the case of *Cape Fear*, that we are in a position to, in Ostwalt's words, 'understand contemporary society, cultural values, and individual beliefs'.[3] Ostwalt's approach may thus be different from mine in certain key respects, but there is nonetheless broad agreement in that it is from an analysis of the redemptive significance of film that one can come to understand a great deal about human existence, and the function of the human individual within society. This is not fundamentally at odds with Ostwalt's hypothesis that, 'It is through popular culture that we learn the values, symbols, and beliefs that inform both religion and society. And it is through immersion in those forms that we incorporate or redefine those values, symbols, and beliefs that define society.'[4]

Although a religious reading of film need not focus exclusively on the specific religious concept of redemption – indeed, Ostwalt has advised against such an approach – I have endeavoured to demonstrate that in view of Martin Scorsese's Christian heritage and the specifically human form of redemption to which his films bear witness, there is a substantial degree to which films such as *Mean Streets, Taxi Driver, Raging Bull* and *Cape Fear* may be seen to constitute a fertile and distinctively Christian site of religious significance. While it would be foolish to suppose that such films are necessarily able to change the lives and perspectives of each individual member of their audience, Ostwalt reasonably conjectures that 'we can assume that a good portion of the millions of people who watch movies are affected or changed in some way and that films can exert influence on attitudes, beliefs, and behaviors'.[5] In the case of Scorsese, for example, his films present especially apt models and indications as to how an individual might live, for his protagonists are authentically human individuals who attempt to wrestle with, and come to a better understanding of, their basic human condition. As with Christ's subjection to extreme physical brutality in the form of his crucifixion, it is significant that Jake La Motta channels the immense physical torture he receives in the boxing ring in order to 'fight', and overcome, the sin and alienation that is intrinsic to human experience. In the case of *Cape Fear*, the family members use the enormous suffering and pain, physical and psychological, that they receive at the hands of Max Cady in order to expiate and absolve themselves of their sins, thereby aiming to lead a life in future that is less destructive and volatile now that they have, arguably, learned from their mistakes.

Although audiences will, of course, read such films in a multiplicity of ways, Scorsese may be said, most pertinently, to have enabled audience members to confront their own misdemeanours – of which the Bowdens' adultery, lies and selfishness may be interpreted as a mirror image of our own – and to apprehend that, the more one endeavours to run away from, or to compound, one's guilt, as in the case of the Bowdens, the more inextricable and potentially cataclysmic the consequences will be, both for oneself and with respect to the lives of those who are in whatever sense *implicated* in that which has been done. It may be a basic message, and certainly one which will not be unfamiliar to many people who have received even a cursory or elementary moral or religious instruction at some point in their lives, but, without in any way *exhorting* an audience how to behave, *Cape Fear* indubitably *illustrates* and *documents* the cause of so much of the alienation, estrangement and malaise that lies at the heart of human experience, and at least *posits* a remedy.

A reversion from redemption to escapism

A fundamental qualification needs to be made at this juncture, however. Despite being acclaimed as one of the most accomplished contemporary film-makers – even as 'the king of American cinema'[6] – Scorsese's work cannot be said to be representative of present-day, mainstream motion pictures. His films may wrestle with, and seek to explore, universal human concerns, albeit in the early days at any rate from a very specific New York Italian–American perspective, but the impact and appeal of his films among film audiences may be seen to be relatively narrow. Even though *Cape Fear* is his most successful film to date, this is not so much because Scorsese has succeeded in combining his religious vision with the sensibilities of a large, mainstream audience as because Universal Pictures, with whom Scorsese had a six-year directing and producing contract, required from him a 'commercial' project in return for their 'risk' in enabling him to make *The Last Temptation of Christ* some three years earlier.[7] Moreover, rather than one of the most fully realized religious films ever made, Terence Rafferty, in an article on *Cape Fear* in *The New Yorker*, published on 2 December 1991, categorizes the film 'a disgrace: an ugly, incoherent, dishonest piece of work',[8] in which the theological motifs utilized by Scorsese 'have been imposed on, rather than discovered in, the material',[9] the effect of which is to increase 'our emotional distance from the story'.[10] In Rafferty's words, 'There's no way to recast this story in Christian terms without reducing it to moral (and aesthetic) nonsense.'[11] And, he argues, in contradistinction to my claim that Cady is an innately religious-orientated instrument and agent of redemption, that 'The idea that Cady is a monster who has just bubbled up out of the unconscious of a "dysfunctional" family seems at first to be just glib, fashionable pop psychology.'[12] Further, rather than that the family is a model, or exemplar, of redemptive significance,

Rafferty reads *Cape Fear* as 'a picture whose sole aim is to give its audience huge, bowel-loosening shocks'[13] under merely the veneer of 'moral seriousness and psychological complexity'.[14]

Nevertheless, without seeking to deny that there are limitations to the extent to which an audience may read *Cape Fear* as a prodigious site of redemptive activity, at least the *opportunity* to apprehend the film as a carrier and conveyor of religious significance is there, as even Rafferty acknowledges in his claim that Scorsese 'has loaded' the film with – albeit 'facile' – 'ideas about guilt and redemption'.[15] In the main, however, the films which tend to attract the largest audiences in contemporary, mainstream cinema are anything but 'religious' pictures, in the spirit of Scorsese's *films noirs*. This, after all, is an age of 'blockbusters' and of 'whizbang technology',[16] which, in Timothy Corrigan's words, are inclined to 'offer an unimaginable audience a minimal amount of textual engagement: they usually either provide an audience with familiar or inoffensive material or with momentary shocks and instant stimulations.'[17] In the spirit of the escapist ethos of pre-Second World War Hollywood cinema, such films are, in effect, 'there to help us through the tedium of inactivity', and may be said to amount, ultimately, to 'an art of illusion',[18] in this case glamorizing death and violence rather than, as in the 1930s, wealth and solidarity. In talking about the redemptive potential of film, therefore, while I have sought to outline how the dark and alienated images and narratives of *films noirs* amount to a more fertile repository of religious significance than the Hollywood propensity to escapism that preceded their output in the early part of the last century, the recent resurgence in Hollywood escapism can be seen to highlight the limitations of my hypothesis. Rafferty might consider *Cape Fear* an altogether 'dumb movie'[19] which, in the final analysis, amounts to little more than 'gut-level, cheap-thrills storytelling',[20] but this criticism surely pertains more reasonably to those pictures which are qualitatively different even from anything Scorsese has produced at his most populist and commercial.

Since the 1970s, indeed, when *film noir* experienced something of a resurgence, it is notable that, as Auster and Quart put it, there has been in Hollywood 'a conspicuous turning away' from films with a serious message 'toward movies stressing entertainment and escapism'.[21] As Scorsese himself experienced, at the end of the 1970s and through the 1980s, 'The whole mood of the country was different. Big money was being made with pictures like *Rocky* and eventually the Spielberg–Lucas films.'[22] It is significant, for example, that Scorsese's musical *New York, New York* (1977) opened on the same day as George Lucas's *Star Wars* in 1977, and was a commercial failure.[23] Ultimately, contemporary films may be seen to be marked not so much by 'complex, challenging narratives with subtle themes, round characters, and ambiguous conclusions'[24] – which, as the experience of *film noir* has shown, are especially amenable to a religious interpretation – but by 'mindless chases and duels, cardboard villains, clear victories, and happy endings',[25] which are designed to appeal to 'the basest instincts of the mass audience'.[26] In the final analysis, as Friedman attests, what matters is 'how the bad guy gets zapped, not why; it is form that hooks us, not function'.[27] Even in a film such as *Terminator 2: Judgment Day* which possesses an ostensibly religious ethos, Fred Pfeil points out that the 'overall regime' is one of 'pleasure',[28] in which the audience is not required to yield too much of its intelligence. While it is possible to read the *Terminator* pictures against the backdrop of the apocalyptic tradition of the Hebrew Bible – and in particular such texts as Jeremiah and Malachi – the crucial difference is that the writings of the Hebrew prophets arose from a long-standing tradition of religious passion[29] whereas, in themselves, 'the films are capacious, largely empty containers'.[30] In spite of 'all the *noir*ish haze and green/blue/black'[31] suffused throughout *Terminator 2*, on the level of narrative, at any rate, 'there is virtually no confusion about what is going on',[32] or as to how the viewer should feel about it. Indeed, in contrast to the ambiguity and cynicism of the classic *noir* protagonist, the audience is left in no doubt as to who is 'good' and who is 'bad', and it is not difficult to ascertain that, eventually, the 'hero', T-800 (Arnold Schwarzenegger) will protect and rescue John Connor (Edward Furlong) from the clutches of T-1000 (Robert Patrick).

In *The Mission* (1986), further, even though a serious attempt is made to explore some of the divisions within the Roman Catholic Church in South America in the eighteenth century, in the form of the resistance of a small group of Jesuits to the authoritarian institution of the Church, the film ultimately succumbs to 'the audience's expectations for entertainment'.[33] Despite the apparent hope of the director, Roland Joffé, that audiences would make a connection with the *contemporary* religious struggle between the Vatican and South and Central American base communities over liberation theology,[34] and in spite of the film's redolence of religious symbolism,[35] the liberties that the film takes with history in order to meet the demands of the mass audience have the effect of thwarting and obviating a religious reading of the film. The film's identification with heroic *individuals*, for instance, may be seen to be out of tune with the insistence of theologians of liberation 'on the primacy of *communities*'.[36] As Margaret Miles attests, this stems from a long Hollywood tradition of focusing on *individual* rather than *ensemble* performances,[37] and the consideration that, although it would have been more appropriate in this instance, a film about a community would be unlikely to do so well at the box office. The history reported in the film is thus, to quote Keith Tribe, 'recognized as Truth by the viewer not by virtue of the 'facts' being correct, but because the image looks right'.[38] Had the criteria been different, Miles suggests that it is unlikely the film would have ended 'in the mandatory carnage of an adventure film'.[39] In delineating what mass audiences want to see, rather than bearing witness to authentic human hopes, concerns and aspirations in the manner of, say, a Scorsese picture, Miles provides the somewhat bleak assessment that, while it would be wrong to rule out the possibility that 'religious films' will continue to generate interest among film audiences, 'attending a Hollywood film about religion is not likely to be a religious *experience* for anyone'.[40]

It is therefore ironic that many of the 'escapist' tendencies which have been so dominant in recent Hollywood film have been apprehended and perceived in religious terms. In line with the spirit of an Alexandrian Christology, M. Darrol Bryant refers to 'the hunger of human beings, in the midst of a technological civilization, to have their lives taken up into a more potent, magical realm',[41] and which is met by the heroic endeavours of film protagonists 'who exercise control in the cinematic world which far exceeds our daily experience'.[42] In Rob Lapsley's words, 'In a runaway world, where subjects increasingly experience their fate as governed by forces outside their control, spectators take flight into Promethean identifications with powerful, apparently self-sufficient figures who are the masters of their own destiny.'[43]

Although his revisionist Western, *Unforgiven*, may be seen to invert the escapist tendency of the traditional Hollywood Western, wherein, to quote Bryant, 'The stranger who rides into town to restore peace and order meets our desire to live in a more ordered world',[44] Clint Eastwood, in an interview for *Time* magazine in January 1978, summed up the process at work in contemporary mainstream cinema. In his words,

> A guy sits alone in the theater. He's young and he's scared. He doesn't know what he's going to do with his life. He wishes he could be self-sufficient, like the man he sees up there on the screen, somebody who can look out for himself, solve his own problems. I do the kinds of roles I'd like to see if I were still digging swimming pools and wanted to escape my problems.[45]

In the 1980s, for instance, the guerrilla warrior John Rambo (Sylvester Stallone) was presented as 'the ultimate fighting machine, with whom no amount of police, national guardsmen, helicopters, antitank weapons and even Doberman Pinschers can cope'.[46] Rambo is a powerful individual avenging a largely passive society in the aftermath of the American failure in Vietnam, inasmuch as he effectively *reverses* the result of the war, at least in the American imagination. With the portrayal of the Vietnamese soldiers being akin to the depiction of the Japanese in film versions of the Second World War, and their fictitious Russian adviser being a caricature of Second World War movie Nazis, Kolker indicates that *Rambo: First Blood, Part Two* (1985) simplistically and straightforwardly defines the existence of social disorder and provides for its correction,[47] with the figure of Rambo speaking 'the discourse of frustration satisfied and fantasies affirmed'.[48] In effect, something is presented as being lost or undone in order that the avenging hero can *reclaim* and *reunite* it, even to the point that, as Kolker points out, the film's resolution is not merely satisfactory but brings 'events back to a better place than where they started or were originally left unfinished'.[49]

Even though the heroic endeavours of the protagonists in so much of contemporary cinema render such individuals in a fundamental sense separate from the rest of humankind, this may be seen to function 'as a device' to fulfil the audience's desire 'for power and recognition *vicariously*'.[50] According to Bryan Burroughs, the 1980s was 'a time when everything – old standards, morals, sometimes even the truth – was sacrificed in the almighty hunt for The Big Deal'.[51] And, according to Fred Steeper, whose firm polled public opinion during the 1988 presidential election campaign in America, 'The upcoming '90s have been prefaced by economic uncertainty due to budget deficits, fear of the hazards of environmental pollution, and sexual doubt fueled by the AIDS crisis . . . There's a sense that the moral fabric of society has been pulled asunder.'[52] Within this context, Andrew Gordon posits that 'We desperately need a renewal of faith in ourselves . . . as men and women, as human beings who count, and so we return temporarily to the simpler patterns of the past',[53] one of the manifestations of which is a resurgence of interest in Hollywood escapism. The scenario is similar to Umberto Eco's diagnosis of the human condition in an industrial society as one 'where man becomes a number in the realm of the organisation which has usurped his decision-making role',[54] in which 'he has no means of production and is thus deprived of his power to decide'.[55] In such a society, Eco attests, 'the *positive hero* must embody to an unthinkable degree the power demands that the average citizen nurtures but cannot satisfy'.[56] In giving voice to 'our deepest longings'[57] and articulating our hopes regarding 'the future of our society and ourselves',[58] such films may be seen, in effect, to represent the fantasy of the assenting viewer, whereby one is given an illusion of power.[59]

It is this very *illusory* quality, however, that, in my interpretation, precludes an effective religious reading of contemporary, blockbuster films. While there is a rational basis to such pictures, insofar as, to quote Hans Küng, it is hardly surprising that in the face of chaos and destruction 'our imagination begins to produce substitute-heroes who can protect us from the inferno',[60] such films bear no relation to external reality, but only to a *fantasy* of how one would *like* reality to be. In Küng's words, 'from James Bond to Superman', contemporary cinema bears witness to 'an illustrious phalanx of superheroes, substitute-Messiahs, and fantasy-redeemers who give us the feeling that we can get away again'.[61] And yet, as Küng acknowledges, the 'average person', in 'his feeling of powerlessness', can, 'with the aid of the drug "superman"', gain relief *for a moment* from the nightmare vision of inferno'.[62] Whereas in *films noirs* there is, characteristically, an authentic portrait of how life *actually* is, the problem with the escapist nature of contemporary Hollywood is that, in not corresponding to the reality of human experience, the figures who appear on the screen amount ultimately to what Don Cupitt calls 'infantile fantasies of omnipotence'.[63] Such films can achieve no more than a *temporary* relief and respite and offer merely 'fleeting moments of unconscious happiness'[64] for the audience from the authentic concerns of the 'real' world, wherein, in the words of Peter Krämer, 'problematic social relationships and painful feelings'[65] are often the norm.

Since the Schwarzenegger or Stallone action hero is single-handedly capable of saving the world from catastrophe, by taking risks and executing stunts which are beyond the competence and means of the average human being, there is a fundamental sense in which the film viewer is being forced to abdicate responsibility in favour of a quasi-messianic, fantasy redeemer-figure who will shoulder our burdens. The confrontation between 'good' and 'evil' which, in much of post-Enlightenment Christian theology, is taken to be an existential and spiritual struggle in the life of each individual person, is *externalized* in many contemporary science-fiction, fantasy and action-adventure films in that it takes the form of an archetypical-mythical, and characteristically violent, duel between the 'good' hero and the forces of evil and destruction with which he (for it invariably is a male) is engaged, and which he will always succeed in combating before the end-credits have started to roll. While the post-Enlightenment age has largely rendered anachronistic the metaphysical polarity of pure good ('God') and absolute evil ('Satan'), the clear-cut and un-ambiguous battle between good and evil that characterizes so many of today's films has prompted Reinhold Zwick to attest that 'The Devil has survived splendidly' in popular film 'despite the fact that Karl Rosenkraz declared him to be totally "superfluous for the arts" almost 150 years ago'.[66] Intellectually out of date such a representation might be, but, in the cinema at any rate, the concept of the Devil 'has shown itself to be resistant to any critical ideological dismantling'.[67]

As Zwick points out, the dualistic distinction between good and evil that is intrinsic to such pictures will always remain attractive to some viewers insofar as there is an extent to which such films suggest that the existence of evil in the world is not something over which human beings ultimately have any control, but that the responsibility for evil lies in external beings and powers that lie beyond human jurisdiction.[68] Consequently, the individual is excused and spared the intrinsically human process of confronting and taking responsibility for the human propensity to sin and error. This is borne out in Zwick's contention that 'Despite all of the evil that washes out onto the viewer from the screen',[69] the film audience 'will, only in the rarest of cases, go home in a state of agitated thought about guilt and forgiveness, freedom and responsibility'[70] – the prerequisite of redemptive activity. In sharp contrast, the trials and afflictions that the *noir* protagonist undergoes address real and authentic human concerns in a world where the simple dualism of 'good' and 'bad' does not correspond to the actuality of human existence, and where such fundamental concerns are far from clear-cut and amenable to analysis in terms of non-human, supernatural agencies and powers.

Concluding remarks: the seeds of change to a more authentic screen protagonist

Nevertheless, while contemporary mainstream cinema is not amenable, on the whole, to a redemptive reading, many of the insights expounded in this book concerning the religious orientation of film in the alienated landscape of *film noir* have the capacity to re-emerge and to play a pivotal role in future film discourse, where there is an earnest attempt to examine human solicitudes, aspirations and emotions. In particular, prevalent though escapism is in contemporary Hollywood film, there are noticeable signs that an authentically human ethos has the capacity to play an important, if not an integral, role in today's cinema. In particular, there are indications of such a human, rather than superhuman, sensibility in some of the post-Rambo Hollywood portrayals of Vietnam. For example, as Auster and Quart point out, *Alamo Bay* (1985) 'became one of the few films to view the war's aftermath with a quiet intelligence and without recourse to extensive murder and mayhem'.[71] The character Shang (Ed Harris) is, indeed, 'much more than a solitary, mad vet seeking revenge on society for some ineffable trauma suffered in Vietnam'.[72] Rather, he is a working man, deeply connected to his work and community. Ironically, as Auster and Quart suggest, the comic-strip nature of Rambo may actually have had the effect –

albeit inadvertently – of producing films which portray the war in a more realistic manner. For, in their words, 'the simple-mindedness and gratuitous violence' of such a cartoon-figure 'may have pushed at least the adults in the audience to seek an antidote in films that could provide a more authentic depiction of the war'.[73]

The power of a film such as Oliver Stone's *Platoon* (1986), for instance, lies in its being 'an antidote to dangerous patriotic cartoons like *Rambo*',[74] in its re-creation of the war's daily agony and in its sense of social realism. The film places the Vietnam experience in 'its proper perspective of climate, terrain, fear, and death',[75] and, in particular,

> its feeling of verisimilitude for the discomfort, ants, heat, and mud . . . of the jungle and brush: the fatigue of patrols, the boredom and sense of release of base camp, the terror of ambushes, and the chaos and cacophony of night firefights. Filmed in tight closeup and medium shots, this powerfully evokes the murderous immediacy of the world into which the GIs were thrust.[76]

Moreover, Stone's protagonist, Chris Taylor (Charlie Sheen), is 'a figure grounded in this world',[77] and whose very ordinariness 'gives Stone the medium to convey the complex, everyday reality of combat in Vietnam'.[78] In the absence of 'one-man' victories by 'asocial, pop-metaphysical supermen'[79] against a multitude of Communist Vietnamese, Auster and Quart even go so far as to suggest that *Platoon* is 'one possible model for individual and perhaps even collective *redemption*'.[80] Although some subsequent Vietnam films, such as *Hamburger Hill* (1987), have, to an extent, moved away from the authenticity of a film such as *Platoon* by their explication of the war in literary and philosophical terms that have the effect of detracting from the tangibility of the conflict, the fact remains that, since the late 1980s, the escapist and fantasy-orientated depiction of the Vietnam experience that suffuses a film such as *Rambo: First Blood, Part Two* has been superseded by a much more human – and potentially religious – perspective. This perspective has arguably reached its apotheosis in Victor Nunez's *Ulee's Gold* (1997), where the cartoon world of John Rambo and the very real struggle of Vietnam veteran Ulysses Jackson (Peter Fonda) to find harmony and atone for the transgressions of the past could not be more distinct.

Even in superheroic comic books, which have traditionally presented their heroes as supernatural and divine figures engaged in cosmic battles between the forces of good and evil, the last few years have conspicuously borne witness to a *humanization* of the comic book superhero, and this has been mirrored in the cinematic representations of such figures as Batman.[81] In particular, Tim Burton's 1989 screen version of *Batman* may be seen to derive its downbeat and austere *noir* tone from the DC comic books and, specifically, from writer-artist Frank Miller's reinterpretation of Batman in the 1986 four issue mini-series *The Dark Knight Returns*, which examines what Forbes calls 'the psyche of an obsessed vigilante in a story usually described as dark'.[82] Such a figure, in contradistinction to the superheroic antics of Superman, is suffused with personal struggles and self-doubts; he questions his ambiguous character and behaviour and endeavours to confront his inner demons. Moreover, as Forbes points out, it is not uncommon to find on the covers of such books the figure of Batman in a *crucifixion* pose, which may be read as analogous to the person of Christ, whose own crucifixion was the epitome of human suffering. Even the figure of Superman, moreover, who traditionally, 'kryptonite aside, was nearly invulnerable'[83] – an interpretation reflected in the four screen versions of *Superman* hitherto produced[84] – even this most supernatural of heroes has undergone a significant transformation in recent years. Indeed, Forbes indicates that at the end of 1992 the best sales figures in DC comics' history was prompted by the 'Death of Superman' storyline, and when he returned a year or so later, he was a more authentically human, vulnerable figure.[85] Even more recently, Forbes observes that 'the first cover image of a crucifix Superman has appeared, and at least one story has played explicitly with crucifixion themes'.[86] The fact that Tim Burton has worked on a reinterpretation of the Superman character for Warner Brothers (though at the time of writing there are no signs such a movie will actually see the light of day) invariably leads to speculation that, as with his screen depiction of Batman in *Batman* (1989) and *Batman Returns* (1992), the new Superman character will embody more authentically human characteristics, even to the extent that he may be seen to bear witness to the Christ-like nature of his recent comic book counterpart.

Moreover, Steven Spielberg, whose films are commonly seen as pertinent examples of populist, escapist entertainment in contemporary cinema is also capable of exploring authentically human and far from fantasy-orientated subjects, as his work on the Holocaust and the aftermath of the D-Day landings of the Second World War, in *Schindler's List* (1993) and *Saving Private Ryan* (1998), respectively, have recently demonstrated. While Indiana Jones (Harrison Ford) constitutes 'an individual of almost supernatural powers',[87] whose dexterity and ability to overcome the most difficult of obstacles sets him apart from everyone else both inside and outside the film's space, Oscar Schindler (Liam Neeson) and Captain Miller (Tom Hanks) are authentically human individuals who have lived through and experienced first-hand some of the greatest atrocities of the twentieth century. In a review of *Saving Private Ryan* in the September 1998 edition of *Sight and Sound*, John Wrathall observes, for instance, that Tom Hanks 'is perfectly cast as an ordinary man doing the best he can in impossible circumstances, and gradually losing his grip'.[88] In lieu of the heroics of Indiana Jones, and of narratives of what Robert Kolker categorizes as 'simple desires fulfilled, of reality diverted into the imaginary spaces of aspirations realized, where fears of abandonment and impotence are turned into fantasy spectacles of security and joyful action',[89] and in which the viewer may be invited to 'become a privileged participant in the illusory world of adventure and salvation',[90] Wrathall attests that *Saving Private Ryan* is 'open to interpretation', which 'in itself is a breakthrough in a Spielberg film'.[91] This ambiguity, moreover, 'is the ultimate proof', Wrathall continues, that Spielberg 'has come of age as an artist'.[92]

While it may, ultimately, be too premature to infer from such recent trends what shape the future of Hollywood cinema will take, the plaudits which films such as *Platoon* and *Saving Private Ryan* have received from critics, and which are mirrored by their box office draw,[93] are evidence that there is a call, in an age of 'high-concept' science-fiction, fantasy and action-adventure films, for films whose domain is 'the soul and not the solar system, the torment of Jake La Motta and not the ecstasy of Rocky, the claustrophobic streets of New York and not Indiana Jones's temple'.[94] Indeed, in an interview published in the *Independent* on 29 May 1998, the film director Alan Rudolph, who has, in the past, branded Hollywood movies 'corporate propaganda', explained that the 'modest goal' with his recent picture, *Afterglow* (1997), is that the film audience may come to 'feel something' not only 'about the characters, but also something about themselves'. Such a film may therefore succeed in 'denting' the cycle of predictability perpetually spun by the Hollywood 'dream merchants' who, Rudolph claims, seek 'to replace your sense of identity with their version of it – they want their logos in your dreams'.[95] While the film struggled to receive a British release, and demonstrates, at least in terms of its limited box office success, that such a character-driven picture does not appeal to mass audiences in the same way as, say, an effects-laden film *à la* James Cameron's *Titanic* (1997), which was on release in the same period,[96] there is some consolation to be drawn from the fact that Hollywood at least acknowledged the quality and calibre of such a film enough to nominate its leading actress, Julie Christie, for an Academy Award®.[97]

There will, invariably, be obstacles and even regressions along the way. Despite, for instance, the religious propensity of Tim Burton's humanization of the Batman 'superhero', which befits an Antiochene Christology, Joel Schumacher's recent additions to the franchise, *Batman Forever* (1995) and *Batman and Robin* (1997), have reverted to the superhuman and transcendent heroics of the comic book. The films which are most susceptible to a religious reading may be the least commercial in today's cinema, but it is their creators' very unwillingness to conform to Hollywood stereotypes that is responsible for what popular and critical success they *do* command. According to Martin Scorsese, when George Lucas saw the rough-cut of his musical, *New York, New York*, he pointed out that 'we could add $10 million to the box-office receipts if we'd give the film a happy ending . . . He was right, but I said it just wouldn't work for this story. I knew that he was going for something that was extremely commercial, but I had to go another way.'[98] Indeed, one of the most prominent characteristics of Scorsese's film – if not its *raison d'être* – is that it stands in opposition to, and takes issue with, the conventions of mainstream Hollywood cinema which, throughout its history, 'has attempted precisely to disguise its illusory nature . . . and therefore present its values and itself as truth, as history, and as reality'.[99] Lucas may have preferred it had *New York, New York* conformed to the escapist sensibility of Hollywood cinema, but the significance of the film is precisely that it *obfuscates*, and even *inverts*, the established 'illusions' of Hollywood through the portrayal of wholly authentic characters and situations. Indeed, against the grain of Hollywood, *New York, New York* presents the experience of individuals who, in the final analysis, are unable and unwilling to compromise career and personal ambitions for the sake of marriage.

Whereas what Robin Garnett refers to as 'the sheer spectacle of song and dance'[100] in the conventional Hollywood musical caused the destructive conflicts that lay at the heart of its characters' lives to be glossed over, if not altogether omitted, in Scorsese's picture not only do Francine Evans (Liza Minnelli) and Jimmy Doyle (Robert De Niro) go their separate ways at the end – having inexorably drawn apart during the course of the film – but the implication is that they are probably *better off* doing so. We may be far removed from the 'joyfully love-sick antics of Gene Kelly singin' in the rain',[101] but, as epitomized in the final shot of Jimmy Doyle walking out of the frame, and leaving behind him a lifeless and artificial city street, Scorsese has *demythologized* the musical genre, and exposed its 'myths' as *illusory, unsustainable* and, even, as *destructive*, conforming as they do to the 'reel' world of the 1940s musical rather than to the real and empirical world of everyday human experience.

As we enter the twenty-first century, popular film appears to be in a reasonably healthy shape. More than twenty years on from *New York, New York*, this authentically human dimension to the musical genre may be found to imbue Mark Herman's *Little Voice* (1998), which, like Scorsese's picture, takes issue with the overtly escapist ethos of the conventional Hollywood 'feel-good' movie. In place of the kind of reconciliation and harmony that traditionally brings closure to a musical comedy, *Little Voice* brazenly concludes on a note of imbalance, with misguided and pitiable – even tragic – figures materially and emotionally bankrupt by the film's denouement. At the time of writing, a number of Christian and non-Christian authors are publishing a number of articles – and with increasing alacrity on the internet[102] – on the theological and spiritual dimensions of such contemporary films as *Pleasantville* (1998), *Magnolia* (1999), *Fight Club* (1999) and *American Beauty* (1999), including discussions of the ways in which these films not only invoke and call to mind particular scriptural motifs and passages but act as an agency through which audiences can come to a fuller understanding of how to address some of the core issues and dilemmas that lie at the heart of human experience, and in particular the universal human experience of sin, alienation and suffering. So long as films continue to be produced which enable an authentic encounter with our basic human condition to take place, in the manner of an Antiochene Christology, then film-makers will continue to be capable of making a serious contribution to theological and religious reflection, and the medium of film should, with increasing authority, come to be accepted by theologians and students of religion as amounting to a viable and fertile repository of religious significance.

Notes

Notes to Chapter 1: Cinema as a contemporary site of religious activity

1   Plato; quoted in Brian Morris, *Anthropological Studies of Religion* (Cambridge, Cambridge University Press, 1987), 1.
2   Plato: 428–347 BCE.
3   Morris, *Anthropological Studies*, 1.
4   Jung; quoted ibid., 172–3.
5   Ibid., 173.
6   Margaret R. Miles, *Image as Insight* (Boston, MA, Beacon Press, 1985), 152.
7   Conrad E. Ostwalt, Jr., 'Religion, film and cultural analysis', in Joel W. Martin and Ostwalt (eds.), *Screening the Sacred* (Boulder, CO, and Oxford, Westview Press, 1995), 157.
8   A. I. C. Heron's words, *A Century of Protestant Theology* (Cambridge, Lutterworth Press, 1985), 139.
9   Ibid.
10 Michael Paul Gallagher, 'Theology, discernment and cinema', in John R. May (ed.), *New Image of Religious Film* (Kansas City, Sheed & Ward, 1997), 156.
11 Peter Williams, *Popular Religion in America* (Englewood Cliffs, NJ, Prentice Hall, 1980), 15.
12 Walter Capps, *Religious Studies* (Minneapolis, Fortress Press, 1995), 336. Of course, it does not automatically follow from Capps's assessment that the fact that religious studies is interdisciplinary guarantees the study of film a pivotal place in the study of religion. However, the fact that a number of films touch on issues relevant to the study of religion in so many key respects certainly warrants consideration by the religious studies scholar.
13 Ibid., 339.
14 J. Macquarrie, *Jesus Christ in Modern Thought* (London, SCM, 1992), 24.
15 R. J. Zwi Werblowsky, *Beyond Tradition and Modernity: Changing Religions in a Changing World* (London, Athlone Press/University of London, 1976), 25.
16 Capps, *Religious Studies*, 342.

17 Ostwalt, 'Religion, film and cultural analysis', 154.
18 Ibid.
19 Mary Pat Kelly, *Martin Scorsese* (New York, Thunder's Mouth Press, 1991), 254. *Raging Bull* is one of the core instances of religion in film, and will be examined in detail in Chap. 7.
20 Margaret R. Miles, *Seeing and Believing* (Boston, MA, Beacon Press, 1996), 25.
21 Ibid.
22 See Karen E. Fields's introduction to E. Durkheim, *The Elementary Forms of Religious Life* (New York, Free Press, 1995), p. xviii.
23 M. Weber, *The Sociology of Religion* (London, Methuen & Co., 1965), 107.
24 Peter Williams, *Popular Religion in America* (Englewood Cliffs, NJ, Prentice Hall, 1980), 11. The Christian belief in the coming Parousia has found social expression in the millenarian movements which developed contemporaneously with the agrarian and industrial revolutions, and it is not insignificant in this regard that Karl Marx expected the 'final crisis of capitalism' (A. J. P. Taylor, introduction to Marx and Engels, *The Communist Manifesto* (Harmondsworth, Penguin, 1967), 36) – which could be read as analogous to the Christian hope in the imminence of the end of all things – to come about in 1848, the infamous 'year of revolutions'.
25 Talcott Parson's words; introduction to Weber, *Sociology of Religion*, p. xxvii.
26 P. B. Plouffe, 'The tainted Adam' (Ph.D. thesis, Univ. of California, Berkeley, 1979), p. ii.
27 F. Hirsch, *The Dark Side of the Screen* (London, Tantivy Press, 1981), 21.
28 R. P. Kolker, *A Cinema of Loneliness*, 2nd edn. (Oxford, Oxford University Press, 1988), 23; my italics.
29 Ibid., 63.
30 Ibid.
31 Mary–Kay Gamel, 'An American tragedy: *Chinatown*', in Martin M. Winkler (ed.), *Classics and Cinema* (Toronto, Bucknell University Press, 1991), 224.
32 Philip French, introduction to the first UK terrestrial screening of *Taxi Driver*, BBC2, 25 August 1995.
33 Kolker, *Cinema of Loneliness*, 64.
34 Winston L. King, 'Religion', in M. Eliade (ed.), *The Encyclopedia of Religion*, vol. 12 (New York, Macmillan Publishing Co., 1987), 284.
35 S. Bruce, *Religion in the Modern World* (Oxford, Oxford University Press, 1996), 188.
36 Ibid.

37   Quoted in R. N. Stromberg, *Redemption by War* (Kansas City, Regents Press, 1982), 55.
38   Quoted ibid. 11.
39   M. G. Witten, *All is Forgiven* (Princeton, Princeton University Press, 1993), 5.
40   King, 'Religion', 292.
41   Ibid.
42   Ibid.
43   Ibid.
44   D. Cupitt, *The Sea of Faith* (London, BBC, 1984), 32.
45   Durkheim, *Elementary Forms*, 429.
46   A. Giddens, *Sociology* (Oxford, Polity Press, 1989), 460.
47   Quoted in Bruce *Religion in the Modern World*, 188.
48   Ibid.
49   Ibid.
50   David Jasper, 'On systematizing the unsystematic: a response', in Clive Marsh and Gaye Ortiz (eds.), *Explorations in Theology and Film* (Oxford, Blackwell, 1997), 244.
51   Ibid., 243.

Notes to Chapter 2: The cultural and religious significance of film

1   Peter Horsfield, 'Teaching theology in a new cultural environment', in Chris Arthur (ed.), *Religion and the Media* (Cardiff, University of Wales Press, 1963),42.
2   Source: *Screen Finance*; published on the British Film Institute website (www.bfi.org.uk/facts/stats).
3   *The Exorcist* was re-released in Scottish cinemas in July 1998, and in the rest of the United Kingdom on 30 October 1998.
4   An elaboration on the controversy surrounding *Last Temptation* is provided in Chapter 6.
5   Scorsese; quoted in David Thompson and Ian Christie, *Scorsese on Scorsese* (London, Faber & Faber, 1989), 124.
6   Robert A. White in John R. May (ed.), *New Image of Religious Film* (Kansas City, Sheed & Ward, 1997), 201.
7   Ibid.
8   Ibid.
9   Ibid., 202.
10   Ibid.
11   *Media Development* (4/1995), 2.
12   Ibid. Examples of such directors are Buñuel, Bergman, Kurosawa and Ray.

13 Marjeet Verbeek, 'Mythological aspects of contemporary film art', *Media Development*, 42/2 (1995), 29.

14 T. van den Berk; quoted ibid.

15 Kevin Jackson (ed.), *Schrader on Schrader and Other Writings* (London, Faber & Faber, 1990), 42. Paul Schrader refers to Bresson's films as an example of transcendental style in film: *Transcendental Style in Film: Ozu, Bresson, Dreyer* (Berkeley, University of California, 1972).

16 Michael Bird, 'Film as hierophany', in John R. May and Michael Bird (eds.), *Religion in Film* (Knoxville, University of Tennessee Press, 1982), 17.

17 Paul Coates, *Film at the Intersection of High and Mass Culture* (Cambridge, Cambridge University Press, 1994), 128.

18 Ibid.

19 Stanley Rothman, 'Is God really dead in Beverly Hills? Religion and the movies', *The American Scholar*, 65/2 (1996), 273.

20 Michael Pye and Lynda Myles; quoted ibid., 274.

21 Ibid.

22 Gaye Ortiz, 'Theology and the silver screen', *The Month* (May 1998), 173.

23 Joel Martin, 'Seeing the sacred on the screen', in Martin and Conrad E. Ostwalt, Jr. (eds.), *Screening the Sacred* (Boulder, CO, and Oxford, Westview Press, 1995), 2.

24 Quoted ibid.

25 John Hill, introduction to Hill and Pamela Church Gibson (eds.), *Oxford Guide to Film Studies* (Oxford, Oxford University Press, 1998), p. xx.

26 Ibid.

27 Ibid.

28 Paul Giles, *American Catholic Arts and Fictions* (Cambridge, Cambridge University Press, 1992), 5.

29 Ibid., 6.

30 Ibid.

31 Boston, MA, Beacon Press, 1996.

32 Ibid., p. ix.

33 Lloyd Baugh, *Imaging the Divine* (Kansas City, Sheed & Ward, 1997), 4.

34 The trend is changing, however. Many of those books on theology and film that have recently been published are edited works, encompassing chapters by a variety of scholars, and taking into consideration a vast range of films, including some very recent films. For example, see Martin and Ostwalt (eds.) *Screening the Sacred* and Marsh and Ortiz (eds.), *Explorations in Theology and Film*.

35 Kansas City, Sheed & Ward, 1997.

[36]   Joseph Marty, 'Toward a theological interpretation and reading of film: incarnation of the Word of God – relation, image, word' (tr. Robert Robinson III), in May (ed.), *New Image of Religious Film*, 137.

[37]   Ibid., 136.

[38]   Ibid.

[39]   Margaret Miles makes this same point, in *Seeing and Believing*, p. xii.

[40]   Michael Paul Gallagher, 'Theology, discernment and cinema', in May (ed.), *New Image of Religious Film*, 156.

[41]   Ibid.

[42]   A number of articles on religion and the Hollywood apocalyptic imagination can be found on the internet *Journal of Religion and Film* (*http://www.unomaha.edu/~wwwjrf*), beginning with Conrad Ostwalt, 'Visions of the end: secular apocalypse in recent Hollywood film', 2/1. Five further articles appear in 4/1.

[43]   Ibid.

[44]   Miles, *Seeing and Believing*, p. xii.

[45]   John Hill, in Hill and Church Gibson (eds.), *The Oxford Guide to Film Studies* (Oxford, Oxford University Press, 1998), pp. xxi–xxii.

[46]   Ibid., p. xx.

[47]   Carl Skrade, 'Theology and films', in J. C. Cooper and Skrade (eds.), *Celluloid and Symbols* (Philadelphia, Fortress Press, 1970), 22.

[48]   Joseph Marty, in May (ed.), *New Image of Religious Film*, 141.

[49]   Ibid., 146.

[50]   Claude Geffré; quoted ibid., 144.

[51]   Joseph Marty; ibid., 142.

[52]   Ibid., 140.

Notes to Chapter 3: Models of redemption evident in films

[1]   Siegfried Kracauer; quoted by Gerald Mast, Marshall Cohen and Leo Braudy (eds.), *Film Theory and Criticism* (Oxford, Oxford University Press, 1992), 4.

[2]   Leo Braudy; quoted ibid., 430. In *An American in Paris* (1951), for instance, Jerry Mulligan (Gene Kelly) rejects his intended professional career as a painter in order to sing and dance, with the result that 'liberated by the implied naturalness of musical expression, the concerns of the "real world" miraculously disappear' (R. S. Garnett, 'Martin Scorsese: a cinema of disillusionment' (MA thesis, Univ. of Kansas, 1991), 24) and evolve into what Thomas Schatz designates as 'an integrated utopian community.' (quoted ibid.).

[3]   Richard Dyer, 'Entertainment and utopia', in Bill Nichols (ed.), *Movies and Methods*, vol. 2 (London, University of California Press, 1985), 229. That there is an intrinsically escapist ethos to such films is borne out by David Thomson's recollection that, when he saw *Meet*

Me in St. Louis (1944) in his youth, it made him wish 'for older sisters, a large fond family, and the precious aura of St. Louis in 1904.' (Thomson, *America in the Dark* (London, Hutchinson, 1978), 21.) Indeed, in more general terms, he explains that 'long before I heard the word escapism I made the journeys the films allowed' (ibid.).

4   Jeffrey Richards, 'Frank Capra and the cinema of populism', in Bill Nichols (ed.), *Movies and Methods*, vol. 1 (London, University of California Press, 1976), 77.

5   Ibid.

6   Joseph Marty, 'Toward a theological interpretation and reading of film', in John R. May (ed.), *New Image of Religious Film* (Kansas City, Sheed & Ward, 1997), 135.

7   Bryant, in John R. May and Michael Bird (eds.), *Religion in Film* (Knoxville, University of Tennessee Press, 1982), 103.

8   Thomson, *America in the Dark*, 14.

9   Ibid.; my italics.

10   Ibid.

11   Ibid., 15.

12   Ibid., 18.

13   Ibid.

14   Ibid., 15.

15   Ibid., 16.

16   Furthermore, writing on 'Cinema, religion and popular culture', M. Darroll Bryant recalls that, back in the 1950s in North Dakota, he 'regularly participated in the weekly Saturday ritual of going to the movies': in May and Bird (eds.), *Religion in Film* 101. This notion of the cinema as some kind of religious ritual is further articulated by film-maker Woody Allen, who took pleasure as a child in entering 'a large, dark place with huge chandeliers', within which memories of 'the outside world' were 'blocked out' (quoted in S. Björkman, *Woody Allen on Woody Allen* (London, Faber & Faber, 1995), 151). He recollects that on 'hot, hazy summer days' in Brooklyn 'there were thousands of movie houses around' which one could enter for just 25 cents, whereupon it was suddenly 'cool and air-conditioned and dark' (ibid., 149), and one moment 'you would see pirates and you would be on the sea', while in the next 'you might be in a penthouse in Manhattan with beautiful people' (ibid., 149). The following day, one might attend another 'movie' house and, similarly, 'one moment you'd be in a battle with the Nazis and in the second feature you'd be together with the Marx Brothers' (ibid.). He refers to the experience as being 'just a total, total joy' and 'the greatest kind of tranquillizer and embalmment you could think of' (ibid.). Woody Allen's own films, furthermore, frequently bear witness to the power and magic of

the cinema, as this chapter illustrates with respect to *Hannah and her Sisters* and *The Purple Rose of Cairo*.

17   John 6: 35.
18   John 4: 10.
19   Richard Maltby, *Hollywood Cinema: An Introduction* (Oxford, Blackwell, 1996), 23.
20   Powdermaker; quoted ibid.
21   Ibid.
22   Ibid.
23   Powdermaker; quoted ibid.
24   Ibid., 24. Irrespective of whether or not the film in question happens to be a romance, such as *Pretty Woman* (1990), or a thriller, such as *Knight Moves* (1992), any attempt to convey genuine human emotions, feelings and solicitudes is obviated by the film's overarching escapist sensibility. In the case of *Pretty Woman*, it is inevitable that the millionaire (Richard Gere) will fall in love with the prostitute (Julia Roberts), and rescue her from a life on the streets, ultimately conforming to its fairy-tale ethos, signalled throughout the film, as a modern-day version of the classic Cinderella story. As for *Knight Moves*, Nigel Floyd, in the *Time Out Film Guide*, refers to this thriller, about a chess champion who is framed for committing a series of murders, as featuring 'a clever opening gambit, a series of predictable moves, and a disappointing end game', and as 'A classic case of all plot and no substance' (p. 434).
25   Quoted in Simon Rose, *Classic Movie Guide* (Glasgow, Harper Collins, 1995), 161.
26   Allen himself uses this word; quoted in Julian Fox, *Woody: Movies from Manhattan* (London, B. T. Batsford, 1996), 170.
27   Ibid. 171, and Maureen Dowd, in Sean B. Girgus, *The Films of Woody Allen* (Cambridge, Cambridge University Press, 1993), 108.
28   Fox, *Woody*, 170–1.
29   Martin Scorsese's words; quoted in Les Keyser, *Martin Scorsese* (New York, Twayne Publishers, 1992), 163–4.
30   From Woody Allen's interview with Stig Björkman, *Woody Allen*, 50.
31   Ibid., 50–1.
32   Margaret R. Miles, *Seeing and Believing* (Boston, MA, Beacon Press, 1996), p.xii.
33   Ibid.
34   Ibid.
35   David John Graham, 'The uses of film in theology', in Clive Marsh and Gaye Ortiz (eds.), *Explorations in Theology and Film* (Blackwell, Oxford, 1997), 39.
36   Girgus, *Films of Woody Allen*, 78.

37 Ibid.
38 Ibid.
39 Ibid., 85.
40 Gary Commins, 'Woody Allen's theological imagination', *Theology Today*, 44 (July 1987), 245.
41 Ibid.
42 Ibid.
43 Slavoj Žižek, '"The thing that thinks": the Kantian background of the noir subject', in Joan Copjec (ed.), *Shades of Noir: A Reader* (London, Verso, 1993), 221.
44 Frank Krutnik, 'Something more than night: tales of the *noir* city', in David B. Clarke (ed.), *The Cinematic City*, (London, Routledge, 1997), 85.
45 Ibid., 87.
46 Ibid.
47 Ibid.
48 Ibid.
49 James Agee; quoted ibid., 88.
50 Krutnik, in Clarke (ed.), *Cinematic City*, 87.
51 Ibid.
52 Quoted in Stephen Brown, 'Optimism, hope, and feelgood movies: the Capra connection', in Marsh and Ortiz (eds.), *Explorations*, 221.
53 A paraphrase of Brown's words, ibid., 222.
54 Quoted ibid.
55 Quoted in James C. Livingston, *Modern Christian Thought* (London, Collier Macmillan, 1971), 222.
56 Ibid.
57 Brown, in Marsh and Ortiz (eds.), *Explorations*, 221.
58 The words of Alisdair Heron, *A Century of Protestant Theology* (Cambridge, Lutterworth Press, 1985), 16.
59 Ibid., 17.
60 Quoted in John Hick (ed.), *The Existence of God* (London, Collier Macmillan, 1964), 108.
61 Ibid., 108.
62 Brown, in Marsh and Ortiz (eds.), *Explorations*, 224.
63 Ibid.
64 Ibid., 225.
65 Jonathan Romney, 'The dark end of the street', *Sight and Sound*, 7/11 (November 1997), London Film Festival special supplement, p. 19.
66 Brown, in Marsh and Ortiz (eds.), *Explorations*, 232.
67 Quoted in Romney, *Sight and Sound*, 16.
68 Ibid.
69 David Parkinson, in *Empire*, 99 (September 1997), 21.

70 Ibid.

71 Such as *Vertigo* (1958).

72 Such as *The Naked Spur* (1953), in which Stewart's character is a man obsessed with the pursuit of revenge, and by which he is ultimately consumed.

73 Maltby, *Hollywood Cinema*, 39.

74 Ibid.

75 This point is made by David Browne, 'Film, movies, meanings', in Marsh and Ortiz (eds.), *Explorations*, 9.

76 Nick Roddick, *Sight and Sound*, 8/12 (December 1998), 26.

77 Maltby, *Hollywood Cinema*, 39.

78 Ibid.

79 Ibid.

80 Many of the films of Steven Spielberg may, indeed, be viewed as vehicles of wish-fulfilment, fantasy and pure magic. As Kolker puts it, his films may be seen to 'speak of a place and a way of being in the world that viewers find more than just comfortable, but desirable and – within the films – available': *A Cinema of Loneliness*, 2nd edn. (Oxford, Oxford University Press, 1988), 238. In an uncomfortable world, Spielberg's pictures could be said to 'create for their viewers comfortable surrogates' (ibid.), where desires are satisfied and an emotional bond is established between the viewer and the picture. At the end of *E.T.*, for instance, in which a friendly extra-terrestrial, who has been stranded in suburban America, returns 'home', the audience may be said to miss 'him', and, as Kolker has observed, is often reduced to tears (ibid., 293). In having established an emotional bond with the alien creature, a certain 'dissatisfaction with the mundane' (ibid.) on the part of the audience can be said to have taken hold, with the magical world realized on the screen – which is given added force in the end scene when the bicycles belonging to E.T.'s human friends magically soar into the air – appearing better than the events and possibilities that belong to the 'real' world.

Notes to Chapter 4: *Film noir* as a repository of theological significance

1 According to John Belton, *film noir* crosses over traditional genre boundaries: '*film noir* is not a genre, but every *film noir* is *also* a genre film', since 'the conventions and systems of expectations that can be found in *films noirs* are those of the various genres to which these films belong – those of the detective film, the melodrama, or the Western'. Belton, *American Cinema/American Culture* (London, McGraw-Hill, 1994), 187.

2 John Tuska, *Dark Cinema* (London, Greenwood Press, 1984), 152.

3   Bruce, Crowther, *Film Noir* (London, Columbus Books, 1988), 7.
4   Tuska, *Dark Cinema*, 109.
5   Paul Schrader makes this observation in his pioneering article, 'Notes on film noir', first publ. 1971; quoted in Kevin Jackson (ed.), *Schrader on Schrader*, 80.
6   Crowther, *Film Noir*, 7.
7   Paul Schrader; quoted in Jackson (ed.), *Schrader on Schrader*, 81.
8   H. A. Williams, *True Resurrection* (London, Mitchell Beazley, 1972), 10.
9   Todd Erickson, 'Kill me again: movement becomes genre', in Alain Silver and James Ursini (eds.), *Film Noir Reader* (New York, Limelight Editions, 1997), 323.
10 Romans 5: 12, 14, 18.
11 From *City of God* 14, 1; quoted in A. C. O'Connor, 'An understanding of sin and redemption in traditional Christianity and in Unification theology' (Ph.D. thesis, Lampeter, 1995), 20.
12 Henry Chadwick; quoted in Maurice Wiles, *The Christian Fathers* (London, SCM, 1966), 99.
13 From *City of God*; quoted by Peter A. Friend, *Cowboy Metaphysics: Ethics and Death in Westerns* (Oxford, Rowman & Littlefield, 1997).
14 Cf. Romans 6: 20.
15 David Thomson, *America in the Dark* (London, Hutchinson, 1978), 177.
16 Ibid., 178.
17 Michael Walker, 'Film noir: introduction', in Ian Cameron (ed.), *The Movie Book of Film Noir* (London, Studio Vista, 1994), 22.
18 Crowther, *Film Noir*, 159.
19 Ibid.
20 Robin Gill provides a serviceable discussion of Luther's theological anthropology, *A Textbook of Christian Ethics* (Edinburgh, T. & T. Clark, 1989), 42.
21 This is cited in, among other sources, Tuska, *Dark Cinema*, p. xxii; James Monaco (ed.), *Virgin Film Guide* (London, Virgin Books, 1992), 69; Simon Rose, *Classic Movie Guide* (Glasgow, Harper Collins, 1995), 40.
22 Thomson, *America in the Dark*, 176.
23 Ibid.
24 Foster Hirsch, *The Dark Side of the Screen* (London, Tantivy Press, 1981), 75.
25 Tuska, *Dark Cinema*, 214.
26 Ibid.
27 Michael Walker, 'Film Noir', calls this Hitchcock's most *noir* film.
28 Monaco (ed.), *Virgin Film Guide*, 1082.
29 Tuska, *Dark Cinema*, 235.

30   Ibid.

31   Ibid., 214. Robert Porfirio refers in this regard to the element of blind chance operative in *film noir*, such as when, in *He Walked by Night* (1948), a car parked on a manhole prevents the protagonist's escape, and he is thus able to be shot down by police in the sewers. In *Nightmare* (1956), a youth becomes the instrument of a murderer's plans simply because he accepted a cough drop in a crowded elevator.

32   Crowther, *Film Noir*, 12.

33   Schrader; quoted in Jackson (ed.), *Schrader on Schrader*, 85.

34   Crowther, *Film Noir*, 181.

35   Ibid.

36   Schrader, in Jackson (ed.), *Schrader on Schrader*, 85.

37   Ibid., 86.

38   Crowther, *Film Noir*, 159.

39   Walker, 'Film Noir', 16.

40   Crowther, *Film Noir*, 9.

41   Tuska, *Dark Cinema*, 135.

42   Ibid.

43   According to the 1934 report of the President of the Motion Picture Producers and Distributors Association in America, Will Hays, at a time of social uncertainty, in relation to the contemporary world-wide economic Depression, 'no medium has contributed more greatly than the film' (quoted in Tuska, *Dark Cinema*, 133) to bolstering and upholding national morale. Hays identified 'the mission of the screen' (ibid.) to be that of prescribing what contemporary 'audiences *ought* to feel' (ibid., p134; my italics), as opposed to reflecting what audiences were actually experiencing and suffering. There was a perception at this time that the popular appeal of the gangster in American culture had reached a dangerous level, with the effect that pressure was put on the film industry to diminish the attractiveness of gangsters in films. *Scarface* (1932), for instance, was subtitled 'Shame of a nation', and, as Paul Plouffe points out, the intention behind this film was to help foster a more suitable audience reaction than was facilitated by such earlier films as *Little Caesar* (1930) and *The Public Enemy* (1931), whose protagonists – played by Edward G. Robinson and James Cagney respectively – could be said to have earned the audience's sympathy through their defiance of the 'system' in an age when the 'system' was widely believed to have created the Depression in which America was then embroiled. (Plouffe, 'The tainted Adam' (Ph.D. thesis, Univ. of California, Berkeley, 1979), 61). In *Scarface*, the protagonist may not be an unsympathetic character, but, at the end, he dies in an unheroic fashion, 'trembling like a coward under the guns of the police' (ibid.).

44 A paraphrase of Hirsch, *Dark Side*, 60.

45 Ibid.

46 Kant, *Religion within the Limits of Reason Alone*; quoted in A. C. O'Connor, 'Understanding of sin and redemption', 36.

47 Ibid., 36.

48 Paul Tillich, *Systematic Theology* (1950); quoted by Walter Kaufmann in Richard Schacht, *Alienation* (London, George Allen & Unwin, 1971), 206.

49 Tillich, *Systematic Theology* (1950); quoted by Mark Kline Taylor, *Paul Tillich: Theologian of the Boundaries* (London, Collins, 1987), 187.

50 James C. Livingston, *Modern Christian Thought* (London, Collier Macmillan, 1971), 150.

51 J. A. Place and L. S. Peterson, 'Some visual motifs of film noir', in Bill Nichols (ed.), *Movies and Methods* vol. 2 (London, University of California Press, 1985), 330.

52 Ibid., 336.

53 Crowther, *Film Noir*, 10.

54 Schrader; quoted in Jackson (ed.), *Schrader on Schrader*, 84.

55 Ibid.

56 Ibid., 85.

57 Place and Peterson, 'Some visual motifs', 335.

58 Ibid.

59 Schrader; quoted in Jackson (ed.), 85.

60 Ibid.

61 Place and Peterson, 'Some visual motifs', 336–7.

62 Ibid., 330.

63 Crowther, *Film Noir*, 8.

64 Ibid.

65 Ibid., 80.

66 Ibid.

67 R. P. Kolker, *A Cinema of Loneliness*, 2nd edn. (Oxford, Oxford University Press, 1988), 340.

68 John G. Cawelti, 'Chinatown and generic transformation in recent American films', in Gerald Mast, Marshall Cohen and Les Braudy (eds.), *Film Theory and Criticism* (Oxford, Oxford University Press, 1992), 499.

69 Thomson, *America in the Dark*, 176.

70 Tuska, *Dark Cinema*, p. xxi.

71 Kolker, *Cinema of Loneliness*, 319.

72 Tuska, *Dark Cinema*, p. xxi.

73 Edward Gallafent, 'Echo Park', in Ian Cameron (ed.), *The Movie Book of Film Noir* (London, Studio Vista, 1994), 259.

74 Ibid., 254.

[75] In contrast, the gangster Marty Augustine is surrounded by a number of henchmen.

[76] Edward Gallafent, 'Echo Park', 260.

[77] Leighton Grist, 'Moving targets and black widows: *film noir* in modern Hollywood', in Cameron (ed.), *Movie Book*, 269.

[78] Ibid. One of the film's most violent moments occurs when Marty Augustine smashes his girlfriend's face with a glass coke bottle in order to teach Marlowe to co-operate.

[79] Kolker makes this point, *Cinema of Loneliness*, 342.

[80] Grist, 'Moving targets', 269.

[81] Ibid.

[82] Kolker, *Cinema of Loneliness*, 319.

[83] Ibid.

[84] Ibid., 343.

[85] Gallafent, 'Echo Park', 265. I elaborate on the significance of the Watergate scandal to the *noir* universe in Chap. 1, p. 6.

[86] Kolker, *Cinema of Loneliness*, 340. As Joan Copjec puts it, 'The world no longer unfolds in nonsimultaneous parts, as in detective fiction; in *film noir* it breaks up into inconsistent and always alien fragments', *Shades of Noir* (London, Verso, 1993), p. ix.

[87] Mary-Kay Gamel, 'An American tragedy: *Chinatown*', in Martin M. Winkler (ed.), *Classics and Cinema* (Toronto, Bucknell University Press, 1991), 212.

[88] Ibid., 213.

[89] Ibid.

[90] Cawelti in Mast, Cohen and Braudy (eds.), *Film Theory and Criticism*, 500; my italics. Public officials have been bought. We learn, for example, that visitors to Noah Cross's ranch 'paid $50,000 each towards the sheriff's re-election', and Cross's thug, Mulvehill, is a corrupt former sheriff. Further, when Gittes says he will sue 'the big boys who are making the payoffs', his employee, Duffy, responds, 'People like that are liable to be having dinner with the judges trying the suit.' Evelyn Mulwray, Cross's daughter, even informs Gittes that her father 'owns the police'.

[91] Gamel, 'American Tragedy', 228.

[92] Cawelti in Mast, Cohen and Braudy (eds.), *Film Theory and Criticism*, 502.

[93] Gamel, 'American Tragedy', 215.

[94] Grist, 'Moving targets', 270.

[95] John May, 'Visual story and the religious interpretation of film', in May and Michael Bird (eds.), *Religion in Film* (Knoxville, University of Tennessee Press, 1982), 37.

[96] Cawelti in Mast, Cohen and Braudy (eds.), *Film Theory and Criticism*,

503. As Gamel ('American Tragedy', 218) points out, in an argument towards the beginning of the film between Noah Cross and Hollis Mulwray that one of Gittes's staff, Walsh, overhears, Walsh thinks he has heard the words 'apple core' (rather than 'Albacore') used, 'suggesting that Los Angeles is another Eden destroyed by greed, but for this original sin there is no redemption'.

97 John May, 'The demonic in American cinema', in May and Bird (eds.), *Religion in Film*, 91.

98 Kolker, *Cinema of Loneliness*, 66.

99 A paraphrase of Kolker, ibid. 66.

100 At the end, we see Moseby at sea, going round and round in circles.

101 Grist, 'Moving targets', 271.

102 F. W. Dillistone, *The Christian Understanding of Atonement* (Welwyn, James Nisbet & Co., 1968), 16.

103 Kolker, *Cinema of Loneliness*, 242.

104 *Virgin Film Guide* (London, Virgin Books, 1992 edn), 151.

105 Kolker, *Cinema of Loneliness*, 242.

106 Dillistone, *Christian Understanding*, 401.

107 Tillich; quoted by Kaufmann, in Schacht, *Alienation*, 206.

108 Dillistone, *Christian Understanding*, 9.

109 Ibid., 11–12.

110 Livingston, *Modern Christian Thought*, 151.

111 Quoted ibid., 314.

112 Kierkegaard, *Either–Or*, vol. 2, p. 175; quoted ibid.

113 The words of Jerry L. Walls, *Hell* (Notre Dame, IN: University of Notre Dame Press, 1992), 119.

114 From Tillich's *Systematic Theology*, 166; quoted in Livingston, *Modern Christian Thought*, 369.

115 Ibid.

116 Leon Morris, *The Atonement: Its Meaning and Significance* (Leicester, Inter-varsity Press, 1983), 128.

117 Ibid.

118 John 1: 5.

119 John 1: 9.

120 John 1: 10.

121 John 1: 12.

122 John 1: 11.

123 According to Geiko Müller-Fahrenholz, *The Art of Forgiveness* (Geneva, WCC Publications, 1997), 28, the light does not *dispel* the darkness – 'it shines out in the midst of it and . . . it becomes visible for those who dare to enter it'.

124 John 11: 5.

Notes to Chapter 5: The theological basis of redemption in *film noir*

1   *Empire*, 80 (February 1996), 29.
2   Ibid.
3   John Wrathall, in *Sight and Sound*, 6/1 (January 1996), 50.
4   Ibid.
5   Carl Skrade, 'Theology and films', in John C. Cooper and Skrade (eds.), *Celluloid and Symbols* (Philadelphia, Fortress Press, 1970),14.
6   Ibid., 21.
7   Ibid.
8   Philip Strick, Review of *The Game*, *Sight and Sound*, 7/11 (November 1997), 41.
9   Derek Elley (ed.), *Variety Movie Guide* (London, Hamlyn, 1994), 353.
10   Ibid.
11   Lesley Stern, *The Scorsese Connection* (London, British Film Institute, 1995), 3.
12   Ibid., 116. This is an experience she says occurs each time she visits the cinema.
13   Todd Erickson, 'Kill me again: movement becomes genre', in Alain Silver and James Ursini (eds.), *Film Noir Reader* (New York, Limelight Editions, 1997), 313.
14   Les Keyser, *Martin Scorsese* (New York, Twayne Publishers, 1992), 201.
15   Ibid.
16   Erickson, 'Kill me again', 325.
17   Scorsese; quoted in David Thompson and Ian Christie (eds.), *Scorsese on Scorsese* (London: Faber & Faber, 1989), 48.
18   Ibid.
19   Ibid., 155.
20   Rob Lapsley, 'Mainly in cities and at night: some notes on cities and film', in David B. Clarke (ed.), *The Cinematic City* (London, Routledge, 1997), 197.
21   Ibid.
22   Ibid.
23   Frank Krutnik, 'Something more than night: tales of the noir city', in David B. Clarke (ed.), *The Cinematic City* (London, Routledge, 1997), 88.
24   Ibid.
25   Ibid. Krutnik does not specify what he means by 'attractions', but it is clearly the case that the authenticity of the *noir* city milieu enables its inhabitants to live a life that, while hardly utopian, is at least free of the illusions and deceptions that an existence predicated on a fantasy world can bring.

26 Quoted in F. W. Dillistone, *The Christian Understanding of Atonement* (Welwyn, James Nisbet & Co., 1968), 158.
27 Ibid.
28 Ibid.
29 Ibid.
30 Ibid., 160.
31 Peter Williams, *Popular Religion in America* (Englewood Cliffs, NJ, Prentice Hall, 1980), 136.
32 J. A. Soggin, *Introduction to the Old Testament* (London, SCM, 1989), 438.
33 Proverbs 10: 15.
34 James C. Crenshaw, *Old Testament Wisdom* (London, SCM, 1982), 79.
35 A paraphrase of J. Blenkinsopp, *Wisdom and Law in the Old Testament* (Oxford, Oxford University Press, 1983), 65.
36 Stephen L. Harris, *Understanding the Bible* (Mountain View, CA, Mayfield, 1985), 172.
37 Ecclesiastes 1: 15.
38 R. B. Y. Scott, *The Way of Wisdom in the Old Testament* (New York, Macmillan, 1971), 170.
39 Ibid.
40 Ecclesiastes 3: 19–20.
41 J. A. Place and L. S. Peterson, 'Some visual motifs of film noir', in Bill Nichols (ed.), *Movies and Methods*, vol. 2 (London, University of California Press, 1985), 330.
42 Ecclesiastes 1: 14.
43 Ecclesiastes 1: 13.
44 Jon Tuska, *Dark Cinema* (London, Greenwood Press, 1994), p. xvi.
45 Ecclesiastes 4: 1–3: 'Again I saw all the oppressions that are practised under the sun . . .'
46 Noah Cross raped his daughter.
47 Scott, *Way of Wisdom*, 171.
48 Tuska, *Dark Cinema*, p. xviii.
49 Ibid.
50 Ibid.
51 Scott, *Way of Wisdom*, 170.
52 Ibid., 183.
53 Ecclesiastes 2: 17.
54 Ecclesiastes 2: 18.
55 Ecclesiastes 2: 20.
56 Scott, *Way of Wisdom*, 184; my italics.
57 Blenkinsopp, *Wisdom and Law*, 65.
58 Ibid., 66.
59 Scott, *Way of Wisdom*, 187.

60 Ibid.

61 Ibid.

62 Ibid., 186.

63 Ibid.

64 Ibid.

65 Ecclesiastes 11: 8; my italics.

66 Scott, *Way of Wisdom*, 186.

67 Quoted in *Time* (15 February 1993); quoted by Robert Jewett, 'Stuck in time: *kairos*, *chronos*, and the flesh in *Groundhog Day*', in Clive Marsh and Gaye Ortiz (eds.), *Explorations in Theology and Film* (Oxford, Blackwell, 1997), 161.

68 Ibid.; my italics.

69 Ibid., 164.

70 Jeffrey Richards, 'Frank Capra and the cinema of populism', in Bill Nichols (ed.), *Movies and Methods*, vol. 1 (London, University of California Press, 1976), 67.

71 Ibid., 77.

72 Harris, *Understanding the Bible*, 155.

73 Ibid., 156.

74 Gary Commins, 'Woody Allen's theological imagination', *Theology Today* (July 1987), 237.

75 Ibid., 236.

76 Ibid., 237.

77 Ibid., 239.

78 Job 40 ff.

79 Commins, 'Woody Allen's theological imagination', 241.

80 Ibid.

81 Ibid., 237.

82 Sean B. Girgus, *The Films of Woody Allen* (Cambridge, Cambridge University Press, 1993), 22.

83 Ibid., 23.

84 Ibid. 246.

85 Ibid.

86 Commins, 'Woody Allen's theological imagination', 246.

87 Girgus, *Films*, 69.

88 Commins, 'Woody Allen's theological imagination', 246.

89 Quoted ibid., 248.

90 Ibid.

91 Girgus, *Films*, 70.

92 Ibid., 126.

93 Ibid., 127.

Notes to Chapter 6: Film protagonists as exemplars of redemptive possibility.

1   Willard G. Oxtoby, 'Reflections on the idea of salvation', in Eric J. Sharpe and John R. Hinnells (eds.), *Man and his Salvation* (Manchester, Manchester University Press, 1973), 26.
2   1 Corinthians 11: 1.
3   Irenaeus; quoted in Peter A. French, *Cowboy Metaphysics: Ethics and Death in Westerns* (Oxford, Rowman & Littlefield, 1997), 19.
4   Ibid.
5   Henry Chadwick, *The Early Church* (London, Penguin, 1990), 228.
6   Paul S. Fiddes, *Past Event and Present Salvation* (London, Darton Longman & Todd, 1989), 10; my italics.
7   Ibid.
8   From *The Origin of Species*; quoted in Alfred C. O' Connor, 'An understanding of sin and redemption in traditional Christianity and in Unification theology' (Ph.D. thesis, Lampeter, 1995), 232.
9   Paul and Linda Badham, *Immortality or Extinction?* (London, SPCK, 1984), 46.
10 Kant (1724–1804), of course, preceded Darwin (1809–82).
11 Quoted in James C. Livingston, *Modern Christian Thought* (London, Collier Macmillan, 1971), 72.
12 Ibid., 74.
13 O'Connor's words, 'Understanding of sin and redemption', 197.
14 Ibid.
15 Vidler's words, in Alec R. Vidler, *The Church in an Age of Revolution: 1789 to the Present Day* (London, Penguin, 1971), 205.
16 Ibid.
17 Ibid.
18 Ibid.
19 Ibid., 211.
20 Livingston, *Modern Christian Thought*, 106.
21 Ibid., 108.
22 Schleiermacher; quoted in O' Connor, 'Understanding of sin and redemption', 196.
23 As to the form that this state of equilibrium took, however, Schleiermacher was uncertain. He was sceptical regarding belief in life after death. In *The Christian Faith*, he suggests that belief in Christ is possible even though Jesus' teaching on the afterlife may be 'figurative, and not to be interpreted strictly . . . [since] he nowhere claims personal survival' (p. 700; quoted in Colleen McDannell and Bernhard Lang, *Heaven: A History* (New Haven, CT, Yale University Press, 1990), 324). Although a state of heavenly bliss could be achieved, 'Schleiermacher was uncertain as to how this occurred after death' (ibid.).

24   John Hick, *The Centre of Christianity* (London, SCM, 1977), 74.
25   Ibid.
26   Ibid.
27   Ibid.
28   Ibid., 87.
29   Ibid.
30   Paul Lakeland, *Postmodernity* (Minneapolis, Fortress Press, 1997), 100.
31   Ibid.
32   Ibid., 74.
33   Hick, *Centre of Christianity*, 87.
34   Ibid., 88.
35   Ibid.
36   Richard Swinburne, *The Existence of God* (Oxford, Clarendon Press, 1979), 215.
37   Hick, *Centre of Christianity*, 88.
38   Oxtoby, 'Reflections', 30.
39   Quoted in ibid., 31.
40   Ibid.; my italics.
41   Bruce Crowther, *Film Noir* (London, Columbus Books, 1988), 8.
42   Fiddes, *Past Event*, 10.
43   Peter Malone, '*Edward Scissorhands:* Christology from a suburban fairy-tale', in Clive Marsh and Gaye Ortiz (eds.), *Explorations in Theology and Film* (Oxford, Blackwell, 1997), 78.
44   Ibid.
45   William R. Telford, 'Jesus Christ movie star: the depiction of Jesus in the cinema', in Marsh and Ortiz (eds.) *Explorations in Theology and Film*, 123.
46   Apollinaris, fragment 45; quoted in Richard Norris, *The Christological Controversy* (Philadelphia, Fortress Press, 1980), 109.
47   Ibid., 20.
48   Fragment 50; quoted ibid. 109; my italics.
49   Alan Richardson, *Creeds in the Making* (London, SCM, 1986), 73.
50   Don Cupitt, *The Sea of Faith* (London, BBC, 1984), 10. Although the essence of Cupitt's point is correct, the qualification needs to be made that it is not solely from its Protestant background that popular culture has inherited its 'craving' for supernatural redeemer-figures. While the influence of Protestant Christianity is strong in Western society, a cursory knowledge of Greek mythology, as well as of such religious traditions as Islam, Judaism and Zoroastrianism, will reveal the presence of such figures. See Fiona Bowie and Christopher Deacy (eds.), *The Coming Deliverer: Millennial Themes in World Religions* (Cardiff, University of Wales Press, 1997) for a detailed examination

of the function of redeemer-figures across a range of world religions and sects. Consider also Brian Morris, *Anthropological Studies of Religion* (Cambridge, Cambridge University Press, 1987), according to whom 'We have yet to discover any society that does not articulate some notions about the sacred and about spiritual beings' (p. 1).

51 Lee Aaron Mason, 'Attitudes to society and politics in the superhero comic' (MA thesis, Lampeter, 1991), 14.

52 Ibid., 1.

53 Quoted by Bruce David Forbes, 'Batman crucified: religion and modern superheroes', *Media Development*, 44/4 (1997), 12.

54 Ibid.

55 This point is made by Neil Hurley, 'Cinematic transfigurations of Jesus', in John R. May and Michael Bird (eds.), *Religion in Film* (Knoxville, University of Tennessee Press, 1982), 76, in view of the fact that Darth Vader is a rebel, a former Jedi (read 'disciple').

56 John 20: 19, 21.

57 John 16: 7.

58 Revelation 6: 8.

59 Ibid.

60 Robert Banks, 'The drama of salvation in George Stevens's *Shane*', in Marsh and Ortiz (eds.), *Explorations in Theology and Film*, 67.

61 This point is made by Conrad Ostwalt, 'Hollywood and Armageddon: apocalyptic themes in recent Hollywood presentation', in Joel M. Martin and Conrad Ostwalt (eds.), *Screening the Sacred* (Boulder, CO, Oxford, Westview Press, 1995), 57.

62 Banks, 'Drama of salvation', 67.

63 Bruce Babington and Peter William Evans, *Biblical Epics* (Manchester, Manchester University Press, 1993), 47.

64 James M. Wall, 'Biblical spectaculars and secular man', in John C. Cooper and Carl Skrade (eds.), *Celluloid and Symbols* (Philadelphia, Fortress Press, 1970), 53.

65 Gaye Ortiz, 'Theology and the silver screen', *The Month* (May 1998), 172.

66 Wall, 'Biblical spectacular', 53.

67 Paul Schrader, who makes this point in *Transcendental Style in Film* (Berkeley, University of California Press, 1972), is critical of this 'abundant' style. As he puts it, the assumption is that 'the film is "real", the spiritual is "on" film, ergo: the spiritual is real' (p. 63).

68 *Variety* review of Scorsese's *The Last Temptation of Christ*; cited in Andy Dougan, *Martin Scorsese* (London, Orion Media, 1997), 129.

69 Babington and Evans, *Biblical Epics*, 117.

70 Forbes, 'Batman crucified', 12; my italics.

71 Romans 5: 12.

72 Norris, *Christological Controversy*, 2.
73 Fiddes, *Past Event*, 125.
74 Ibid.
75 Ibid., 126.
76 A paraphrase of Lloyd Baugh, *Imaging the Divine* (Kansas City, Sheed & Ward, 1997), 18.
77 Ibid.
78 Ibid., 26.
79 Ibid., 30.
80 Baugh provides these figures, ibid., 25.
81 Wall provides this figure, 'Biblical spectaculars', 52.
82 Baugh, *Imaging the Divine*, 25.
83 Peter Malone, *Movie Christs and Antichrists* (New York, Crossroads, 1990), 43.
84 Ibid., 39.
85 Quoted in Baugh, *Imaging the Divine*, 20.
86 Babington and Evans, *Biblical Epics*, 134.
87 Ibid.
88 Ibid.
89 Quoted in Baugh, *Imaging the Divine*, 52.
90 Les Keyser's words; quoted in ibid.
91 Quoted in ibid.
92 Ibid., 54.
93 Ibid., 55. Baugh is, though, critical of Scorsese's film on the whole, on the grounds that it has more in common with Scorsese's other films than with the Jesus of the Gospels. Jesus is, for instance, according to Baugh, somewhat neurotically dependent upon Judas, in a manner consonant with the troubled masculine protagonist of *Mean Streets*, who is dependent upon another, somewhat wayward and reckless character for his salvation to be achieved. (I discuss *Mean Streets* in detail in Chapter 7).
94 Babington and Evans, *Biblical Epics*, 158.
95 Ibid.
96 Ibid.
97 Ibid.
98 Ibid.
99 Les Keyser, *Martin Scorsese* (New York, Twayne Publishers, 1992), 176.
100 Ibid.
101 Babington and Evans, *Biblical Epics*, 151.
102 Ibid., 132.
103 Ibid., 153.
104 Lawrence S. Friedman, *The Cinema of Martin Scorsese* (Oxford, Roundhouse, 1997), 162.

[105] Ibid.
[106] R. V. Sellers, *Two Ancient Christologies* (London, SPCK, 1940), 137.
[107] Friedman, *Cinema*, 153.
[108] John 11: 35.
[109] John 11: 33.
[110] Mark 3: 5.
[111] Mark 3: 21.
[112] Matthew 10: 34–6.
[113] Mark 11: 15.
[114] Mark 11: 17.
[115] Ibid.
[116] Mark 11: 13–14.
[117] Telford, 'Jesus Christ movie star', 138.
[118] Jonathan Rosenbaum, 'Raging Messiah', *Sight and Sound*, 57/4 (Autumn 1988), 281.
[119] Ibid.
[120] Ibid., 282.
[121] H. A. Williams, *True Resurrection* (London, Mitchell Beazley, 1972), 89.
[122] For it is invariably a 'he'; in the examples cited in this book, the *noir* protagonist is a male.
[123] Ibid.
[124] Conrad Ostwalt, 'Religion, film and cultural analysis', in Martin and Ostwalt (eds.), *Screening the Sacred*, 157.
[125] Joel Martin, 'Seeing the sacred on screen', in Martin and Ostwalt (eds.), *Screening the Sacred*, 1.
[126] Ibid.
[127] Ostwalt's words, 'Religion, film and cultural analysis', 157.
[128] Quoted in Margaret R. Miles, *Seeing and Believing* (Boston, MA, Beacon Press, 1996), 7.
[129] Ibid., 193.
[130] Ibid.
[131] Ian Maher, 'Liberation in *Awakenings*', in Marsh and Ortiz (eds.), *Explorations in Theology and Film* (Oxford, Blackwell, 1997), 98.
[132] Ibid., 113.
[133] Ibid.
[134] Stephen Brie and David Torevell, 'Moral ambiguity and contradiction in *Dead Poets Society*', in Marsh and Ortiz (eds.), *Explorations in Theology and Film*, 169.
[135] My italics.
[136] Ibid., 173.
[137] Ibid.
[138] Ibid.

139 Louise Sweet on *Awakenings*, *Monthly Film Bulletin*, 58/686 (March 1991), 73.

140 Ibid.

141 Ibid.

142 Richard Combs on *Dead Poets Society*, *Monthly Film Bulletin*, 56/668 (September 1989), 272.

143 Ibid., 273.

144 Ibid.

145 Rudolf Bultmann in Hans-Werner Bartsch (ed.), *Kerygma and Myth*, vol. 1 (London, SPCK, 1953), 36.

146 Ibid.

147 Neil P. Hurley on 'Alfred Hitchcock', in John R. May and Michael Bird (eds.), *Religion in Film* (Knoxville, University of Tennessee Press, 1982), 67.

148 Ibid.

149 Ibid.

150 Paul Plouffe, 'The tainted Adam' (Ph.D. thesis, University of California, Berkeley, 1979).

151 The words of Ihan Hassan; quoted ibid., 2.

152 Plouffe makes this point, ibid., 70.

153 Ibid., 164.

154 J. P. Tellotte in Todd Erickson, 'Kill me again: movement becomes genre', in Alain Silver and James Ursini (eds.), *Film Noir Reader* (New York, Limelight Editions, 1997), 326.

155 Ibid.

156 Ibid.

157 Paul Giles, *American Catholic Arts and Fictions* (Cambridge, Cambridge University Press, 1992), 334.

158 Eric Rohmer and Claude Chabrol, quoted ibid., 326.

159 Ibid., 326–7.

160 Neil Hurley, 'Alfred Hitchcock', 177.

161 Giles, *American Catholic Arts and Fictions*, 327.

162 Ibid.

163 Ibid., 332.

164 Neil Hurley, *Theology through Film* (New York, Harper & Row, 1970), 19.

165 Ibid.

166 Ibid.; my italics.

167 Gustavo Gutierrez, *A Theology of Liberation* (London, SCM, 1974), 37.

168 Ibid.

169 Gutierrez; quoted in Hugo Assmann, *Practical Theology of Liberation* (London, Search Press, 1975), 16.

Notes to Chapter 7: Redemption through the cinema of Martin Scorsese

1   Rosalie Savage, 'The *film noir* savior' (MA thesis, Clemson University, 1995), 1.
2   Les Keyser, *Martin Scorsese* (New York, Twayne Publishers, 1992), p. xii.
3   David Jasper, 'On systematizing the unsystematic: a response', in Clive Marsh and Gaye Ortiz (eds.), *Explorations in Theology and Film* (Oxford, Blackwell, 1997), 235.
4   Ibid., 244.
5   Ibid., 243.
6   Lawrence S. Friedman, *The Cinema of Martin Scorsese* (Oxford, Roundhouse, 1997), 10.
7   Andy Dougan, *Martin Scorsese* (London, Orion Media, 1997), 28.
8   Mary Pat Kelly, *Martin Scorsese* (New York, Thunder's Mouth Press, 1991), 11.
9   Scorsese; quoted in Paul Giles, *American Catholic Arts and Fictions* (Cambridge, Cambridge University Press, 1992), 335.
10 Martin Scorsese, 'In the streets', in Peter Occhiogrosso (ed.), *Once a Catholic: Prominent Catholics and Ex-Catholics Discuss the Influence of the Church on Their Lives and Works* (Boston, MA, Houghton Mifflin, 1987), 92.
11 Savage, '*Film noir* savior', 9.
12 Kelly, *Scorsese*, 11.
13 Andrew Greeley, 'Religion and attitudes toward the environment', *Journal for the Scientific Study of Religion*, 32 (1993), 21.
14 Martin Palmer, 'Ecology – prophetic or pathetic?', in Cyril Rodd (ed.), *New Occasions Teach New Duties* (Edinburgh, T. & T. Clark, 1995), 181.
15 Keyser, *Scorsese*, 41.
16 Quoted in Giles, *American Catholic Arts*, 341.
17 See ibid. 350 and Savage, '*Film noir* savior', 10.
18 Savage, '*Film noir* savior', 10.
19 Michael Bliss; quoted ibid.
20 Ibid.
21 Ibid., 11.
22 Savage's words, '*Film noir* savior', 11.
23 David John Graham, 'Redeeming violence in the films of Martin Scorsese', in Marsh and Ortiz (eds.), *Explorations in Theology and Film*, 91.
24 See Leviticus 16: 23–34.
25 Quoted in Dougan, *Scorsese*, 14.
26 Cited by Friedman, *Cinema*, 12.

27   Ibid., 31.
28   Savage, '*Film noir* savior', 28.
29   Ibid.
30   Giles, *American Catholic Arts*, 336.
31   Ibid.
32   Friedman, *Cinema*, 31.
33   Kelly, *Scorsese*, 69.
34   Quoted in Dougan, *Scorsese*, 19.
35   Ibid.
36   Savage, '*Film noir* savior', 24; my italics.
37   David Denby, 'Mean streets: the sweetness of hell', *Sight and Sound*, 43/1 (Winter 1973/4), 48.
38   Friedman, *Cinema*, 34.
39   Quoted in David Thompson and Ian Christie (eds.), *Scorsese on Scorsese* (London, Faber & Faber, 1996), 48.
40   Ibid.
41   Ibid.
42   John Berger, 'Every time we say goodbye', *Sight and Sound*, 1/2 (June 1991), 17.
43   Ibid.
44   Ian Christie, 'Martin Scorsese's testament', *Sight and Sound*, 6/1 (January 1996), 8.
45   Nicholas Pileggi; quoted in Thompson and Christie (eds.), *Scorsese on Scorsese*, 199.
46   Quoted by Christie in *Sight and Sound*, 6/1 (January 1996), 9.
47   Ibid. Also quoted in Thompson and Christie (eds.), *Scorsese on Scorsese*, 202.
48   Graham, 'Redeeming violence', 94.
49   Jasper, 'Systematizing the unsystematic', 240.
50   Bruce Crowther, *Film Noir* (London, Columbus Books, 1988), 165.
51   Foster Hirsch, *The Dark Side of the Screen* (London, Tantivy Press, 1981), 207.
52   In Hirsch's words, 'A place of all–night movies and of sex for sale, the crumbling, dank city is an inferno in which steam drifts up from holes in the street and blinking neon lights perform their own demented dance of death; the city is a symbol of the anti–hero's tortured state of mind.' (Hirsch, p207).
53   Richard Bauckham; quoted in Jerry L. Walls, *Hell* (Notre Dame Press, IN, University of Notre Dame Press, 1992), 2.
54   Matthew 8: 12; 18: 9.
55   *Paradise Lost*, IV, 75; quoted in Walls, *Hell*, 142.
56   Ibid., 142.
57   Ibid., 145.

58 Ibid.
59 Walls, *Hell*, 152.
60 Savage, '*Film noir* savior', 45.
61 Lesley Stern, *The Scorsese Connection* (London, British Film Institute, 1995), 32.
62 Ibid., 48.
63 M. K. Connelly, *Martin Scorsese* (Jefferson, NC, McFarland & Co., 1993), 42.
64 James Monaco, *Virgin Film Guide* (London, Virgin Books, 1992), 938.
65 This occurs when, at the beginning, we see Travis's eyes reflected through the mirrors and lights of his cab.
66 Walls, *Hell*, 6.
67 Friedman, *Cinema*, 63.
68 Ibid., 61.
69 Quoted in Thompson and Christie (eds.), *Scorsese on Scorsese*, 62.
70 Quoted in Keyser, *Scorsese*, 81.
71 Ibid.
72 Stern, *Scorsese Connection*, 51.
73 Ibid.
74 Friedman, *Cinema*, 73.
75 Ibid.; my italics.
76 Quoted in Keyser, *Scorsese*, 82.
77 Friedman, *Cinema*, 82.
78 Keyser, *Scorsese*, 78.
79 Hebrews 9: 12: 'he entered once for all into the Holy Place, taking not the blood of goats and calves but his own blood, thus securing an eternal redemption'.
80 Quoted in H. E. W. Turner, *The Patristic Doctrine of Redemption: A Study of the Development of Doctrine during the First Five Centuries* (London, A. R. Mowbray & Co., 1952), 107.
81 Some scholars have argued that Jesus literally engaged with and confronted this sinful world in the sense that he was a political and revolutionary Messiah. See, for example, S. G. F. Brandon, *Jesus and the Zealots: A Study of the Political Factor in Primitive Christianity* (Manchester, Manchester University Press, 1967), who argued that there was a close association between Christ and the Zealot movement of the first century CE. While this picture of Christ is not accepted by most scholars (Oscar Cullmann says Jesus was sceptical of all political power and, as the Sermon on the Mount indicates, constantly rejected violence), it does allow one to make one particularly pertinent connection between Jesus and Travis – that the redeemer not only *suffers* violence; he has the capacity to *inflict* it.
82 Savage, '*Film noir* savior', 58.

83   Ibid., 57; my italics.
84   Paul Badham makes this point in 'In search of heaven', in Tony Moss (ed.), *In Search of Christianity* (London, Firethorn Press, 1986), 124–36. Badham continues, however, that 'in this case it is hard to see why it should be of any interest now, apart perhaps as a historical belief about the founder of Christianity. By contrast, the Christian tradition itself has seen the resurrection of Jesus as important precisely as a guarantee of a destiny in which we may expect to share.'
85   Cited ibid.
86   Colin L. Westerbeck, Jr., 'Beauties and the beast: *Seven Beauties/Taxi Driver*', *Sight and Sound*, 45/3 (Summer 1976), 135.
87   Ibid.
88   Ibid.
89   Quoted in Kelly, *Scorsese*, 89. Schrader also discussed this period in his life in a *Kaleidoscope* feature on *Taxi Driver*, 'God's lonely man', produced by Paul Quinn for BBC Radio 4; broadcast Saturday, 14 June 1997, at 7.20 p.m.
90   Friedman, *Cinema*, 62.
91   Quoted ibid.
92   Ibid., 71.
93   Westerbeck, 'Beauties and the beast', 138; my italics.
94   Quoted in Thompson and Christie (eds.), *Scorsese on Scorsese*, 63.
95   Westerbeck, 'Beauties and the beast', 135.
96   Ibid.
97   Ibid., 139.
98   Ibid.
99   Ibid.
100 Ibid.
101 Friedman, *Cinema*, 115.
102 Quoted ibid.
103 In *Soho News* (19 November 1980); cited in Keyser, *Scorsese*, 112; my italics.
104 Friedman, *Cinema*, 115.
105 Ibid., 113.
106 Paul Giles, *American Catholic Arts and Fiction* (Cambridge, Cambridge University Press, 1992), 341.
107 Ibid.
108 Quoted in Friedman, *Cinema*, 122.
109 Michael Blowen; quoted in Keyser, *Scorsese*, 115.
110 Ibid.
111 Giles, *American Catholic Arts*, 341.
112 Ibid.
113 Ibid., 122.

[114] Ibid., 343.

[115] Friedman, *Cinema*, 126.

[116] Quoted in Thompson and Christie (eds.), *Scorsese on Scorsese*, 77.

[117] John 9: 25.

[118] Quoted in Keyser, *Scorsese*, 112; my italics. Furthermore, according to Mark Le Fanu ('Looking for Mr De Niro', in *Sight and Sound*, 55/1 (Winter 1985/6), 49), although on the surface the story could not be less intellectual, *Raging Bull* 'finds access, through the poetry and seriousness of its treatment, to a region of universality denied to many works of more obviously "intelligent" provenance.'

[119] Friedman, *Cinema*, 113.

[120] Quoted in Dougan, *Scorsese*, 60, 63.

[121] Friedman, *Cinema*, 115.

[122] Quoted in Thompson and Christie (eds.), *Scorsese on Scorsese*, 76–7.

[123] Quoted in Friedman, *Cinema*, 115; my italics.

[124] Ibid.

[125] Ibid.

[126] Quoted in Keyser, *Scorsese*, 115.

[127] Quoted in Kelly, *Scorsese*, 254.

[128] Keyser makes this point, *Scorsese*, 115.

[129] Jonathan Rosenbaum, 'Raging Messiah', *Sight and Sound*, 57/4 (Autumn 1988), 281.

[130] Quoted in Dougan, *Scorsese*, 65; my italics.

[131] Ibid.

[132] Friedman, *Cinema*, 168. After Universal Pictures enabled Scorsese to make *The Last Temptation of Christ* in 1988, by contributing $6 million to the budget, Thompson and Christie explain that 'there was an understanding that Scorsese would go on to make more commercial films for them' (*Scorsese on Scorsese*, 165). It is within this context that *Cape Fear* was born. The studio owned the rights to the picture, which began a six-year directing/production deal between Universal and Scorsese.

[133] Pam Cook, 'Scorsese's masquerade', *Sight and Sound*, 1/12 (April 1992), 15.

[134] Woody Allen; quoted in Stig Björkman, *Woody Allen on Woody Allen* (London, Faber & Faber, 1995), 50.

[135] One of the most conspicuous signs of reworking in Scorsese's version are the cameo appearances by Robert Mitchum and Gregory Peck, who played the central characters in the original *Cape Fear*. This time, however, Gregory Peck, instead of playing the morally unreproachable Sam Bowden is Cady's somewhat shady attorney, Lee Heller, while Mitchum – Cady in the 1962 picture – is Lieutenant Elgart, who decides to bring Cady to the police station to be strip-searched.

[136] Jenny Diski, 'The shadow within', *Sight and Sound*, 1/10 (February, 1992), 12.

[137] Ibid.

[138] Slavoj Žižek, ' "The thing that thinks": the Kantian background of the noir subject', in Joan Copjec (ed.), *Shades of Noir* (London, Verso, 1993), 208.

[139] Scorsese and Spielberg actually swapped projects. Scorsese was interested in adapting Thomas Keneally's book, *Schindler's Ark*, but which Spielberg went on to film (as *Schindler's List*, 1993). Conversely, Spielberg passed on a remake of J. Lee Thompson's *Cape Fear*, a project which came to be taken on by Scorsese.

[140] Quoted in Friedman, *Cinema*, 164.

[141] Savage, '*Film noir* savior', 67.

[142] Ibid., 13.

[143] Stern, *Scorsese Connection*, 180.

[144] Ibid.

[145] Ibid., 179.

[146] Ibid., 183.

[147] Quoted in Thompson and Christie (eds.), *Scorsese on Scorsese*, 169.

[148] Ibid., 166.

[149] Friedman, *Cinema*, 164.

[150] Ibid.

[151] Savage, '*Film noir* savior', 68.

[152] David John Graham, 'The uses of film in theology', Marsh and Ortiz (eds.), *Explorations in Theology and Film*, 92.

[153] Job 1: 13–2: 8.

[154] Job 7: 7–10.

[155] Paul Badham, *Christian Beliefs about Life after Death* (London, SPCK, 1978), 13. It is important to stress, however, that not all scholars read Job in this way. Despite the existence of suffering, the text does not posit a future life, where Job will be recompensed for his suffering on earth. Rather, the text indicates that suffering is a divine discipline, the appropriate response to which is humble acceptance. There is no explanation for Job's suffering which humankind can fathom. See Job 40: 8–9. The ultimate answer is not theodicy but piety and faith, which transcend rational and intellectual analysis.

[156] Cf. John Hick, *Death and Eternal Life* (Basingstoke, Macmillan, 1985), 159.

[157] Ibid.

[158] Stern, *Scorsese Connection*, 184.

[159] Kelly, *Scorsese*, 287.

[160] Ibid.; my italics.

[161] Savage, '*Film noir* savior', 80.

162 Quoted in Thompson and Christie (eds.), *Scorsese on Scorsese*, 171.
163 Savage, '*Film noir* savior', 179.
164 According to 1 John 4: 7–21, God *is* love.
165 Judges 2: 11, 12.
166 Judges 2: 14.
167 Judges 2: 16.
168 Judges 2: 19–20.
169 Robin Stuart Garnett, 'Martin Scorsese: a cinema of disillusionment' (MA thesis, University of Kansas, 1991), 183.
170 Diski, 'Shadow within', 13. Sam Bowden faces disbarment for his illegal methods to get rid of Cady – in particular, for arranging for Cady to be beaten to a pulp, with bicycle chains and baseball bats, by three hired thugs. In one of the film's most violent episodes, Cady manages to outwit them, and succeeds in beating the three hired men to a pulp.
171 Garnett, 'Scorsese', 183.
172 For instance, according to a review of *Cape Fear*, when the film was released on laserdisc, in the October 1996 edition of *Empire* (vol. 88), 'For the most part this is chillingly effective, only to give way to out-of-place histrionics in the final half-hour.' (p130).
173 In Thompson and Christie (eds.), *Scorsese on Scorsese*, 171.
174 Ibid., 174.
175 Savage, '*Film noir* savior', 13. Savage also expresses reservations about whether Travis is really redeemed at the end of *Taxi Driver*, in that '[a]lthough Travis desires spiritual redemption for Iris, the city, and himself through his own self-sacrifice, he fails in his savior role since his sacrifice is not completed by his own death' (p. 57). In response I would say that, as in the case of *Cape Fear*, the ending may be ambiguous, but the fact that the protagonist is still living at the end of the film hardly discounts the possibility that he has undergone a redemptive experience.
176 Savage, '*Film noir* savior', 81.
177 Origen, *On First Principles*, 3. 6. 9; cited in Brian E. Daley, *The Hope of the Early Church* (Cambridge, Cambridge University Press, 1991), 49.
178 *On First Principles*, 3. 3. 6; cited in Henry Bettenson (ed.), *The Early Christian Fathers* (Oxford, Oxford University Press, 1991), 257; my italics.
179 Ibid.
180 Brian Hebblethwaite, *The Christian Hope* (Marshall, Morgan & Scott, 1984)
181 Daley, *Hope*, 49; my italics.
182 J. N. D. Kelly, *Early Christian Doctrines* (London, Adam & Charles Black, 1958), 473.

Notes to Chapter 8: Redemption or regression? The escapist ethos of contemporary film

1 Conrad E. Ostwalt, 'Religion, film and cultural analysis', in Joel W. Martin and Ostwalt (eds.), *Screening the Sacred* (Boulder, CO, and Oxford, 1995), 159.
2 Ibid.
3 Ibid.
4 Ibid.
5 Ibid., 157.
6 Scorsese; quoted in David Thompson and Ian Christie (eds.), *Scorsese on Scorsese* (London, Faber & Faber, 1996), p. xvii.
7 See Chapter 7, note 132.
8 Terence Rafferty, 'Mud', *The New Yorker* (2 December 1991), 156.
9 Ibid., 158.
10 Ibid.
11 Ibid.
12 Ibid.
13 Ibid., 159.
14 Ibid.
15 Ibid., 156.
16 Lawrence S. Friedman, *The Cinema of Martin Scorsese* (Oxford, Roundhouse, 1997), 7.
17 Timothy Corrigan, *A Cinema without Walls* (London, Routledge, 1992), 30.
18 David Jasper, 'On systematizing the unsystematic: a response', in Clive Marsh and Gaye Ortiz (eds.), *Explorations in Theology and Film* (Oxford, Blackwell, 1997), 235.
19 Rafferty, 'Mud', 158.
20 Ibid.
21 Albert Auster and Leonard Quart, *How the War was Remembered* (New York, Praeger Publishers, 1988), 85.
22 Scorsese; quoted in Les Keyser, *Martin Scorsese* (New York, Twayne Publishers, 1992), 123.
23 In Scorsese's own words, 'The film was not successful, and I was very depressed' (quoted in Thompson and Christie (eds.), *Scorsese on Scorsese*, 76).
24 Keyser, *Scorsese*, 123.
25 Ibid.
26 Ibid.
27 Friedman, *Cinema*, 7.
28 Fred Pfeil, 'Home fires burning: family noir in *Blue Velvet* and *Terminator 2*', in Joan Copjec (ed.), *Shades of Noir* (London, Verso, 1993), 238.

[29] Jasper, 'Systematizing the unsystematic', 238.
[30] Ibid.
[31] Pfeil, 'Home fires burning', 242.
[32] Ibid.
[33] Margaret R. Miles, *Seeing and Believing* (Boston, MA, Beacon Press, 1996), 52.
[34] This point is made by Miles, ibid.
[35] For example, as Miles points out (ibid., 56), most of the white men and Indians live below the falls, while the primitive Indians and virtuous Christian whites live above them. She refers to this as a geographical Genesis, with 'above the falls' and 'below the falls' to be read as 'before' and 'after' the Fall, respectively.
[36] Ibid., 52; my italics.
[37] Ibid.
[38] Quoted by Miles, ibid., 55.
[39] Ibid., 55.
[40] Ibid., 67; my italics.
[41] M. Darroll Bryant, 'Cinema, religion and popular culture', in John R. May and Michael Bird (eds.), *Religion in Film* (Knoxville, University of Tennessee Press, 1982), 109.
[42] Ibid.
[43] Rob Lapsley, 'Mainly in cities and at night: some notes on cities and film', in David B. Clarke (ed.), *The Cinematic City* (London, Routledge, 1997), 198.
[44] Bryant, 'Cinema, religion and popular culture', 109.
[45] Ibid., 110.
[46] Auster and Quart, *How the War was Remembered*, 93.
[47] Robert Philip Kolker, *A Cinema of Loneliness*, 2nd edn. (Oxford, Oxford University Press, 1988), 252.
[48] Ibid.
[49] Ibid., 263.
[50] Lee Mason, 'Attitudes to society and politics in the superhero comic' (MA thesis, Lampeter, 1991), 11; my italics. The actual context of Mason's argument is superhero comic books.
[51] Quoted by Todd Erickson, 'Kill me again: movement becomes genre', in Alain Silver and James Ursini (eds.), *Film Noir Reader* (New York, Limelight Editions, 1997), 312.
[52] Quoted ibid.
[53] Andrew Gordon, '*Star Wars*: a myth for our time', in Martin and Ostwalt (eds.), *Screening the Sacred*, 82.
[54] Quoted in Mason, 'Attitudes to society', 11.
[55] Ibid.
[56] Ibid.; my italics.

57   Gordon, '*Star Wars*', 82.
58   Ibid.
59   Kolker, *Cinema of Loneliness*, 255.
60   Hans Küng, *Eternal Life?* (London, Collins, 1984), 254.
61   Ibid.
62   Ibid.; my italics.
63   Don Cupitt, *The Sea of Faith* (London, BBC, 1984), 10.
64   Peter Krämer, 'Would you take your child to see this film? The cultural and social work of the family-adventure movie', in Steve Neale and Murray Smith (eds.), *Contemporary Hollywood Cinema* (London, Routledge, 1998), 304.
65   Ibid.
66   Reinhold Zwick, 'The problem of evil in contemporary film', in John R. May (ed.), *New Image of Religious Film* (Kansas City, Sheed & Ward, 1997), 76.
67   Ibid.
68   In Zwick's words, 'A dualistic contemplation of evil will always be attractive because it frees the individual to a great extent from the claims of freedom, inasmuch as it puts guilt and responsibility into the hands of another, namely, the tempter' (ibid., 76).
69   Ibid., 83.
70   Ibid.
71   Auster and Quart, *How the War was Remembered*, 123.
72   Ibid.
73   Ibid.
74   Ibid., 137.
75   Ibid.
76   Ibid., 132.
77   Ibid., 139.
78   Ibid.
79   Ibid.
80   Ibid., 139; my italics.
81   I am referring here to Tim Burton's *Batman* (1989) and *Batman Returns* (1992), rather than the more recent *Batman Forever* (1995) and *Batman and Robin* (1997), directed by Joel Schumacher.
82   Bruce David Forbes, 'Batman crucified: religion and modern super-heroes', *Media Development*, 44/4 (1997), 11.
83   Ibid., 12.
84   1978, 1980, 1983, 1987.
85   Ibid.
86   Ibid.
87   Kolker, *Cinema of Loneliness*, 281.
88   John Wrathall, in *Sight and Sound*, 8/9 (September 1998), 34.

89   Kolker, *Cinema of Loneliness*, 265.
90   Ibid., p281.
91   Wrathall, *Sight and Sound*, 8/9 (September 1998), 35.
92   Ibid. There are many critics, however, who write favourably about Spielberg's earlier films. For instance, Warren Buckland challenges the idea that so much of contemporary cinema is simply a sequence of emptily expensive, aesthetically impoverished spectacles. Spielberg's 'blockbusters', he maintains, 'have their own complex structure', and their popularity should not 'preclude them from being considered as serious objects worthy of study.' 'A close encounter with *Raiders of the Lost Ark:* notes on narrative aspects of the New Hollywood blockbuster', in Neale and Smith (eds.), *Contemporary Hollywood Cinema*, 175.
93   In the case of *Platoon*, despite costing only $6 million to make, the film went on to gross over $100 million world-wide. See Simon Rose, *Classic Movie Guide* (Glasgow, Harper Collins, 1995), 92.
94   Keyser, *Scorsese*, 147.
95   These quotations are taken from the *Independent* interview with James Mottram, 29 May 1998.
96   At the UK box office in 1998, *Titanic* grossed an unprecedented £68,971,523, while *Afterglow* grossed only £65,923 (figures cited in *Empire*, 115 (January 1999), 130).
97   Julie Christie was nominated in the category of Best Performance by an Actress in a Leading Role.
98   Quoted in Thompson and Christie (eds.), *Scorsese on Scorsese*, 69.
99   Robin Stuart Garnett, 'Martin Scorsese: a cinema of disillusionment' (MA thesis, University of Kansas, 1991), 55.
100 Ibid., 42.
101 Ibid., 142.
102 For example, see *www.unomaha.edu/~wwwjrf/*, *www.christiananswers.net/spotlight/reviews/*, *www.christiancritic.com/movies/* and *www.hollywoodjesus.com*.

Bibliography

Assmann, Hugo, *Practical Theology of Liberation* (London, Search Press, 1975).

Auster, Albert, and Quart, Leonard, *How the War was Remembered: Hollywood and Vietnam* (New York, Praeger Publishers, 1988).

Babington, Bruce, and Evans, Peter William, *Biblical Epics: Sacred Narrative in the Hollywood Cinema* (Manchester, Manchester University Press, 1993).

Badham, Paul, *Christian Beliefs about Life after Death* (London, SPCK, 1978).

Badham, Paul, 'In search of heaven', in Tony Moss (ed.), *In Search of Christianity* (London, Firethorn Press, 1986).

Badham, Paul, and Linda Badham, *Immortality or Extinction?* (London, SPCK, 1984).

Banks, Robert, 'The drama of salvation in George Stevens's *Shane*', in Clive Marsh and Gaye Ortiz (eds.), *Explorations in Theology and Film: Movies and Meaning* (Oxford, Blackwell, 1997), 59–71.

Bartholomew, Michael, 'The moral critique of Christian orthodoxy', in Gerald Parsons (ed.), *Religion in Victorian Britain*, vol. 2: *Controversies* (Manchester, Manchester University Press, 1988), 166–90.

Baugh, Lloyd, *Imaging the Divine: Jesus and Christ-Figures in Film* (Kansas City, Sheed & Ward, 1997).

Belton, John, *American Cinema/American Culture* (London, McGraw-Hill, 1994).

Berger, John, 'Every time we say goodbye', *Sight and Sound*, 1/2 (June 1991), 14–17.

Bettenson, Henry (ed.), *The Early Christian Fathers* (Oxford, Oxford University Press, 1991).

Bird, Michael, 'Film as hierophany', in John R. May and Michael Bird (eds.), *Religion in Film* (Knoxville, University of Tennessee Press, 1982), 3–22.

Björkman, Stig, *Woody Allen on Woody Allen* (London, Faber & Faber, 1995).

Blenkinsopp, J., *Wisdom and Law in the Old Testament* (Oxford, Oxford University Press, 1983).

Bloch, Ernst, *The Principle of Hope*, vol. 1 (Oxford, Blackwell, 1986).

Brandon, S. G. F., *Jesus and the Zealots: A Study of the Political Factor in Primitive Christianity* (Manchester, Manchester University Press, 1967).

Brie, Stephen, and Torevell, David, 'Moral ambiguity and contradiction in *Dead Poets Society*', in Clive Marsh and Gaye Ortiz (eds.), *Explorations in Theology and Film: Movies and Meaning* (Oxford, Blackwell, 1997), 167–80.

Brown, Stephen, 'Optimism, hope, and feelgood movies: the Capra connection', in Clive Marsh and Gaye Ortiz (eds.), *Explorations in Theology and Film: Movies and Meaning* (Oxford, Blackwell, 1997), 219–32.

Browne, David, 'Film, movies, meanings', in Clive Marsh and Gaye Ortiz (eds.), *Explorations in Theology and Film: Movies and Meaning* (Oxford, Blackwell, 1997), 9–19.

Bruce, Steve, *Religion in the Modern World: From Cathedrals to Cults* (Oxford, Oxford University Press, 1996).

Bryant, M. Darroll, 'Cinema, religion and popular culture', in John R. May and Michael Bird (eds.), *Religion in Film* (Knoxville, University of Tennessee Press, 1982), 101–14.

Bultmann, Rudolf, 'New Testament and theology', in Hans-Werner Bartsch (ed.), *Kerygma and Myth*, vol. 1 (London, SPCK, 1953), 1–44.

Cahill, P. Joseph, *Mended Speech: The Crisis of Religious Studies and Theology* (New York, Crossroad, 1982).

Capps, Walter, *Religious Studies: The Making of a Discipline* (Minneapolis, Fortress Press, 1995).

Cawelti, John G., 'Chinatown and generic transformation in recent American films', in Gerald Mast, Marshall Cohen and Leo Braudy (eds.), *Film Theory and Criticism* (Oxford, Oxford University Press, 1992), 498–511.

Chadwick, Henry, *The Early Church* (London, Penguin, 1990).

Chow, Rey, 'Film and cultural identity', in John Hill and Pamela Church Gibson (eds.), *The Oxford Guide to Film Studies* (Oxford, Oxford University Press, 1998), 169–75.

Christie, Ian, 'Martin Scorsese's testament', *Sight and Sound*, 6/1 (January 1996), 7–11.

Coates, Paul, *Film at the Intersection of High and Mass Culture* (Cambridge, Cambridge University Press, 1994).

Cochrane, J. Scott, 'The Wizard of Oz and other mythic rites of passage', in John R. May (ed.), *Image and Likeness: Religious Visions in American Film Classics* (Paulist Press, 1982), 79–86.

Collins, Jim, 'Genericity in the 90s: eclectic irony and the new sincerity', in Jim Collins, Hilary Radner and Ava Preacher Collins (eds.), *Film Theory Goes to the Movies* (London, Routledge, 1993), 242–63.

Combs, Richard, Review of *Dead Poets Society,* in *Monthly Film Bulletin,* 56/668 (September 1989), 272–3.

Commins, Gary, 'Woody Allen's theological imagination', in *Theology Today,* 44 (July 1987), 235–49.

Connelly, Marie Katheryn, *Martin Scorsese: An Analysis of his Feature Films* (Jefferson, NC, McFarland & Co., 1993).

Cook, Pam, 'Scorsese's masquerade', *Sight and Sound,* 1/12 (April 1992), 14–15.

Cooper, John C., 'The image of man in the recent cinema', in John C. Cooper and Carl Skrade (eds.), *Celluloid and Symbols* (Philadelphia, Fortress Press, 1970), 25–39.

Copjec, Joan, 'Introduction', to Joan Copjec (ed.), *Shades of Noir: A Reader* (London, Verso, 1993), pp. vii–xii.

Corrigan, Timothy, *A Cinema without Walls: Movies and Culture after Vietnam* (London, Routledge, 1992).

Creed, J. M., *The Divinity of Jesus Christ* (London and Glasgow, Collins, 1964).

Crenshaw, James L., *Old Testament Wisdom: An Introduction* (London, SCM, 1982).

Crowther, Bruce, *Film Noir: Reflections in a Dark Mirror* (London, Columbus Books, 1988).

Cullmann, Oscar, *Salvation in History* (London, SCM, 1967).

Cupitt, Don, *The Sea of Faith* (London, BBC, 1984).

Daley, Brian E., *The Hope of the Early Church: A Handbook of Patristic Eschatology* (Cambridge, Cambridge University Press, 1991).

Danielou, Jean, *Origen,* tr. by Walter Mitchell (New York, Sheed & Ward, 1955).

Davies, Douglas, 'Christianity', in Jean Holm and John Bowker (eds.), *Human Nature and Human Destiny: Themes in Religious Studies Series* (London, Pinter, 1994), 39–70.

Deacy, Christopher, 'An application of the religious concept of redemption through *film noir*', *Scottish Journal of Religious Studies,* 18/2 (Autumn 1997), 199–212.

Deacy, Christopher, 'The Christian concept of redemption and its application through the films of Martin Scorsese', *Religious Studies and Theology,* 17/1 (1999), 46–70.

Deacy, Christopher, 'Fantasy and redemption: religious possibility in *Little Voice*', *Journal of Religion and Film* (*http://www.unomaha.edu/~wwwjrf/*), 4/2 (2000).

Deacy, Christopher, 'Integration and rebirth through confrontation: *Fight Club* and *American Beauty* as contemporary religious parables', *Journal of Contemporary Religion,* 16/3 (2001).

Deacy, Christopher, 'Redemption and film: cinema as a contemporary site of religious activity', *Media Development,* 47/1 (2000), 50–4.

Deacy, Christopher, 'Screen Christologies: an evaluation of the role of Christ-figures in film', *Journal of Contemporary Religion*, 14/3 (1999), 325–37.

Denby, David, 'Mean streets: the sweetness of Hell', *Sight and Sound*, 43/1 (Winter 1973/4), 48–50.

Dillistone, F. W., *The Christian Understanding of Atonement* (Welwyn, James Nisbet & Co., 1968).

Diski, Jenny, 'The shadow within', *Sight and Sound*, 1/10 (February 1992), 12–13.

Donald, James (ed.), *Fantasy and the Cinema* (London, British Film Institute, 1989).

Dougan, Andy, *Martin Scorsese: The Making of his Movies* (London, Orion Media, 1997).

Durgnat, Raymond, *The Strange Case of Alfred Hitchcock* (London, Faber & Faber, 1974).

Durkheim, Emile, *The Elementary Forms of Religious Life*, tr. Karen E. Fields (New York, Free Press, 1995).

Dyer, Richard, 'Entertainment and utopia', in Bill Nichols (ed.), *Movies and Methods*, vol. 2 (London, University of California Press, 1985), 220–32.

Elley, Derek (ed.), *Variety Movie Guide* (London, Hamlyn, 1994).

Erickson, Todd, 'Kill me again: movement becomes genre', in Alain Silver and James Ursini (eds.), *Film Noir Reader* (New York, Limelight Editions, 1997), 307–29.

Ferm, Vergilius (ed.), *An Encyclopedia of Religion* (Westpoint, CT, Greenwood Press, 1976).

Fiddes, Paul S., *Past Event and Present Salvation: The Christian Idea of Atonement* (London, Darton Longman & Todd, 1989).

Floyd, Nigel, Review of *Knight Moves*, in John Pym (ed.), *Time Out Film Guide* (London, Penguin, 1997), 434.

Forbes, Bruce David, 'Batman crucified: religion and modern superheroes', in *Media Development*, 44/4 (1997), 10–12.

Fore, William F., 'Moving images challenge theology', in *Media Development*, 42/4 (1995), 7–10.

Forshey, Gerald E., *American Religious and Biblical Spectaculars* (Westport, CT, Praeger Publishers, 1992).

Fox, Julian, *Woody: Movies from Manhattan* (London, B. T. Batsford, 1996).

French, Peter A., *Cowboy Metaphysics: Ethics and Death in Westerns* (Oxford, Rowman & Littlefield, 1997).

French, Philip, Introduction to the first UK terrestrial television screening of *Taxi Driver* (BBC2, 25 August 1995).

Friedman, Lawrence S., *The Cinema of Martin Scorsese* (Oxford, Roundhouse, 1997).

Gallafent, Edward, 'Echo Park: film noir in the seventies', in Ian Cameron (ed.), *The Movie Book of Film Noir* (London, Studio Vista, 1994), 254–66.

Gallagher, Michael Paul, 'Theology, discernment and cinema', in John R. May (ed.), *New Image of Religious Film* (Kansas City, Sheed & Ward, 1997), 151–60.

Gamel, Mary-Kay, 'An American tragedy: Chinatown', in Martin M. Winkler (ed.), *Classics and Cinema* (Toronto, Bucknell University Press, 1991), 209–31.

Garnett, Robin Stuart, 'Martin Scorsese: A cinema of disillusionment' (MA thesis, University of Kansas, 1991).

Giddens, Anthony, *Sociology* (Oxford, Polity Press, 1989).

Giles, Paul, *American Catholic Arts and Fictions: Culture, Ideology, Aesthetics* (Cambridge, Cambridge University Press, 1992).

Gill, Robin (ed.), *A Textbook of Christian Ethics* (Edinburgh, T. & T. Clark, 1989).

Girgus, Sean B., *The Films of Woody Allen* (Cambridge, Cambridge University Press, 1993).

Goethals, Gregor T., *The Electronic Golden Calf: Images, Religion, and the Making of Meaning* (Cambridge, MA, Cowley Publications, 1990).

Gordon, Andrew, '*Star Wars*: a myth for our time', in Joel W. Martin and Conrad E. Ostwalt Jr. (eds.), *Screening the Sacred: Religion, Myth and Ideology in Popular American Film* (Boulder, CO, & Oxford, Westview Press, 1995), 73–82.

Graham, David John, 'Redeeming violence in the films of Martin Scorsese', in Clive Marsh and Gaye Ortiz (eds.), *Explorations in Theology and Film: Movies and Meaning* (Oxford, Blackwell, 1997), 87–95.

Graham, David John, 'The uses of film in theology', in Clive Marsh and Gaye Ortiz (eds.), *Explorations in Theology and Film: Movies and Meaning* (Oxford, Blackwell, 1997), 35–43.

Greeley, Andrew, 'Religion and attitudes toward the environment', *Journal for the Scientific Study of Religion*, 32 (1993), 19–28.

Grist, Leighton, 'Moving targets and black widows: film noir in modern Hollywood', in Ian Cameron (ed.), *The Movie Book of Film Noir* (London, Studio Vista, 1994), 267–85.

Gutierrez, Gustavo, *A Theology of Liberation* (London, SCM, 1974).

Harris, Stephen L., *Understanding the Bible* (Mountain View, CA, Mayfield, 1985).

Hebblethwaite, Brian, *The Christian Hope* (Hants, Marshall, Morgan & Scott, 1984).

Heron, Alasdair I. C., *A Century of Protestant Theology* (Cambridge, Lutterworth Press, 1985).

Hick, John, *Philosophy of Religion* (Englewood Cliffs, NJ/Hemel Hempstead, Prentice-Hall, 1973).

Hick, John (ed.), *The Existence of God* (London, Collier Macmillan, 1964).

Hick, John, *The Centre of Christianity* (London, SCM, 1977).

Hick, John, *Death and Eternal Life* (Basingstoke, Macmillan, 1985).

Hill, John, 'General introduction' to John Hill and Pamela Church Gibson (eds.), *The Oxford Guide to Film Studies* (Oxford, Oxford University Press, 1998), pp. xix–xxii.

Hirsch, Foster, *The Dark Side of the Screen: Film Noir* (London, Tantivy Press, 1981).

Hoberman, J., 'Sacred and profane', *Sight and Sound*, 1/10 (February 1992), 8–11.

Hollows, Joanne, 'Mass culture theory and political economy', in Joanne Hollows and Mark Jancovich (eds.), *Approaches to Popular Film* (Manchester, Manchester University Press, 1995), 15–36.

Hoover, Stewart M., 'Mass media and religious pluralism', in Philip Lee (ed.), *The Democratization of Communication* (Cardiff, University of Wales Press, 1995), 185–98.

Horsfield, Peter, 'Teaching theology in a new cultural environment', in Chris Arthur (ed.), *Religion and the Media* (Cardiff, University of Wales Press, 1993), 41–53.

Hurley, Neil P., *Theology through Film* (New York, Harper & Row, 1970).

Hurley, Neil P., 'Alfred Hitchcock', in John R. May and Michael Bird (eds.), *Religion in Film* (Knoxville, University of Tennessee Press, 1982), 177–81.

Hurley, Neil P., 'Cinematic transfigurations of Jesus', in John R. May and Michael Bird (eds.), *Religion in Film* (Knoxville, University of Tennessee Press, 1982), 61–78.

Jackson, Kevin (ed.), *Schrader on Schrader and Other Writings* (London, Faber & Faber, 1990).

Jasper, David, 'On systematizing the unsystematic: a response', in Clive Marsh and Gaye Ortiz (eds.), *Explorations in Theology and Film: Movies and Meaning* (Oxford, Blackwell, 1997), 235–44.

Jewett, Robert, 'Stuck in time: kairos, chronos, and the flesh in Groundhog Day', in Clive Marsh and Gaye Ortiz (eds.), *Explorations in Theology and Film: Movies and Meaning* (Oxford, Blackwell, 1997), 155–65.

Kaleidoscope feature on *Taxi Driver:* 'God's lonely man', produced by Paul Quinn (BBC Radio 4, 14 June 1997).

Kelly, J. N. D., *Early Christian Doctrines* (London, Adam & Charles Black, 1958).

Kelly, Mary Pat, *Martin Scorsese: A Journey* (New York, Thunder's Mouth Press, 1991).

Keyser, Les, *Martin Scorsese* (NewYork,Twayne Publishers, 1992).

King, Noel, 'Hermeneutics, reception, aesthetics, and film inter-pretation', in John Hill and Pamela Church Gibson (eds.), *The Oxford Guide to Film Studies* (Oxford, Oxford University Press, 1998), 212–23.

King, Winston L., 'Religion', in Mircea Eliade (ed.), *The Encyclopedia of Religion*, vol. 12 (NewYork, Macmillan Publishing Co., 1987), 282–93.

Kolker, Robert Phillip, *A Cinema of Loneliness*, 2nd edn. (Oxford, Oxford University Press, 1988).

Krutnik, Frank, *In a Lonely Place: Film Noir, Genre, Masculinity* (London, Routledge, 1991).

Krutnik, Frank, 'Something more than night: tales of the noir city', in David B. Clarke (ed.), *The Cinematic City* (London, Routledge, 1997), 83–109.

Küng, Hans, *Eternal Life?*, tr. Edward Quinn (London, Collins, 1984).

Lakeland, Paul, *Postmodernity: Christian Identity in a Fragmented Age* (Minneapolis, Fortress Press, 1997).

Lapsley, Rob, 'Mainly in cities and at night: some notes on cities and film', in David B. Clarke (ed.), *The Cinematic City* (London, Routledge, 1997), 186–208.

Le Fanu, Mark, 'Looking for Mr De Niro', *Sight and Sound*, 55/1 (Winter 1985/6), 46–9.

Livingston, James C., *Modern Christian Thought: From the Enlightenment to Vatican II* (London, Collier Macmillan, 1971).

McDannell, Colleen, and Lang, Bernhard, *Heaven: A History* (New Haven, CT,Yale University Press, 1990).

Macquarrie, John, *An Existentialist Theology* (London, SCM, 1955).

Macquarrie, John, *Studies in Christian Existentialism* (London, SCM, 1966).

Macquarrie, John, *Jesus Christ in Modern Thought* (London, SCM, 1992).

Maher, Ian, 'Liberation in *Awakenings*', in Clive Marsh and Gaye Ortiz (eds.), *Explorations in Theology and Film: Movies and Meaning* (Oxford, Blackwell, 1997), 97–113.

Malone, Peter, *Movie Christs and Anti-Christs* (New York, Crossroad, 1990).

Malone, Peter, '*Edward Scissorhands*: Christology from a suburban fairy-tale', in Clive Marsh and Gaye Ortiz (eds.), *Explorations in Theology and Film: Movies and Meaning* (Oxford, Blackwell, 1997), 73–86.

Maltby, Richard, *Hollywood Cinema: An Introduction* (Oxford, Blackwell, 1996).

Marsh, Clive, 'Film and theologies of culture', in Clive Marsh and Gaye Ortiz (eds.), *Explorations in Theology and Film: Movies and Meaning* (Oxford, Blackwell, 1997), 21–34.

Marsh, Clive, 'Religion, theology and film in a postmodern age: a response to John Lyden', in *Journal of Religion and Film* (*http://www.unomaha.edu/~wwwjrf*), 2/1 (1997).

Marsh, Clive, and Ortiz, Gaye, 'Theology beyond the modern and the postmodern: a future agenda for theology and film', in Clive Marsh and Gaye Ortiz (eds.), *Explorations in Theology and Film: Movies and Meaning* (Oxford, Blackwell, 1997), 245–55.

Marshall, I. Howard, 'The development of the concept of redemption in the New Testament', in Robert Banks (ed.), *Reconciliation and Hope: New Testament Essays on Atonement and Eschatology* (Grand Rapids, MI, William B. Eerdmans, 1974), 153–69.

Martin, Joel W., and Ostwalt Jr., Conrad E., 'Mythological criticism', in Joel W. Martin and Conrad E. Ostwalt Jr. (eds.), *Screening the Sacred: Religion, Myth and Ideology in Popular American Film* (Boulder, CO & Oxford, Westview Press, 1995), 65–71.

Martin, Joel W., 'Redeeming America: Rocky as ritual racial drama', in Joel W. Martin and Conrad E. Ostwalt Jr. (eds.), *Screening the Sacred: Religion, Myth and Ideology in Popular American Film* (Boulder, CO & Oxford, Westview Press, 1995), 125–33.

Martin, Joel W., 'Seeing the sacred on the screen', in Joel W. Martin and Conrad E. Ostwalt Jr. (eds.), *Screening the Sacred: Religion, Myth and Ideology in Popular American Film* (Boulder, CO & Oxford, Westview Press, 1995), pp. 1–12.

Martin, Thomas M., *Images and the Imageless* (Cranbury, NJ, Associated University Press, 1981).

Marty, Joseph, 'Toward a theological interpretation and reading of film: incarnation of the Word of God – relation, image, word' (tr. Robert Robinson III), in John R. May (ed.), *New Image of Religious Film* (Kansas City, Sheed & Ward, 1997), 131–50.

Mason, Lee Aaron, 'Attitudes to society and politics in the superhero comic' (MA thesis, SDUC, Lampeter, 1991).

Mast, Gerald, Cohen, Marshall and Braudy, Leo (eds.), *Film Theory and Criticism* (Oxford, Oxford University Press, 1992).

May, John R., 'The demonic in American cinema', in John R. May and Michael Bird (eds.), *Religion in Film* (Knoxville, University of Tennessee Press, 1982), 79–100.

May, John R., 'Visual story and the religious interpretation of film', in John R. May and Michael Bird (eds.), *Religion in Film* (Knoxville, University of Tennessee Press, 1982), 23–43.

Miles, Margaret R., *Image as Insight: Visual Understanding in Western Christianity and Secular Culture* (Boston, MA, Beacon Press, 1985).

Miles, Margaret R., *Seeing and Believing: Religion and Values in the Movies* (Boston, MA, Beacon Press, 1996).

Monaco, James (ed.), *Virgin Film Guide* (London, Virgin Books, 1992).

Morris, Brian, *Anthropological Studies of Religion* (Cambridge, Cambridge University Press, 1987).

Morris, Leon, *The Atonement: Its Meaning and Significance* (Leicester, Inter-Varsity Press, 1983).

Mottram, James, 'The eccentric great uncle', *Independent* (29 May 1998); reproduced in Chapter programme note on *Afterglow*, 31 July–6 August 1998 (Chapter, Market Road, Canton, Cardiff CF1 1QE).

Müller-Fahrenholz, Geiko, *The Art of Forgiveness: Theological Reflections on Healing and Reconciliation* (Geneva, WCC Publications, 1997).

Neale, Steve, and Smith, Murray (eds.), *Contemporary Hollywood Cinema* (London, Routledge, 1998).

Norris, Richard, *The Christological Controversy* (Philadelphia, Fortress Press, 1980).

O'Connor, Alfred C., 'An understanding of sin and redemption in traditional Christianity and in Unification theology (Ph.D. thesis, SDUC, Lampeter, 1995).

Orr, John, *Contemporary Cinema* (Edinburgh, Edinburgh University Press, 1998).

Ortiz, Gaye, 'Theology and the silver screen', *The Month: A Review of Christian Thought and World Affairs* (May 1998), 171–4.

Ortiz, Gaye, and Roux, Maggie, 'The Terminator movies: hi-tech holiness and the human condition', in Clive Marsh and Gaye Ortiz (eds.), *Explorations in Theology and Film: Movies and Meaning* (Oxford, Blackwell, 1997), 141–54.

Ostwalt, Jr., Conrad E., 'Hollywood and Armageddon: apocalyptic themes in recent Hollywood presentation', in Joel W. Martin and Conrad E. Ostwalt, Jr. (eds.), *Screening the Sacred: Religion, Myth and Ideology in Popular American Film* (Boulder, CO, and Oxford, Westview Press, 1995), 55–63.

Ostwalt, Jr., Conrad E., 'Religion, film and cultural analysis', in Joel W. Martin and Conrad E. Ostwalt, Jr., (eds.), *Screening the Sacred: Religion, Myth and Ideology in Popular American Film* (Boulder, CO, and Oxford, Westview Press, 1995), 152–9.

Ostwalt, Jr., Conrad E., 'Visions of the end: secular apocalypse in recent Hollywood film', *Journal of Religion and Film* (*http://www.unomaha. edu/~wwwjrf*), 2/1 (1997).

Oxtoby, Willard G., 'Reflections on the idea of salvation', in Eric J. Sharpe and John R. Hinnells (ed.), *Man and his Salvation: Studies in Memory of S. G. F. Brandon* (Manchester, Manchester University Press, 1973), 17–37.

Palmer, Martin, 'Ecology: prophetic or pathetic?', in Cyril Rodd (ed.), *New Occasions Teach New Duties: Christian Ethics for Today* (Edinburgh, T. & T. Clark, 1995), 173–85.

Parkinson, David, Obituary of James Stewart, in *Empire*, 99 (September 1997), 21.

Perdue, Leo G., *Wisdom and Cult: A Critical Analysis of the Views of Cult in the Wisdom Literatures of Israel and the Ancient Near East* (Missoula, MT, Scholars Press, 1977).

Petrie, Duncan, *Cinema and the Realms of Enchantment* (London, British Film Institute, 1993).

Pfeil, Fred, 'Home fires burning: family noir in *Blue Velvet* and *Terminator 2*', in Joan Copjec (ed.), *Shades of Noir: A Reader* (London, Verso, 1993), 227–59.

Place, J. A., and Peterson, L. S., 'Some visual motifs of *film noir*', in Bill Nichols (ed.), *Movies and Methods*, vol. 2 (London, University of California Press, 1985), 325–38.

Plouffe, Paul Bernard, 'The tainted Adam: the American hero in film noir' (Ph.D. thesis, University of California, Berkeley, 1979).

Porfirio, Robert G., 'No way out: existential motifs in the *film noir*', *Sight and Sound*, 45/4 (Autumn 1976), 212–17.

Pyle, Forest, 'Making cyborgs, making humans: of Terminators and Blade Runners', in Jim Collins, Hilary Radner and Ava Preacher Collins (eds.), *Film Theory Goes to the Movies* (London, Routledge, 1993), 227–41.

Rafferty, Terence, 'Mud', *The New Yorker* (2 December 1991), 156–9.

Richards, Jeffrey, 'Frank Capra and the cinema of populism', in Bill Nichols (ed.), *Movies and Methods*, vol. 1 (London, University of California Press, 1976), 65–77.

Richardson, Alan, *Creeds in the Making* (London, SCM, 1986; 1st publ. 1935).

Robinson, J. A. T., *Honest to God* (London, SCM, 1963).

Roddick, Nick, 'Show me the culture!', *Sight and Sound*, 8/12 (December 1998), 22–6.

Rose, Simon, *Classic Movie Guide* (Glasgow, Harper Collins, 1995).

Rosenbaum, Jonathan, 'Raging Messiah', *Sight and Sound*, 57/4 (Autumn 1988), 281–2.

Rothman, Stanley, 'Is God really dead in Beverly Hills? Religion and the movies', *The American Scholar*, 65/2 (1996), 272–8.

Savage, Rosalie, 'The *film noir* savior: themes of redemption and atonement in Martin Scorsese's *Mean Streets*, *Taxi Driver*, and *Cape Fear*' (MA thesis, Clemson University, 1995).

Schacht, Richard, *Alienation* (London, George Allen & Unwin, 1971).

Schillaci, Anthony, 'Bergman's vision of good and evil', in John C. Cooper and Carl Skrade (eds.), *Celluloid and Symbols* (Philadelphia, Fortress Press, 1970), 75–88.

Schrader, Paul, *Transcendental Style in Film: Ozu, Bresson, Dreyer* (Berkeley, University of California, 1972).

Schrader, Paul, 'Notes on *film noir*', in Kevin Jackson (ed.), *Schrader on Schrader and Other Writings* (London, Faber & Faber, 1990), 80–94.

Scott, Julie F., 'The truth is out there: the renewal of the western religious consciousness', *Scottish Journal of Religious Studies*, 18/2 (Autumn 1997), 115–27.

Scott, R. B. Y., *The Way of Wisdom in the Old Testament* (New York, Macmillan, 1971).

Sellers, R.V., *Two Ancient Christologies* (London, SPCK, 1940).

Skrade, Carl, 'Theology and films', in John C. Cooper and Carl Skrade (eds.), *Celluloid and Symbols* (Philadelphia, Fortress Press, 1970), 1–24.

Soggin, J. A., *Introduction to the Old Testament* (London, SCM, 1989).

Stark, Rodney, and Bainbridge, William Sims, *The Future of Religion* (Berkeley, University of California Press, 1985).

Stern, Lesley, *The Scorsese Connection* (London, British Film Institute, 1995).

Stevenson, J., *A New Eusebius*, rev. W. H. C. Frend (Cambridge, Cambridge University Press, 1992).

Stoddart, Helen, 'Auteurism and film authorship theory', in Joanne Hollows and Mark Jancovich (eds.), *Approaches to Popular Film* (Manchester, Manchester University Press, 1995), 37–52.

Stout, Daniel A., and Buddenbaum, Judith M., *Religion and Mass Media: Audiences and Adaptations* (London, Sage, 1996).

Strick, Philip, Review of *The Game*, in *Sight and Sound*, 7/11 (November 1997), 41–2.

Stromberg, Roland N., *Redemption by War: The Intellectuals and 1914* (Kansas City, University Press of Kansas, 1982).

Sunshine, Linda (ed.), *The Illustrated Woody Allen Reader* (London, Jonathan Cape, 1993).

Sweet, Louise, Review of *Awakenings*, in *Monthly Film Bulletin*, 58/686 (March 1991), 72–3.

Swinburne, Richard, *The Existence of God* (Oxford, Clarendon Press, 1979).

Taylor, Mark Kline, *Paul Tillich: Theologian of the Boundaries* (London, Collins, 1987).

Telford, William R., 'Jesus Christ movie star: the depiction of Jesus in the cinema', in Clive Marsh and Gaye Ortiz (eds.), *Explorations in Theology and Film: Movies and Meaning* (Oxford, Blackwell, 1997), 115–39.

Thompson, David, and Christie, Ian (eds.), *Scorsese on Scorsese* (London, Faber & Faber, 1989; 2nd edn., 1996).

Thomson, David, *America in the Dark: Hollywood and the Gift of Unreality* (London, Hutchinson, 1978).

Tudor, Andrew, *Theories of Film* (London, Martin Secker & Warburg, 1975).

Turner, Graeme, *Film as Social Practice* (London, Routledge, 1993).

Turner, H. E. W., *The Patristic Doctrine of Redemption: A Study of the*

Development of Doctrine during the First Five Centuries (London, A. R. Mowbray & Co., 1952).

Tuska, Jon, *Dark Cinema: American Film Noir in Cultural Perspective* (London, Greenwood Press, 1984).

Tyler, Parker, *Magic and Myth of the Movies* (London, Secker & Warburg, 1971).

Verbeek, Marjeet, 'Mythological aspects of contemporary film art', *Media Development*, 42/2 (1995), 29–31.

Vidler, Alec R., *The Church in an Age of Revolution: 1789 to the Present Day* (London, Penguin, 1971).

Virgin Film Guide (London, Virgin Books, 1992 edn.).

von Rad, Gerhard, *Wisdom in Israel* (London, SCM, 1970).

Wagner, Robert W., 'Film, reality, and religion', in John C. Cooper and Carl Skrade (eds.), *Celluloid and Symbols* (Philadelphia, Fortress Press, 1970), 127–39.

Walker, Michael, '*Film noir*: introduction', in Ian Cameron (ed.), *The Movie Book of Film Noir* (London, Studio Vista, 1994), 8–38.

Wall, James M., 'Biblical spectaculars and secular man', in John C. Cooper and Carl Skrade (eds.), *Celluloid and Symbols* (Philadelphia, Fortress Press, 1970), 51–60.

Walls, Jerry L., *Hell: The Logic of Damnation* (Notre Dame, IN, University of Notre Dame Press, 1992).

Weber, Max, *The Sociology of Religion*, tr. Ephraim Fischoff (London, Methuen & Co., 1965).

Wells, David F., *The Search for Salvation* (Leicester, Inter-Varsity Press, 1978).

Werblosky, RJ Zwi, *Beyond Tradition and Modernity: Changing Religions in a Changing World* (London, Athlone Press/University of London, 1976).

Westbrook, Caroline, Review of laserdisc version of *Cape Fear*, in *Empire*, 88 (September 1996), 130.

Westerbeck, Colin L., 'Beauties and the beast: *Seven Beauties/Taxi Driver*', *Sight and Sound*, 45/3 (Summer 1976), 134–9.

White, Robert A., 'The role of film in personal religious growth', in John R. May (ed.), *New Image of Religious Film* (Kansas City, Sheed & Ward, 1997), 197–212.

Wiles, Maurice, *The Christian Fathers* (London, SCM, 1966).

Wiles, Maurice, *The Making of Christian Doctrine* (Cambridge, Cambridge University Press, 1967).

Williams, Harry A., *True Resurrection* (London, Mitchell Beazley, 1972).

Williams, Peter W., *Popular Religion in America: Symbolic Change and the Modernization Process in Historical Perspective* (Englewood Cliffs, NJ, Prentice Hall, 1980).

Willis, Andrew, 'Cultural studies and popular film', in Joanne Hollows and Mark Jancovich (eds.), *Approaches to Popular Film* (Manchester, Manchester University Press, 1995), 173–91.

Witten, Marsha G., *All is Forgiven: The Secular Message in American Protestantism* (Princeton, NJ, Princeton University Press, 1993).

Wood, Robin, 'An introduction to the American horror film', in Bill Nichols (ed.), *Movies and Methods*, vol. 2 (London, University of California Press, 1985), 195–220.

Wrathall, John, Review of *Seven,* in *Sight and Sound*, 6/1 (January 1996), 50.

Wrathall, John, Review of *Saving Private Ryan* in *Sight and Sound*, 8/9 (September 1998), 34–5.

Zahrnt, Heinz, *The Question of God*, tr. R. A. Wilson (London, Collins, 1969).

Žižek, Slavoj, ' "The thing that thinks": the Kantian background of the *noir* subject', in Joan Copjec (ed.), *Shades of Noir: A Reader* (London, Verso, 1993), 199–226.

Zwick, Reinhold, 'The problem of evil in contemporary film', in John R. May (ed.), *New Image of Religious Film* (Kansas City, Sheed & Ward, 1997), 72–91.

Filmography

Afterglow (Alan Rudolph, 1997)
After Hours (Martin Scorsese, 1985)
Alamo Bay (Louis Malle, 1985)
American Beauty (Sam Mendes, 1999)
An American in Paris (Vincente Minnelli, 1951)
Apocalypse Now (Francis Ford Coppola, 1979)
Armageddon (Michael Bay, 1998)
As Good as it Gets (James L. Brooks, 1997)
The Asphalt Jungle (John Huston, 1950)
Awakenings (Penny Marshall, 1990)
Batman (Tim Burton, 1989)
Batman and Robin (Joel Schumacher, 1997)
Batman Forever (Joel Schumacher, 1995)
Batman Returns (Tim Burton, 1992)
The Best Years of our Lives (William Wyler, 1946)
The Big Sleep (Howard Hawks, 1946)
Blackboard Jungle (Richard Brooks, 1955)
Blow-Up (Michelangelo Antonioni, 1966)
Blue Velvet (David Lynch, 1986)
Born on the Fourth of July (Oliver Stone, 1989)
Cape Fear (J. Lee Thompson, 1962)
Cape Fear (Martin Scorsese, 1991)
Casino (Martin Scorsese, 1995)
Chinatown (Roman Polanski, 1974)
Close Encounters of the Third Kind (Steven Spielberg, 1977)
The Color of Money (Martin Scorsese, 1986)
Contact (Robert Zemeckis, 1997)
The Conversation (Francis Ford Coppola, 1974)
Cool Hand Luke (Stuart Rosenberg, 1967)
Crimes and Misdemeanors (Woody Allen, 1989)
Darling (John Schlesinger, 1965)
Dead Man Walking (Tim Robbins, 1995)
Dead Poets Society (Peter Weir, 1989)
Deep Impact (Mimi Leder, 1998)
Detour (Edgar G. Ulmer, 1946)

The Diary of a Country Priest/Le Journal d'un curé de campagne (Robert Bresson, 1950)

Double Indemnity (Billy Wilder, 1944)

Duck Soup (Leo McCarey, 1933)

Edward Scissorhands (Tim Burton, 1990)

End of Days (Peter Hyams, 1999)

E.T. the Extra-Terrestrial (Steven Spielberg, 1982)

The Exorcist (William Friedkin, 1973; rereleased 1998)

Field of Dreams (Phil Alden Robinson, 1989)

Fight Club (David Fincher, 1999)

The Game (David Fincher, 1997)

The Glenn Miller Story (Anthony Mann, 1953)

The Godfather (Francis Ford Coppola, 1972), *The Godfather Part II* (Francis Ford Coppola, 1974), *The Godfather Part III* (Francis Ford Coppola, 1990)

Gold Diggers of 1933 (Mervyn LeRoy, 1933)

GoodFellas (Martin Scorsese, 1990)

Grand Canyon (Lawrence Kasdan, 1991)

The Greatest Story ever Told (George Stevens, 1965)

Groundhog Day (Harold Ramis, 1993)

Hamburger Hill (John Irvin, 1987)

Hannah and her Sisters (Woody Allen, 1986)

He Walked by Night (Alfred Werker, 1948)

I Confess (Alfred Hitchcock, 1953)

In a Lonely Place (Nicholas Ray, 1950)

It's a Wonderful Life (Frank Capra, 1946)

I Want to Live! (Robert Wise, 1958)

Jesus of Nazareth (TV) (Franco Zeffirelli, 1977)

Jurassic Park (Steven Spielberg, 1993)

King of Kings (Nicholas Ray, 1961)

Kiss me Deadly (Robert Aldrich, 1955)

Knight Moves (Carl Schenkel, 1992)

Kundun (Martin Scorsese, 1997)

The Last Temptation of Christ (Martin Scorsese, 1988)

Laura (Otto Preminger, 1944)

Little Voice (Mark Herman, 1998)

The Long Goodbye (Robert Altman, 1973)

Love and Death (Woody Allen, 1976)

M (Fritz Lang, 1933)

The Maltese Falcon (Roy Del Ruth, 1931)

Manhattan (Woody Allen, 1979)

Mean Streets (Martin Scorsese, 1973)

Meet John Doe (Frank Capra, 1941)

Meet Me in St Louis (Vincente Minnelli, 1944)
Midnight Cowboy (John Schlesinger, 1969)
The Mission (Roland Joffé, 1986)
Mr Deeds Goes to Town (Frank Capra, 1936)
Mr Smith Goes to Washington (Frank Capra, 1939)
Mrs Brown (John Madden, 1997)
The Naked Spur (Anthony Mann, 1953)
New York, New York (Martin Scorsese, 1977)
Night and the City (Jules Dassin, 1950)
Nightmare (Maxwell Shane, 1956)
Night Moves (Arthur Penn, 1975)
North by Northwest (Alfred Hitchcock, 1959)
On Dangerous Ground (Nicholas Ray, 1951)
One Flew Over The Cuckoo's Nest (Milos Forman, 1975)
Out of the Past (Jacques Tourneur, 1947)
Pale Rider (Clint Eastwood, 1985)
The Paradine Case (Alfred Hitchcock, 1947)
Platoon (Oliver Stone, 1986)
Play it Again, Sam (Herbert Ross, 1972)
Pleasantville (Gary Ross, 1998)
Possessed (Curtis Bernhardt, 1947)
The Postman Always Rings Twice (Tay Garnett, 1946)
Pretty Woman (Garry Marshall, 1990)
The Purple Rose of Cairo (Woody Allen, 1985)
Raging Bull (Martin Scorsese, 1980)
Raiders of the Lost Ark (Steven Spielberg, 1981)
Rambo: First Blood, Part Two (George Pan Cosmatos, 1985)
Rebel without a Cause (Nicholas Ray, 1955)
The Red Desert (Michelangelo Antonioni, 1964)
Rock Around the Clock (Fred F. Sears, 1956)
Rocky (John G. Avildsen, 1976)
Saving Private Ryan (Steven Spielberg, 1998)
Scarlet Street (Fritz Lang, 1945)
Schindler's List (Steven Spielberg, 1993)
Seven (David Fincher, 1995)
Shane (George Stevens, 1953)
Short Cuts (Robert Altman, 1993)
Somewhere in the Night (Joseph L. Mankiewicz, 1946)
Stardust Memories (Woody Allen, 1980)
Star Wars (George Lucas, 1977); *Star Wars: The Phantom Menace* (George
  Lucas, 1999)
La Strada/The Road (Federico Fellini, 1954)
Strange Days (Kathryn Bigelow, 1995)

Superman (Richard Donner, 1978); *Superman II* (Richard Lester, 1980); *Superman III* (Richard Lester, 1983); *Superman IV: The Quest For Peace* (Sidney J. Furie, 1987)

Taxi Driver (Martin Scorsese, 1976)

Titanic (James Cameron, 1997)

Top Hat (Mark Sandrich, 1935)

Twelve Monkeys (Terry Gilliam, 1995)

Unforgiven (Clint Eastwood, 1992)

Vertigo (Alfred Hitchcock, 1958)

Waterworld (Kevin Reynolds, 1995)

White Heat (Raoul Walsh, 1949)

Wild at Heart (David Lynch, 1990)

The Wings of the Dove (Iain Softley, 1997)

The Wizard of Oz (Victor Fleming, 1939)

Wolf (Mike Nichols, 1994)

The Woman in the Window (Fritz Lang, 1944)

Yankee Doodle Dandy (Michael Curtiz, 1942)

Index

DATE DUE
